Deeper Splendor

Deeper Splendor

Spirituality and Personality in Modern Literature

ROBERT P. VANDE KAPPELLE

WIPF & STOCK · Eugene, Oregon

DEEPER SPLENDOR
Spirituality and Personality in Modern Literature

Wipf & Stock
An Imprint of Wipf and Stock Publishers
199 W. 8th Ave., Suite 3
Eugene, OR 97401

www.wipfandstock.com

PAPERBACK ISBN: 978-1-6667-3790-5
HARDCOVER ISBN: 978-1-6667-9796-1
EBOOK ISBN: 978-1-6667-9797-8

MARCH 2, 2022 10:59 AM

The vocation of the poet

is to evoke the holy.

—Martin Heidegger

Many times man lives

Between his two eternities.

—William Butler Yeats

All we need to do is cleanse the doors of perception,

and we shall see things as they are—infinite.

—William Blake

Contents

Preface | ix

CHAPTER 1
Spirituality and Personality | 1

CHAPTER 2
Jungian Personality and Spirituality Theory | 14

CHAPTER 3
Hermann Hesse's Four Ways of Functioning | 27

CHAPTER 4
Fyodor Dostoevsky's *The Brothers Karamazov* | 43

CHAPTER 5
Jane Austen's *Sense and Sensibility*
and Charlotte Brontë's *Jane Eyre* | 62

CHAPTER 6
Nathaniel Hawthorne's *The Scarlet Letter*
and Thomas Hardy's *Tess of the D'Urbervilles* | 82

CHAPTER 7
Charles Dickens's *Bleak House*
and William Thackeray's *Vanity Fair* | 102

CHAPTER 8
George Eliot's *Middlemarch* and Virginia Woolf's *Orlando* | 123

CHAPTER 9
E. M. Forster's *A Passage to India* | 145

CHAPTER 10
Ralph Ellison's *Invisible Man* and
José Vasconcelos's *The Cosmic Race* | 160

APPENDIX
Franz Kafka's *The Metamorphosis* | 179

Bibliography | 191

Index | 195

Preface

In the late 1960s, when I enrolled in the Master of Divinity (MDiv) program at Princeton Theological Seminary as a first-year student, I expected to learn about biblical studies, theology, ethics, and church history. I was surprised, therefore, to learn that the task of spirituality is not to achieve correct doctrine or proper polity, or even to attain effective Christian leadership, but to help believers best answer the question, "What does it mean to be human?" It is this question, integrative in nature, which drives our study of spirituality and personality in modern literature. But why focus on modern literature? Shouldn't we concentrate on spirituality and theology, or spirituality and philosophy, or spirituality and social change? While those approaches can be helpful, there can be no social change without individual change, and in my experience, one of the best devices for studying transformative spirituality is great literature.

Appropriately, *Deeper Splendor* is a companion volume to *Deep Splendor*, my study of spirituality in modern literature. As I state in the preface to that earlier book, love of great literature made me a better husband and parent, a healthier cleric, and a more effective teacher, for it kept me open to lifelong learning, an advantage I imparted to many students along the way. Literature also contributed significantly to my wellbeing, for it helped me outgrow fundamentalist and dualist perspectives and kept me open to spiritual growth and ongoing transformation.

The restoration of wonder is the beginning of the inward journey toward the awaiting God. Literature, as all art, is a gift of divine grace, a pathway to mystery. Each literary experience is slightly beyond our horizon of understanding. What a gift literature is! When it enhances spirituality, each literary moment confounds in order to keep us going and growing. In the past, when people asked me what I do in my retirement years, I responded, "I write about theology and spirituality." Now, when asked, I respond, "I write about spirituality and the arts." *Deeper Splendor* is another volume in this series.

NOTE FOR LEADERS AND PARTICIPANTS

Deeper Splendor is useful for individual or group study. As you read this book, consider journaling as a way to grow spiritually. A good place to start is with your hopes and dreams. As you reflect and write, be honest with your thoughts and feelings, without ignoring your fears. Transparency facilitates the process of becoming healthy and whole.

As you read this book, it will be helpful for you to become acquainted with the extraordinary literature examined in each chapter. While I have included summary, overview, or synopsis of the literature for each chapter, I encourage you to read the original material when possible. Because some of this literature is difficult, dense, or lengthy, consider selecting one or two authors or works you initially find most interesting, intriguing, or compelling, and obtain copies from an available library or through purchase. Later, you may wish to add to that list. In this regard, be aware that reading and analyzing great literature can be daunting, but if you stay with it, your ability to read, analyze, understand, and benefit from this experience will expand your horizons and enrich your life.

Each chapter concludes with questions for discussion or reflection. Write the answers to each question in your journal, in addition to the questions below, which are appropriate for each chapter. If you are reading this book in a group setting, be prepared to share your answers with others in the group. If your study is private, I encourage you to write answers to each question in your journal for review and further reflection. Leaders may select questions from these lists that they deem most helpful to group discussion.

1. After reading this chapter, what did you learn about spirituality?

2. In your estimation, what is the primary insight gained from this chapter?

3. For personal reflection: Does this chapter raise any issues you need to handle or come to terms with successfully? If so, how will you deal with them?

Chapter 1

Spirituality and Personality

SPIRITUALITY AND PERSONALITY ARE INTERRELATED, and to examine one without the other is like viewing reality with one eye instead of two, or like hearing with just one ear; the result is partial, incomplete, and distorted. Like cyclists on a tandem, personality and spirituality travel together through the journey of life. Riding in tandem, they are deeply influenced by conditions both internal (goals, moods, desires) and external to the self. When one leans, the other leans; where one starts, the other starts; if one stops, the other stops. Though not identical, they strive to be in sync, balancing one another in profound and intimate ways. Personality takes the lead, and where personality goes, spirituality follows, though not blindly or passively. Spirituality has its own voice, and when its desires are addressed and heeded, personality thrives. When the two disagree, they must communicate, or the consequences can be disastrous. Cooperation always enhances the ride.

Ultimately, spirituality is about one's relationship with God—not with an idea of God, but actually with God. While such a statement might seem mystical or unrealistic, it is both practical and realistic, if we understand God not as a concept or person, but as a stand-in for everything—Reality, truth, and the essence of our universe. What I have in mind, however, is not pantheism but panentheism, the view that God is in all things yet distinct and not a "thing" at all. What this means is that God is not simply another way of speaking of reality, for God is reality with a face—Reality with Personality—which is the only way most of us relate to others. For relationship to occur, there must be personality.

It is important that we understand God correctly, because our image of God influences, even determines, our self-image. There is an absolute connection between how we see God and how we see ourselves, between how we relate to ourselves, to others, and to the world around us and within us. This is why good theology, healthy psychology, and holistic spirituality can make a major difference in how we live with ourselves and with others.

Therapists, life coaches, and spiritual directors tell a common story, that most people's operative image of God is initially a subtle combination of their parents and other early authority figures. Without a healthy and mature spiritual journey nurtured by prayer, contemplation, empathy, and a supportive community, much of religion is largely childhood conditioning, vital and valuable in itself but often limited and distorted. Skeptics and atheists rightly react against such religion because it is childish and fear-based, yet they argue against a caricature of faith, deriding views of God and forms of spirituality I too cannot endorse.

As we learn from philosophy and psychology and find illustrated in great literature, whatever we receive is received in the manner of the receiver. What this means theologically is that what we believe about God and how we view reality is greatly dependent upon our parents and other early authority figures. If our father was punitive, our God is usually punitive. If our mother was cold and withdrawn, we assume God is cold and withdrawn. If authority in our lives came primarily through males, we probably assume and even prefer a male image of God, even if our hearts desire otherwise.

In our conception of the nature of God lies the kernel of the spiritual life. Until we discover the God in which we believe, we will never fully accept and understand ourselves. Such lack of acceptance and understanding means that the polarities of our nature will keep us frustrated and fragmented, preventing the wholeness and integration we seek and need for health and happiness. As we develop physically, intellectually, and emotionally, we must also grow toward a mature spirituality that includes reason, faith, and inner experience we can trust. A mature God creates mature people: a big God creates big people; a small God creates small people; a loving God creates loving people; a punitive God creates punitive people. As our theology is mirrored in our spirituality, our self-image is mirrored in our political views as well: good theology makes for good politics and positive social relationships; bad theology makes for stingy politics, a reward/punishment mindset, xenophobia, and highly controlled relationships.

As views of God influence self-image, the reverse is equally true, for self-knowledge is the path to knowledge of God (the ultimate or the divine). While this correlation is affirmed by the world's major religions, they disagree, however, on the nature of reality and the self, thereby differing on how self-knowledge is acquired. While Western religions assume an evolutionary cosmogony with a beginning and a goal, Eastern religions assume a static, self-contained, eternal cycle of events. Furthermore, the Western mindset finds meaning externally, in a purposeful universe, whereas the Eastern mind finds meaning and fulfillment internally, within the psyche. In his autobiography, *Memories, Dreams, Reflections*, Carl Jung finds himself agreeing with both perspectives, distinguishing between the Western mindset, which he describes as "predominantly extraverted," and the Eastern mindset, found to be "predominantly introverted." Meaning, he concludes," is both without and within."[1]

While Eastern religions attribute divine significance to the human self, this perspective is foundational to Western religions as well. Ancient Christians affirmed it, though mainstream medieval and Reformation Christians suppressed it by emphasizing externalized and objectified truth. Thankfully, this understanding continued in the mystical tradition and is affirmed by those who promote spiritual formation.

While there is plenty of evidence in the world to conclude that there is something fundamentally flawed with humanity, the biblical creation story declares that humans are created in the "image and likeness" of God and out of generative love. If this is true, this means that the human family of origin is divine. That original goodness is the place to which humans always seek to return. There are many detours along the way, and many "devils" planting the same doubt suggested to Jesus at his baptism, questioning his divine descent (see Matt 4:3, "*If* you are the Son of God" . . .). Due to a lack of mysticism and a contemplative mind, many Christians still have no knowledge of the soul's objective union with God (see 2 Pet 1:4). They delight in affirming that all humans are fallen and depraved. Such a negative starting point hardly results in loving, dignified, or responsive people.

The great illusion we must all overcome is not our unworthiness, but rather the illusion of separateness. It is almost the only task of religion— to communicate not worthiness but union, to reconnect people to their

1. Jung, *Memories, Dreams, Reflections*, 317.

original identity "hidden with Christ in God" (Col 3:3). The Bible calls that state of separateness "sin," and its total undoing is stated frequently as God's clear job description: "Beloved, we are God's children now; what we will be has not yet been revealed. What we do know is this: when he is revealed, we will be like him, for we will see him as he is" (1 John 3:2).

The true purpose of religion is to help us recognize and recover the divine image in ourselves and in everyone else. Whatever we call it, this "image of God" is absolute and unchanging. There is nothing we can do to increase or decrease it. It is not ours to decide who has it or does not have it. It is pure and total gift, given equally to all. Once we have this straight, nothing can stop us and no one can take it away from us.

There is a Jewish proverb, "Before every person there marches an angel proclaiming, 'Behold, the image of God.'" Unselfish, sacrificial living is not about ignoring, denying, or destroying ourselves. It is about discovering our true self—the self that looks like God—and living life from that grounding. Many people are familiar with that part of Jesus' summary of the law of Moses that tells us to love our neighbor as we love our self. What this means is that loving the self is essential. If we fail in that, we fail our neighbor as well. Proper self-love and proper self-understanding are also essential to spirituality. However, getting that starting point straight is not always easy. As Jung noted, "The most terrifying thing is to accept oneself completely." Because most of us are unwilling or unable to accept negative aspects of our personality or of our experience, these repressed elements surface in unpredictable and unhealthy ways. As we will discover, this phenomenon is central to much of the literature discussed in this study.

QUICK-CHANGE ARTISTRY

One of television's most popular variety shows is *America's Got Talent*, an amateur talent competition featuring acts ranging from singing and dancing to comedy, magic, stunts, and other genres. Each participant attempts to stay in the competition by impressing a panel of judges. The winner receives a large cash prize and a chance to headline a show in Las Vegas. One of the finalists during the 2021 season was a quick-change artist named Léa Kyle, a twenty-five-year-old French magician from Bordeaux. With blinding speed and in near-mystical fashion, Léa was able to swap outfits in a matter of seconds while strutting across the stage displaying handmade costumes.

Americans love costumes, and annually on October 31, the eve of the Christian All Saints' Day, it is traditional for children to dress in Halloween costumes and go trick-or-treating around their neighborhood. Halloween costumes allow children to role-play by dressing up like a favorite movie or cartoon character. Children have active imaginations, and they love to dress up like scary creatures or exotic characters. Among the best-known and longest lasting superhero characters are Superman, Batman, Captain America, Spider-Man, Catwoman, Wonder Woman, and Wonder Girl, all appropriately costumed. Superheroes live double lives, ordinary people with superpowers they only use occasionally for the common good. Superheroes come from a wide array of backgrounds and origins; some derive their status from advanced technology, while others possess non-human abilities to achieve their tasks.

While role-playing and make-believe are intrinsic to the field of entertainment, adaptability, malleability, flexibility, and versatility are valued and useful in most occupations and relationships. In the past, young people went to college or into a trade expecting to commit to a lifetime of service in one or at most two careers, but that is no longer the case. Having served a dual role as professor and chaplain at Washington & Jefferson College for thirty-four years, in the latter years of my tenure I remember hearing Dr. Tori Haring-Smith, president of the college from 2005 to 2017, tell incoming students at the annual matriculation ceremony that no longer were they coming to a liberal arts college to prepare for one lifetime career but rather for an average of seven career changes during their lifetime. The college's job, she told first-year students, is not to prepare you for stability and conformity but rather for uncertainty and change. While resilience and commitment retain their value in this new scenario, versatility and adaptability are paramount. Like Léa Kyle, learners today must be able to adjust quickly to new circumstances while remaining calm and proficient in each role they undertake and with each costume they wear. In our postmodern occupational setting, preparation, commitment, and confidence must be paired with versatility and adaptability.

How does one prepare for uncertainty and change? As I learned recently during visits with my holistic chiropractor, the most effective way to stimulate physical change is through neurological rehab. Traditional chiropractic manipulation, like medication, can alleviate pain and bring temporary relief, but for enduring transformation, the mind must be retrained. Cortical efficiency—the speed and accuracy of how the brain handles incoming tasks—is essential to physical wellbeing because the central nervous system (brain and spinal cord) controls and coordinates every cell tissue and organ in the body.

Hearing this explanation during an evaluation session with the chiropractor made sense. However, my training in spirituality induced me to recognize that integrating physiology, kinesiology, and neurology are still not enough for whole body healing. The final step, the chiropractor acknowledged, is spiritual, for a holistic approach to wellness requires a balance of science and spirituality. If the mind controls the body and can change it, I wondered, isn't the ultimate source of healing and transformation the spirit? If humans are quadripartite creatures—consisting comprehensively of four parts: body, mind, soul, and spirit—is not "spirit" the ultimate agent of the self? This realization, of course, underlies all religious conversionism. As you may recall, in his discussion with Nicodemus in John 3:3, Jesus informs the rabbi that in order to enter God's kingdom, he had to be "born from above," which Nicodemus understands to mean, "being born again." That misunderstanding only makes sense in the Greek, not in Aramaic, the language Jesus would have used. However, what Jesus meant was that in order to enter the kingdom of God—that is, in order to experience God's wholeness here and now—humans must be born twice, once physically (of water) and then again spiritually (of Spirit). As our mind controls our body, so our spirit controls our mind. By inference, then, there can be no holistic or ultimate change in our Self—our body, emotions, or personality—without transformational impetus from "above," that is, from the Spirit.

SPIRITUALITY: THE JOURNEY OF LIFE

While we can define religion or theology with some degree of meaning and specificity, the word "spirituality" is often used traditionally with little or no clear meaning, or in a broad and vague manner. For our purposes, I reconnect the term with its root meaning, that is, with Spirit, or as the ancient Hebrews did, with the "wind" or "breath" of God. To be spiritual is to breathe deeply and harmoniously with Reality (Infinity). Spirituality, then, is a hopeful, creative, life-filled path, a Spirit-filled way of living.

Spirituality, traditionally defined by Christians as "life in the Spirit," encompasses the journey of life from a distinct perspective. To quote Matthew Fox, "The path that spirituality takes is a path away from the superficial into the depths; away from the 'outer person' into the 'inner person'; away from the privatized and individualistic into the deeply communitarian."[2] Spirituality is the journey of life "from God, to God, and with God." As a result, it is also a journey toward Self. In other words, the process of coming to know or to experience God is also the process of knowing oneself. Through this process, one comes to differentiate between one's temporary or False Self, which we call the ego, and one's permanent or True Self, that part of us made in the image of God and made for ongoing or everlasting relationship with God. In the end, we discover that we know God by being known, much like one loves by being loved.

The central defining characteristic of spirituality is an individual's sense of connection to a greater whole. At its heart, spirituality involves an emotional experience of awe and reverence. Such experience is highly desired, fervently sought, endlessly disagreed upon, and thoroughly fascinating. Why did our ancestors have such a wonderful idea of God? Because they lived in an awesome world. They wondered at the magnificence of whatever it was that brought the world into being. This led to a sense of adoration. This adoration, this gratitude, we call religion. Now, as the outer world is diminished, our inner world is drying up. The task of spirituality is to help us regain our sense of awe and reverence, beginning with a profound commitment to nature and continuing with an equal commitment to the whole of humanity and every living creature. If we do not love what is visible around us, how can we love God, whom we cannot see? (1 John 4:19–20).

DEATH AND RESURRECTION OF THE SELF

Life's ultimate adventure, its grandest game and greatest challenge, is the spiritual transformation (rebirth) of the self. As I discuss in *Walking on Water*, the role of authentic spirituality is letting go of the False Self, one's incomplete self trying to pass for one's True Self. Our True Self, our inherent soul, is that part of us that sees reality accurately, truthfully. It is divine breath passing through us, dwelling with us. Our False Self is the egoic self that is limited and constantly changing. It masquerades as true and permanent but in reality is passing, tentative, and fearful of change. It is that part of us that will eventually die. The role of true spirituality, of mature religion, is to help speed up this process of dying to the False Self.

2. Fox, *Creation Spirituality*, 12.

Not surprisingly, we cannot accomplish—or even understand—what we have not been told to look for or to expect. This staggering change of perspective—that our ego is not our True Self—is what Jesus came to convey to humanity. It led Thomas Merton, the Trappist monk who first suggested use of the term False Self, to his radical rediscovery of the meaning of Jesus' teaching that his followers must lose their False Self in order to discover their True Self (see Mark 8:35).

Unfortunately, many traditionalists today remain quite rigid in their thinking because they have been taught that belief requires adherence to the religious status quo, and with it unquestioned obedience to the guardians of tradition. Such people are often moral and productive—even model citizens—but they underrate the centrality of paradox or mystery to the faith traditions they espouse. When many religious practitioners observe rituals faithfully without experiencing spiritual transformation at any deep level, religion becomes a duty that actually prevents transformation from taking place. This has been going on for centuries, and in all faith traditions.

Mature religion talks about the death of any notion of a separate, False Self, while recognizing that only a deep security in a larger love will give you the courage to do that. The True Self can let go because it is secure at its core. Our False Self, however, does not let go easily. As Jesus and other great spiritual teachers made clear, there is a self that must be found and another that must be renounced. This teaching is found in each gospel (see Matt 10:39; 16:25; Mark 8:35; Luke 9:24), but is central to John's gospel, where it is coupled with "dying to the self": "unless a grain of wheat falls into the earth and dies, it remains just a single grain; but if it dies, it bears much fruit" (John 12:24). Hence, "those who love their life lose it [that is, their False Self], and those who hate their life [their False Self] in this world will keep it [their True Self] for eternal life" (John 12:25; see also 1 Cor 15:36–37, 42).

In one way or another, almost all religions say that you must die before you die—and then you will know what dying means, and what it does not mean. What it means, of course, is the relinquishment of selfish, possessive living, of egoic existence. The ego self is the self before death; some form of death—psychological, spiritual, relational, or physical—is the only way we will loosen our ties to our small and separate False Self. Only then does it return in a new shape, which we call the soul, the True Self, or the Risen Christ.

There are four major splits from reality that we have all made in varying degrees to create our False Self:

- We split from our shadow self[3] and pretend to be our idealized self
- We split our mind from our body and soul, and live in our minds
- We split life from death and try to live without any "death"
- We split ourselves from other selves and try to live apart, superior, and separate[4]

Each of these illusions must be overcome, either in this world or at the moment of physical death. Spirituality, pure and simple, is overcoming these splits from Reality. Anything less than the death of the False Self is inadequate religion. The False Self must die for the True Self to live, or, as Jesus put it, "If I do not go, the Advocate [the Holy Spirit] will not come to you" (John 16:7). Theologically speaking, what this verse is telling us is that Jesus (a good person) still had to die for the Christ (the universal presence) to arise. This is the pattern of transformation, where the letting go of the original indispensable self results in the arrival of a better reality.

Your True Self sees truthfully and will live forever. Your False Self is constantly changing and will eventually die. Your False Self is your necessary warm-up, the ego part of you that establishes your separate identity, especially in the first half of life. It is your incomplete self trying to pass for your whole self. The role of true spirituality, of mature religion, is to help speed up this process of dying to the False Self. Whatever one calls it, true spirituality is the form of living embodied by Jesus and taught by the Buddha. Such calm, egoless approach to life is invariably characteristic of people at the highest levels of doing and loving in all cultures and religions. These are the ones we call sages or holy ones.

---

3. The shadow self, something everyone possesses, represents the least developed part of one's personality. The shadow uses relatively childish and primitive forms of judgment and perception, often as an escape from the conscious personality and in defiance of conscious standards. As noted above, one's shadow includes "good" qualities as well as "bad" or "shameful" qualities that one denies. As one makes room for one's polarities, one becomes healthier and more open to transforming grace.

4. Rohr, *Diamond*, 29.

TYPES OF SPIRITUALITY

Urban Holmes, Dean of the School of Theology at The University of the South in Sewanee, Tennessee from 1973 until his death in 1981, presents a helpful typology for the spiritual life in his insightful book *A History of Spirituality*. His book provides a tool and a method by which to conceptualize and name spiritual experience within a basic framework, particularly useful in helping to position one's own religious experience within the context of the experience of others.

Holmes suggests two appropriate ends for the spiritual life: a speculative spirituality that focuses on the illumination of the mind, and an affective spirituality that focuses on the illumination of the heart. He further suggests two appropriate means toward those ends: a kataphatic means—an indirect way of knowing in which our relationship with God is mediated—and an apophatic means—a direct way of knowing, in which our relationship with God is not mediated.

Holmes calls his model the "Circle of Sensibility," and in it he delineates four styles of prayer, later configured as schools of spirituality. By "sensibility" he refers to the possibilities within individuals and communities as they seek to understand the experience of God and its meaning for our times. Holmes proposes the use of two intersecting lines placed within a circle. The vertical line creates a north-south axis, with Speculative (Mind or Intellect) at the north pole and Affective (Heart or Emotion) at the south pole. The horizontal line creates an east-west axis, with Kataphatic (God as Revealed: known through images) at the west and Apophatic (God as Mystery: known mystically) at the east. The circle, thus divided, contains four quadrants. Each quadrant contains one of the four schools of spirituality, which he labeled "speculative-kataphatic" (Type I spirituality), "affective-kataphatic" (Type II spirituality), "affective-apophatic" (Type III spirituality), and "speculative-apophatic" (Type IV spirituality). Each quadrant should look to its diagonal spirituality for growth and balance.

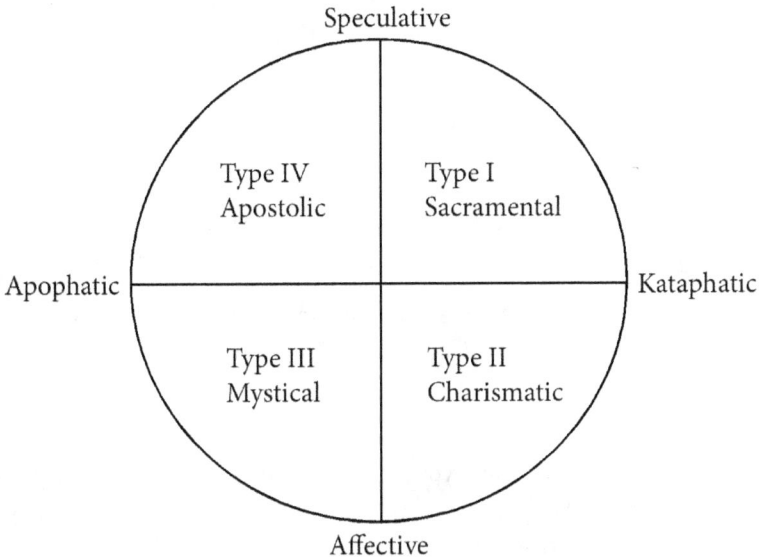

Type I spirituality, an intellectual "thinking" spirituality, has been identified as "sacramental." Its primary aim is to aid persons in fulfilling their vocation in the world. This spirituality favors what it can see, touch, and vividly imagine [Type I's diagonal (growth) quadrant is Type III]. Type II spirituality, a sensate, heartfelt approach to spirituality, has been identified as "charismatic." Its primary aim is to achieve holiness of life through personal renewal [Type II's diagonal (growth) quadrant is Type IV]. Type III spirituality, which emphasizes being and direct experience of God, has been identified as "mystical." Its primary aim is union with the Holy, an unattainable goal, a journey that nevertheless continually impels the disciple onward [Type III's diagonal (growth) quadrant is Type I]. Type IV spirituality, a visionary, almost crusading type of spirituality, has been identified as "apostolic." Its primary aim is to obey God's will completely. Its major concerns are witness to God's reign and striving for justice and peace [Type IV's diagonal (growth) quadrant is Type II].

Like theology and spirituality, great literature is a vast mirror. As all art, literature simultaneously draws us inward and outward. Great literature often describes and interprets spiritual journeys, portraying them as "growing up" or "coming of age." Through plot, narrative, and characterization, great literature beckons us to grow inward and outward, helping us understand who we are and how self-image influences others and society as a whole.

QUESTIONS FOR DISCUSSION AND REFLECTION

In addition to the questions listed at the end of the preface, answer the following questions, writing your answers in a journal. If you are in a group study, be prepared to share your answers with those in the group.

1. Central to any study on spirituality and personality is the question, "What does it mean to be human?" In your estimation, how does spirituality influence one's humanity? Can one be human and not be spiritual? Why or why not?

2. Are you satisfied with your current spiritual state? If not, where would you like to head spiritually, and what adjustments do you need to make to get there?

3. How do you describe God? Do you support the traditional understanding of God as personal, all-powerful, and all-knowing? What are the benefits and limitations of such a description of God?

4. What is your earliest memory or thought about God? As you consider your childhood understanding of God, to what extent was it connected with your parents or other early authority figures?

5. What is your current view or understanding of God? To what extent has it changed over time? Can you identify circumstances or experiences in your life that led to changes in your view of God? In your answer, be as specific as possible.

6. In one sentence, define spirituality. In your estimation, how does personality influence spirituality.

7. In your estimation, can humans experience God directly and personally, or only indirectly and impersonally? If you have had an experience or encounter with God, how would you describe it?

8. Assess the validity and meaning of the statement, "There is an absolute connection between how we see God, how we see ourselves, and how we relate to others and to the world around us."

9. Assess the validity and meaning of the statement, "The true purpose of religion is to help us recognize and recover the divine image in ourselves and in everyone else."

10. Explain the role of versatility and adaptability in healthy spirituality.

11. Explain the role of "spirit" (that is, of one's True Self) in spiritual healing and transformation.

12. Using Holmes's spiritual typology, which quadrant best describes your current spiritual stance? Which quadrant best represents your "growing edge"? Explain your answer.

Chapter 2

Jungian Personality
and Spirituality Theory

PEOPLE ARE NATURALLY DIFFERENT from one another in fundamental ways: they want different things, have different aims, think and learn differently, and believe differently. And of course, how they act and emote is governed by individual needs, desires, and beliefs. In many cases, differences in others trigger a negative response. Seeing others differing from us, we often conclude that when they differ in behavior or response, it is due to some malady or flaw on their part. In that case, the task, at least for those near us, would seem to be to correct their flaws, making them more like us. Such a task, however, is doomed from the start. Our attempts to change others, whether spouse, sibling, lover, co-worker or friend, can culminate in change, but the result is a distortion and not a transformation. Besides, trying to change others is futile and counterproductive, in that most differences are essentially good.

The developments of psychology in the twentieth century were amazing. Behaviorists, cognitivists, constructivists, and others studied the nature of human beings. Most of these theories tried to answer the question whether human personality is determined by nature (i.e. heredity) or nurture (i.e. environment or learning). Theories that claim human personality is a function of nature (or heredity) are called temperament theories. Temperament is that aspect of our personalities that is genetically based and therefore innate. That does not mean that a temperament theory rules out the role of environment; rather, a temperament theory does not focus on environment. It should also be noted that the issue of temperament is much older than psychology itself. It has a history of at least five thousand years.

People's involvement with the notion of "temperament" can be traced back to the traditions of ancient Egypt and Mesopotamia, where the health of the human body was considered to be connected with the four basic elements of nature—air, soil, water, and fire. The four elements, in turn, were related to body fluids (also called humors). In ancient Greek medicine, Hippocrates (c. 370 BCE) was the first to classify people according to their dominant body fluids: blood, black bile, phlegm, and yellow bile. The density of the fluids within individuals was believed to determine their personality. For Hippocrates, people could be classified as "cheerful," "somber," "calm," or "enthusiastic." The Roman physician Galen (c. 190 CE), who developed the ideas of Hippocrates, constructed a taxonomy of human behavior combining the four basic elements of nature with a matrix of hot/cold and dry/wet. Where all the elements were balanced, the individual was said to possess a balanced personality. Another possibility was that one element dominated the rest. This resulted in four less-balanced personality types, which Galen called Sanguine, Melancholic, Phlegmatic, and Choleric.

The sanguine individual, in which blood predominates, is claimed to be cheerful and optimistic, pleasant to be with, and comfortable with his or her work. The melancholic type, in which black bile or gall predominates, is said to be sad, depressed, and pessimistic. The phlegmatic type, in which phlegm predominates, is said to be slow, dull, and calm. The choleric type, said to have an excess of bile, is quick, passionate, hot-tempered, and often aggressive. While we might question the specifics of Galen's bodily fluids, the personal element seems to have some merit, for we all know individuals that fit one of these four temperaments, particularly if we replace Galen's terms with more familiar ones: sanguine with cheerful, melancholic with broody, phlegmatic with calm, and choleric with excitable.

Nearly six hundred years before Galen, Plato had written in *The Republic* of four kinds of character that clearly corresponded with the four temperaments attributed to Hippocrates. Plato was more interested in the individual's contribution to society than in underlying temperament, and so he named the Sanguine temperament the Artisan, endowed with artistic sense (driven by imagery and likely drawn to the arts, crafts, and creativity in general) and playing an aesthetic role in society. He named the Melancholic temperament the Guardian, endowed with common sense (driven by honor, duty, and trust in others and drawn to traditional leadership roles) and playing a caretaking role in society. He named the Phlegmatic temperament the Rationalist, endowed with reasoning ability (driven by cold and calm reason and likely drawn to logical, mathematical fields) and playing the role of logical investigator in society. And he named the Choleric temperament the Idealist, endowed with intuitive sensibility (driven by intuition and insight and likely drawn to activities involving ethics, relationships, and establishing harmony) and playing a moral role in society. A generation after Plato, Aristotle defined character in terms of happiness and not, as his mentor Plato had done, in terms of virtue. Aristotle identified four sources of happiness: sensual pleasure, acquiring assets, logical investigation, and moral virtue.

Writing about the year 180 CE, Irenaeus, Bishop of Lyons correlated the four gospels with the four living creatures of Ezekiel 1 and Revelation 4 as well as to four chief characteristics of Christ himself. The gospel according to Matthew corresponds to the Man, because it emphasizes Christ's humanity, especially by beginning with his genealogy; Mark corresponds to the Lion, because it emphasizes Christ's divine kingship; Luke corresponds to the Bull, because in this gospel Christ is presented as the servant and the sacrificial offering on behalf of sin; and John corresponds to the Eagle, because its clarity of vision pierces the highest things. Though not explicit in Irenaeus, these groups of four can be correlated to the four temperaments quite easily. While Irenaeus doesn't specifically draw the connection between Plato's temperaments and the Four Evangelists (gospels), he does adopt Plato's system, giving the four temperaments his own labels, which are more behavioral and less role-oriented. Artisans he labeled "spontaneous," Guardians he called "historical," Rationals he termed "scholarly," and Idealists he named "spiritual."

These ancient claims survived until the twentieth century, when they found their way to modern psychology. Modern psychologists proposed their own views of the four temperaments and coined different terms to refer to them. Although the terms used by each psychologist may differ from the ones used by others, they present essentially the same ideas. In 1905 Erich Adickes said that humans are divided into four world views: Innovative, Traditional, Skeptical, and Doctrinaire. In 1914 Eduard Spränger wrote of four "value attitudes" that distinguish one personality from another: Artistic, Economic, Theoretic, and Religious. A few years later Ernst Kretschmer took a slightly different approach and proposed that both normal and abnormal behavior can be understood in terms of four "character styles": Hypomanic, Depressive, Anesthetic, and Hyperesthetic. In 1947 Eric Fromm attributed four different "orientations" to the four styles: Exploitative, Hoarding, Marketing, and Receptive. That same year Hans Eysenck, best known for his work on intelligence and personality, identified two major dimensions of human personality: Neuroticism (the tendency to experience negative emotions) and Extraversion (the tendency to enjoy positive events, especially social ones). Upon pairing these two dimensions, he noted that the results were similar to the four ancient temperaments.

The belief that people are fundamentally alike appears to be a twentieth century notion. The idea is probably related to the growth of democracy in the Western world. If we are equals, we must be alike. Classical psychologists such as Freud, Adler, Sullivan, Fromm, and their followers affirmed the idea of singular motivation. Whatever the drive, whether motivated by Eros, power, social solidarity, or the search after Self, each personality school made one instinct primary for everybody.

In 1923, Swiss psychiatrist Carl Jung (1875–1961) disagreed with the prevailing temperament theories, publishing his views in his work *Psychological Types*. In his writing, Jung sought a way to explain why people differ from one another and why large numbers of people are similar to one another but different from others. Can similarities and differences be sorted into reliable patterns that can improve our knowledge of self and others? Jung's break with his mentor Sigmund Freud propelled him to find an explanation for why their close working relationship had deteriorated into an epic parting of the ways. Noting that people differ in fundamental ways, even though they all possess the same instincts to drive them from within, Jung determined that preference, rather than instinct, is central to personality.

Since Jung wrote in German for a largely specialized audience of psychologists, his theory of personality type found scant enthusiasm among ordinary people interested in personality theory. In the 1940s, when the Second World War broke out, two women, Isabel Myers and her mother Katherine Cook Briggs, sought a type indicator that might identify the kind of job for the war effort that non specialists could perform naturally and effective. The result became the Myers-Briggs Type Indicator (MBTI), a questionnaire that took the results of preferences in four areas—extraverted or introverted, sensing or intuitive, thinking or feeling, and judging or perceiving—to sort people into one of sixteen possible personality types in terms of Jungian type theory, thereby developing an instrument globally considered the gold standard for personality inventory.

According to the MBTI, differences in people result from

- where they prefer to focus their attention (Extraversion or Introversion) —E or I

- the way they prefer to take in information (Sensing or Intuition)—S or N

- the way they prefer to make decisions (Thinking or Feeling)—T or F

- how they orient themselves to the external world (Judging or Perceiving) —J or P

These preferences produce sixteen different kinds of people, interested in different things and drawn to different fields. Each type has its own inherent strengths as well as its likely blind spots. One's preference for a given function is characteristic, and so people may be "typed" by this preference. He noted that personality, like spirituality, can never be determined by someone else. It can be influenced by others, as in the case of parents and other authority figures, but ultimately, the choice is our own.

According to Jung, personality and spirituality are interrelated, spirituality flowing out of individuality. Thus, all human seekers think about the trajectory of their life, wondering where they are along the path of life. In Jung's model of the self, there are several levels from which we may attempt to answer the question. Each level represents a different stage of individuation and thus a different vantage point. And there is never a final perspective, only lifelong negotiations between adaptation and a more complete balance.

Jung's model of the self includes three major levels he calls (1) the persona, (2) the conscious realm, centered in the ego, and (3) the unconscious realm, consisting of both a personal and a collective unconscious. The *persona* can be regarded as a mask, for it is an appendage developed early in life, containing all that society would like us to be. As a mask, it received the rewards of society, and we are invited to identify it as our own self. However, there is the tug of the True Self, centered in the unconscious, and from these countervailing forces the conscious ego between them gains in strength and assumes command.

The self, or psyche, is centered in the unconscious but embraces the conscious as well. The unconscious is far larger than the conscious, for it is the repository of instinctual images or archetypes that are an integral part of the human psyche, and which are discernible in certain dreams and in important motifs found in world mythology and religion. According to depth psychology, archetypes function as ruling images that influence our thoughts, instincts, and behavior. Jungian archetypes include the father, the mother, the eternal child, the hero, the virgin, the wise old man, the trickster, the devil, and the God image. These universal archetypes recur in different ways and form part of what Jung called the "collective unconscious."

For Jung, the God archetype is the soul's function that drives us toward committing ourselves to something or someone. Furthermore, it integrates our being by initiating our desire for the absolute. It says to us, "become who you are, and all that you are." In the journey toward psychic wholeness, Jung stressed the God archetype's role in integrating opposites, including the conscious and unconscious, the one and the many, good (by embracing it) and evil (by forgiving it), masculine and feminine, the small self (the ego) and the Big Self (the True or eternal Self). This True Self (the Christ Self) consciously abides in union with the divine Presence within us (see John 14:7).

Jung saw the unconscious as the seat of the "numinous," where the God archetype resides (the Latin word *numen* is simply another word for the Divine). Something numinous is awesome or wondrous, an object, event, or experience that pulls us toward transcendence. Jung thus offered a foundation for affirming humans as ensouled beings, recognizing that the human soul or spirit shares much with transcendent reality. This essential insight overcomes the gap between divine and human transcendence and immanence. This is likely what Augustine had in mind when he declared, "God is more intimate to me than I am to myself."

Each of us has a life story, a narrative that influences our spiritual self-understanding. We have been blessed and wounded along the way. Our reactions to these experiences create in us patterns of response that operate out of what Jung called the personal unconscious, unknown to us. Much material in the personal unconscious is too painful to bring to conscious memory, so it remains latent, awaiting healing moment. Jung believed we all have a tendency toward wholeness, that the self or psyche is self-regulating. Through the years of our story, unresolved issues land in the personal unconscious, combining with content from deeper regions of our unconscious and our *shadow* (the shadow consists of those opposing aspects of self that are difficult to acknowledge or own and that counter our conscious identity). We are likely to project this negativity onto others rather than to face or negotiate an integration of shadow and self.

In the natural world, all substantial objects cast a shadow. Such shadows are intrinsically neither good nor bad—they just are. As Jung made clear, our psychological "shadow" is part of our unconscious, which is neither good nor bad, but simply hidden. Jung described the shadow as "the source of the highest good: not only dark, but also light; not only bestial, semi-human, and demonic, but superhuman, spiritual," and, in Jung's terminology, "divine." Wild beasts and angels reside in the same wilderness, and it takes the Spirit to "drive" us there (see Mark 1:12–13).

The struggle of our life story—our spiritual journey—reveals the human longing to bring the self to wholeness, which Jung calls individuation. Wholeness comes into being when the collective elements of persona and the unconscious move into closer interplay with the strengthened ego, which is capable of managing the richness of polarities at work. What Jung calls the *animus* and *anima*—the male qualities in the female and the female qualities in the male—reside in the unconscious as well, always longing for reinforcement and maturing so that individuals can become more balanced and relationships between the sexes can deepen.

Jung spoke frequently of the first and second halves of life. The first half of life is focused on ego, while the second half requires going inward and letting go of ego. Wholeness is not achieved by cutting off a portion of one's being, however, but by integration of the contraries—our conscious and our shadow side. For Jung, a person must have a dark side to be whole. The two halves of life spiritually correlate with the two major tasks to human life. The first task is to build a strong "container" or identity; the second is to find the contents that the container is meant to hold. The first task is obvious, one we take for granted as the purpose of life: surviving successfully. Many cultures across history, most empires in antiquity, and the majority of individuals in the modern period have focused on first half of life tasks, because of a lack of vision, and because it is all they have time for. We all want to complete successfully the task that life first hands us: establishing an identity, a home, a career, relationships, friends, community, and security, all foundational for getting started in life.

Most of us are never told that we can set out from the known and the familiar to take on a further journey. Our institutions, including our churches, are almost entirely configured to encourage, support, reward, and validate the tasks of the first half of life. Shocking and disappointing as it may be, we are more struggling to survive than to thrive, more focused on "getting through" or trying to get to the top than finding out what is really at the top or was already at the bottom. As wilderness guide Bill Plotkin puts it, many of us learn to do our "survival dance," but we never get to our actual "sacred dance."

Perhaps this is the symbolic meaning of Moses breaking the first tablets of the law, only to go back up the mountain and have them redone by Yahweh (Exod 32:19–35). The second set of tablets emerged after a face-to-face encounter with God, which changes everything. Our first understanding of law must fail us and disappoint us. Only after breaking the first tablets of the law is Moses a real leader and prophet. Only afterward does he see God's glory (Exod 33:18–19), and only afterward does his face "shine" (Exod 34:29–30). It might just be the difference between the two halves of life. As Richard Rohr states it, "we grow spiritually much more by doing something wrong than by doing it right." The Dalai Lama said much the same thing: "Learn and obey the rules very well, so you will know how to break them properly." All the world's religions at the mature levels say the same thing. In the beginning, we tend to think that God really cares about postures in worship, sacred times and places, and the wording of our prayers. Once we reach the level of constant communion, when we discover the God of unconditional love, we discover that the techniques, formulas, sacraments, and rituals are just a dress rehearsal for the real thing, a conscious and loving existence. This is the highest form of worship and praise.

When we speak of the second half of life, we are not thinking in a strictly chronological way. Some young people, especially those who have experienced early suffering, trauma, or life-altering events, may already be there, and some older folks will never reach it. Women, generally more nurturing and compassionate than men and less competitive and violent by nature, are naturally inclined to this reality, though many are prevented, either by duty, obligation, or opportunity, from engaging fully with it.

It takes most of us a long time to discover "the task within the task," as Richard Rohr calls us, a deeper meaning or purpose underlying one's activities or motivation. It is when we begin to pay attention, and seek integrity precisely in "the task within the task," that we begin to move from the first to the second half of our own lives.

The second half of life journey has been likened to the postcritical phase of life or a second simplicity. Paul Ricoeur speaks of it as a second naiveté or a second childhood. Whatever we call it, I believe this condition is the goal of mature adulthood and mature religion. First naiveté is the earnest and dangerous innocence we sometimes admire in young zealots, but it is also the reason we should not elect them or follow them as leaders. It is probably necessary to be impetuous when we are young, taking risks and eliminating most doubt. In the long run such approaches to life are not wise. Mature wisdom is content to live with mystery, doubt, and "unknowing," and in such living ironically resolves that very mystery to some degree. It takes a great deal of learning to finally "learn ignorance," as so many religious sages discovered. As T. S. Eliot puts it in the *Four Quartets*: "We had the experience but missed the meaning." This means, at least in part, that people in the second half of life need not expect to have the same experiences as others; rather, simple meaning now suffices.

This new coherence, a unified field that embraces paradox, is precisely what gradually characterizes a second half of life person. It feels like a return to simplicity after having learned from all the complexity. Finally one understands that "everything belongs," even the sad, absurd, and futile parts. In the second half of life we can devote ourselves to integrating even the painful parts of our life into the now unified field, including people who are different or marginalized. If you can forgive yourself for being imperfect and falling, you can now do it for just about everybody else.

Some people seem to have missed the joy and clarity of the first simplicity, perhaps avoided the interim complexity, and finally lost the great freedom and magnanimity of the second simplicity as well. We need to hold together all of the stages of life, and for some reason it all becomes quite "simple" as we approach our later years.

As previously noted, the transformation that brings us to the second half of life is often more about unlearning than learning. Perhaps it is simply a more profound learning. Life is more spacious now, the boundaries of the container having been enlarged by transformative experiences and relationships. For many people, the second half of life is characterized by seven transformational qualities:[1]

1. Less fearful and therefore less hostile. Because one has less need to eliminate the negative or fearful from one's life, there is less need to

1. The following points are adapted from Rohr, *Falling Upward*, 118–125.

punish other people. Superiority complexes have been shown to be useless, ego based, counterproductive, and often entirely wrong.

2. Less combative. By the second half of life one has learned that most frontal attacks simply add to the amount of evil within. Along with an inflated self-image, they incite retaliation from those one has attacked.

3. Less needful of attention. When "elders" speak, they need few words to make their point. Second simplicity has its own kind of brightness and clarity, but much of it is expressed nonverbally, and only when really needed. In the first half of life, one is defined through differentiation; now one looks for commonality. One does not need to dwell on the differences between people or exaggerate the problems. Creating dramas has become boring.

4. Less assertive. In the second half of life it is good just to be a part of the general dance. We do not have to stand out or be better than others; life is more participatory than assertive, and there is no need for strong or further self-definition.

5. Less self-concerned. At this stage we no longer have to prove that we are the best, that our ethnicity is superior, our religion the only one accepted by God, or that our role and place in society deserve special treatment.

6. Less dogmatic. People in the second half of life are less condemning. They no longer see God as small, punitive, or tribal. They once defended signposts; now they have arrived where the signs pointed. One's growing sense of spaciousness is no longer found mostly "out there" but especially "in here." The inner and the outer have become one. In the second journey, we have less final opinions about things and people as we allow them to delight or sadden us. We no longer need to change or adjust other people in order to be happy ourselves. Ironically, we are more than ever before in a position to change others—but we do not need to—and that makes all the difference. Now we aid and influence others simply by being who we are.

7. Less possessive. At this stage we are no longer preoccupied with accumulating additional goods and services; rather, our desire and effort should be to pay back to the world some of what we have received. Our concern is not so much to have what you love but to love what

you have—here and now. This is such a monumental change from the first half of life that it is almost the litmus test of whether one is in the second half of life at all.

For those who have experienced spiritually and fully their first and second half of lives, a sense of restlessness develops, sometimes formulated in the question, "Is there more?" Is there a third half of life?" For Jung, there is a third half. It generally occurs late in life, in the facing of one's death, for by embracing one's mortality opposites are reconciled, resulting in detachment and nondual wholeness.

A helpful way to conceptualize the difference between first and second half of life spirituality is by contrasting the apple with the onion. While apples have a core, onions have layers but no core. In first half of life spirituality, truth and meaning have a core, and people in this mindset frequently ask of an idea, thought, perspective, or ideology, "But what is the point? What is the takeaway or key concept?" That, of course, is the apple approach. However, people in a second half of life mindset are not looking for final thoughts or takeaways, but rather seek moments of insight and awareness, onion layers to meaning rather than apple cores.

If there is a third half of life or a third spiritual journey, as some suggest, how might it be conceptualized or symbolized? If the apple can be said to symbolize first half of life spirituality and the onion the second half of life mindset, might not the orange best represent life's third half? Once we get past the orange's rind or outer skin, we realize that oranges combine qualities of apples and onions in that they are typically divided into segments, sheathed in skin membranes containing juice and small seeds. As with apple cores, new trees can be grown from orange seeds, and like onions, oranges contain layers or segments yet lack cores.

Great literature, including religious scriptures, is like an orange in that it feeds both first and second half of life spirituality while attracting readers ever deeper into the newness and wholeness of the third journey. While exploring first and second half of life issues, great literature transcends both dimensions when it beckons readers to integrate cores and layers—matter and spirit, meaning and mystery, knowing and unknowing—nudging readers toward that amalgam called the third half of life.

SYMBOLS, ARCHETYPES, AND THE SPIRITUAL JOURNEY

Religion (*re-ligio* meaning re-binding) is not doing its job if it only reminds us of our distance, our unworthiness, our sinfulness, and our inadequacy before God's greatness. Whenever religion increases the gap, it becomes antireligion instead. Such gap creating between God and creation is actually diabolical (*dia balein*, Greek for "to throw apart"). What we need, of course, are adequate symbols (*sym bolon*, "throwing together"), and that, precisely, is what the New Testament provides: an entirely symbolic way of understanding Reality.

When Carl Jung spoke of Jesus as "the Archetype of the Self," he meant that what happened in the life of Jesus happens always and everywhere.[2] Discovering in the Jesus story a map of the unconscious human journey, he feared that Western civilization could lose this pattern, and that the results would be disastrous. Jesus is our "Savior," then, because he is the one who charts and guides us on the necessary path. The contours of that path can be summed up in the twin concepts of death and resurrection, for they serve as the template for full and authentic human life, what Jesus called "abundant life" (John 10:10).

When Jesus called his disciples, he was not asking others to join a new security system, a religious club, denomination, or order. He did not invite them to a belief system, but rather to a lifestyle: "Follow me." Where faith was elicited, it was in the form of trust, not belief. When he called his first disciples, Jesus was talking about further journeys to people who were already settled, socially and religiously.

People concerned with spirituality are seekers. They do not possess truth; rather, truth possesses them. Our task is to let our heart speak its truth. As my friend, Jess reminds me, "the minute we stop learning, we rent our house to an old person." Truth is never ours, for we have not arrived, nor will we ever, at least not until we see, to use the apostle Paul's metaphor, "face to face." For the time being, we are an unfinished painting, though the painting we are becoming is indeed wonderful. In the interim, let us use great literature as the brush and paint, and our curiosity and receptivity as the canvas.

2. Jung, *AION*, 5.70, 115–16, 124; 12.283.

QUESTIONS FOR DISCUSSION AND REFLECTION

In addition to the questions listed at the end of the preface, answer the following questions, writing your answers in a journal. If you are in a group study, be prepared to share your answers with those in the group.

1. Explain the difference between temperamental and behaviorist theories of personality.

2. In your estimation, does "healthy" spirituality require or view as desirable the goal of achieving a "balanced" personality? Explain your answer.

3. Explain and assess Aristotle's theory of happiness.

4. Explain how Jung's theory of personality challenges or disagrees with classical personality theory.

5. Explain the role "preference" plays in Jungian personality theory.

6. Explain Jung's notion of individuation, and the role it plays in healthy spirituality.

7. Explain and assess the relationship between the personal and collective unconscious in Jungian analytical psychology.

8. Explain and assess the role of the "God archetype" in Jungian psychology, and its influence on the self's "shadow."

9. Explain and assess the role of the *animus* and *anima* in Jungian psychology.

10. Do you consider yourself to be in the first or second half of your spiritual journey? In your estimation, can a person revert spiritually from the second to the first half of life? Explain your answer.

11. Of the seven transformational qualities associated with second half of life spirituality, which do you find most attractive and which least attractive? Explain your answer.

12. Explain and assess the possibility or desirability of a third half of life or third half of life spirituality.

13. Explain and assess the role of the "Jesus archetype" in Jungian spirituality.

Chapter 3

Hermann Hesse's
Four Ways of Functioning

IN THE CLOSING CHAPTER of *Deep Splendor*, I examine the life and work of the German novelist Hermann Hesse (1877–1962), showing how his auto-biographical novel *Demian* (1919) illustrates his use of romantic narrative, or what Princeton professor Ralph Freeman called the "lyrical novel," as a tool for analyzing the self and the meaning of personal identity, exploring them in contemporary terms. In German literature, the episodic narrative is widespread and, as we find in Hesse's work, protagonists serving as the writer's mask wander through worlds of spiritual encounter. "Almost all of the prose works I have written are biographies of the soul," Hesse asserted, "monologues in which a single individual is observed in relation to the world and to his [or her] own ego."

According to Hesse's characterization, it is possible to divide people practically into four ways of functioning, with talents and inclinations typical of artisans, poets, thinkers (scientists, mathematicians, philoso-phers, and theologians), and mystics. In his principal novels, Hesse's char-acters are essentially wanderers, living in the liminalities of life, somewhere between "our world" and "the other world," caught in the dichotomy of darkness and light, nature and supernature. What possibilities for living are there for such wanderers between these worlds? A life as a mystic, an intellectual, or an artist? These are the possibilities Hesse tests aesthetically in *Siddhartha*, *Steppenwolf*, and *Narcissus and Goldmund*, creating novels whose protagonists present possible solutions to the dilemmas of human existence.

Hesse was born in a small village in southern Germany, on the edge of the Black Forest. A poet and painter as well as a novelist, Hesse is best known as the author of *Demian, Siddhartha* (1922), *Steppenwolf* (1927), *Narcissus and Goldmund* (1930), and *The Glass Bead Game* (1943). In 1946, the Nobel Prize in Literature honored his body of work. Hesse grew up in a Pietist Lutheran household, within a religious sect that insulated members into small, deeply thoughtful groups. His maternal grandparents served as missionaries in India, where Hesse's mother was born. His grandfather, a linguist, acquired a large library of books about Eastern thought and became a master of Indian languages. Hesse's father, after briefly working as a missionary in India, returned to Germany to work in a religious publishing house.

As a child, Hesse was subjected to many religious influences, both to the narrow views of Protestantism and to the wider scope of Eastern religions and philosophies. Both views were formative of his later thought; his interest in Buddhism led eventually to the publication of his influential *Siddhartha*, a masterpiece that deals with the self-discovery of an Indian named Siddhartha during the time of the Buddha. Hesse's home was frequently the scene of visitations from foreigners, ranging from Buddhists to Americans. At his disposal was his grandfather's rich library. Hesse later stated that all of his writing was spiritual autobiography, religious not in an orthodox sense but in a larger, universal way.

After writing several minor works, he achieved literary success in 1904 with the publication of *Peter Camenzind*; from then on, Hesse knew he could make a living as a writer. This novel became popular throughout Germany, and was praised by Sigmund Freud as one of his favorite reading. Financially independent, Hesse secretly married Maria Bernoulli and they began a family, eventually having three sons. In 1914, Hesse became associated with pacifist writers and even wrote essays against growing nationalism in Germany. For the first time, he found himself in the middle of serious political conflict, attacked by the German press, the recipient of hate mail, and distanced from old friends.

A turning point in Hesse's life occurred in 1916, when his father's death, coupled with the illness of his son Martin and his wife's schizophrenia, led him to receive psychotherapy treatments in a Swiss sanatorium. From 1916 to 1917, he underwent more than seventy sessions with J. B. Lang, a disciple of the famous psychiatrist Carl Jung, eventually coming to know Jung personally. The result was beneficial for Hesse, leading him to new creative heights. The works following this period, particularly *Demian*—written during a three-week period in 1917—cannot be fully understood without recognizing the Jungian influence. After 1919, we cannot appreciate Hesse without a knowledge of such terms as "unconscious," *anima*, and "archetype." By the time Hesse returned to private life, his marriage had failed. After his wife's severe episode of psychosis, their home was divided and their children were accommodated in boarding houses or by relatives. In 1922, his novel *Siddhartha* was published, and the following year he divorced his wife and adopted Swiss citizenship.

In 1924 Hesse married the Swiss writer Lisa Wenger, but that marriage failed as well. The years 1924–1927 saw the publication of various autobiographical works, including *Steppenwolf*, and in 1930 Hesse married Ninon Dolbin, forming a solid relationship that endured until his death in 1962. During World War II, Hesse again became the subject of German ostracism because of his anti-nationalist views. In the late 1930s, German journals stopped publishing his works, which the Nazis eventually banned altogether. However, after receiving the Nobel Prize in 1946, his writings again became popular in Germany. Hesse's works had long enjoyed popularity outside of Germany, especially in southern Europe and Latin America. However, he remained virtually unknown in the United States until the 1960s, when he became a cult hero, particularly within the youth culture, which identified with his alienated protagonists. His works became bestsellers, and *Steppenwolf* became a virtual Bible for the 1960s counter-culture. *Siddhartha* and *Demian*, particularly, were added to the curricula of many progressive high schools and colleges. By the early 1970s, Hesse became the most widely read and translated European author of the twentieth century.

When Hesse first published *Demian*, he did so pseudonymously, using the pen name Emil Sinclair. He did so on account of his anti-nationalist views, to avoid the disfavor with which he was held by the German public. Had he published the novel under his real name, it would have been ignored. Under this guise, however, it was not only a success, but Sinclair was also awarded the Fontane Prize for new authors. When the truth became known, Hesse could not accept the prize, for he was already an established author. Even his friend, the renowned Thomas Mann, could not believe that this was the work of Hermann Hesse, so radical was the departure from his earlier work.

HERMANN HESSE'S AESTHETIC SENSIBILITY
(SENSATION) IN *NARCISSUS AND GOLDMUND*

Having undergone Jungian therapy, Hesse clearly displays the influence of Carl Jung in his writing. In his 1930 novel, *Narcissus and Goldmund*, Hesse's characters embody classic Jungian psychological types or personalities, Narcissus representing the thinker and Goldmund the artist or sensor. Near the end of the story, the two friends are reunited: Narcissus has become the abbot of the cloister at Mariabronn, and Goldmund has returned after years of wandering to serve as the cloister's artist. As they converse, Narcissus tells Goldmund, "In our student days, I sometimes told you that I thought you were an artist. In those days I thought you might become a poet; in your reading and writing you had a certain dislike for the intangible and the abstract, and a special love for words and sounds that had sensuous poetic qualities, words that appealed to the imagination."[1]

As they converse, Narcissus notes how much he has learned from his former pupil, "I'm beginning to understand what art is. Formerly it seemed to me that, compared to thinking and science, [art] could not be taken altogether seriously. . . . Only now do I realize how many paths there are to knowledge and that the path of the mind is not the only one and perhaps not even the best one. It is my way, of course, and I'll stay on it. But I see that you, on the opposite road, on the road of the senses, have seized the secret of being just as deeply and can express it in a much more lively fashion than most thinkers are able to do." Listening attentively, Goldmund responds, "Now you understand that I can't conceive of thoughts without images."[2] Earlier, Narcissus had affirmed a clear distinction between the two forms of conception: "Thinking and imagining have nothing whatsoever in common. Thinking is done not in images but with concepts and formulae. At the exact point where images stop, philosophy begins."[3]

At this point in Hesse's narrative, it is natural for readers to refer to Jung's personality theory, particularly as conceptualized in the Myers-Briggs Type Indicator. As we have learned, the MBTI sorts people into various personality types, based upon where people prefer to focus their attention (Extraversion or Introversion), the way they prefer to take in information (Sensing or Intuition), the way they prefer to make decisions (Thinking or

1. Hesse, *Narcissus and Goldmund*, 279.
2. Hesse, *Narcissus and Goldmund*, 293.
3. Hesse, *Narcissus and Goldmund*, 279.

Feeling), and how they orient themselves to the external world (Judging or Perceiving). These preferences produce sixteen different kinds of people, interested in different things and drawn to different fields. Each type has its own inherent strengths as well as its likely blind spots.

For Hesse, various interpretations of the artist's relationship with personal experience turn primarily on the opposition of sense and intellect, which are associated with polarities such as darkness and light, mother and father, and sensuality and ascetic control. In *Narcissus and Goldmund*, these polarities are expressed by the German terms *Geist* and *Seele*. *Geist* (both spirit and intellect) ranges from the regulating, paternal force of control to the destructive power of rationalistic culture; its counterpart, *Seele* (both sensuality and soul) is associated with sexuality, debauchery, sense experience, and the mother image or the collective unconscious. In *Narcissus and Goldmund*, integration takes place chiefly through *Seele*.

For Hesse, sexuality—the world of the senses—must be experienced in its wholeness. Sexuality makes possible artistic integration, but it must be wedded to the ordering intellect or else chaos results, which is the lesson of *Narcissus and Goldmund*. Although Hesse experienced *Geist* and thought it indispensable to artistic creation, he nowhere allowed it to triumph in the end.

A reciprocal tension of *Geist* and *Seele*, then, is woven into the fabric of Hesse's narratives. On the way to this union of Goldmund and Narcissus in a heightened self, Hesse's characters often reenact Christian salvation through immersion in sensuality. This search for fulfillment is shown in many ways—in *Demian*, it occurs in Sinclair's final vision at the moment of his death. On occasions where resolution approaches, *Seele* is raised from a psychological to a metaphysical level of existence, from a sensual to a transcendental plane.

In *Narcissus and Goldmund*, the two protagonists are modeled after cultural archetypes: Narcissus represents the patriarchal world order of an anthropocentric culture, whose societal hierarchy is based on male authority, maintained by social and sexual repression, and focused on spiritual values centered on the Christian God the Father residing in heaven. Goldmund, by contrast, is associated with the matriarchal myth of a gynocentric utopia, whose ideal state is characterized by female authority based on social equality and sexual permissiveness and centered in the natural world, which finds its symbolic representation in the pagan Mother Goddess living on earth.

Early memories of Goldmund's mother are passed down to Goldmund by his father and are tainted by paternal resentment and patriarchal prejudice: "She had been a dancer, a wild beautiful woman of noble, though poor birth. . . . But after a few years of domesticated and ordered existence, she had remembered her old tricks and crafts, had started to make trouble and seduce men . . . had acquired the reputation of a witch, and . . . finally disappeared forever."[4] From time immemorial, men have desired women's youthful beauty and associated women with the divine, as Goldmund does. Meanwhile, they often demonized them as wicked sorceresses in league with the devil, as evidenced in the persistent witch hunts throughout the Middle Ages and in puritanical societies. Narcissus encourages Goldmund to reconnect with his own true and undistorted memories of his early years: "You've forgotten your childhood; it cries for you from the depths of your soul. It will make you suffer until you heed it."[5]

It is in the world of his dreams that Goldmund begins to recover his childhood. Enchantingly, these dreams "resurrected not only the beloved past: childhood and mother love, the radiantly golden morning of life, but in them also the future swung, menacing, promising, beckoning, dangerous. At times these dreams, in which mother, Virgin, and mistress all fused into one, seemed horrendous crimes to him afterwards, blasphemies, deadly, unpardonable sins; at other times he found in them nothing but harmony and release . . . but these were mother secrets, they came from her, led to her . . . "[6] In these dreams, oedipal fantasies of maternal love merge with Christian pangs of conscience about sin and damnation, only to crystallize in the image of the mythic Mother Goddess, reaching out to her son and embracing him as lover.

In her double function of mistress and mother, woman embodies for Hesse the libidinal force that represent the *Urgrund*, the primal foundation in which salvation and aesthetic reconciliations are found. We all, Hesse states in his introduction to *Demian*, "come out of the same abyss." In the womb—the matrix of experience—integration is grounded.

Just as Hesse had benefitted from psychotherapy before writing *Demian*, he now has Narcissus fulfil the role of therapeutic guide who encourages Goldmund to trust and follow his deepest dreams. Narcissus might not sanction all of Goldmund's daring dreams, but with his friend's

4. Hesse, *Narcissus and Goldmund*, 56.

5. Hesse, *Narcissus and Goldmund*, 44.

6. Hesse, *Narcissus and Goldmund*, 59–60.

encouragement, Goldmund opens a new door to modern self-understanding. With God, Goldmund becomes co-creator of life on earth: Occasionally he would "dream of swimming fish and flying birds, and each fish or bird was his creature, depended on him, could be guided like a breath, radiated from him like an eye, like a thought, returned to him."[7] In many ways, Goldmund's mellifluous dream imagery, free-floating sexual energies, and wandering spirit antedate the psychedelic consciousness that emerged at the end of the 1960s, propagated by Timothy Leary's slogan: "Turn on, tune in, drop out." A positive aspect of Goldmund's sense of alienation, and intricately linked with it, is his awakening concern for the welfare of all creatures, particularly empathy with the suffering of animals and humans alike.

Another aspect of spirituality found in this novel is Goldmund's fixation on images. In this respect, he is the counterpart of Narcissus, who tells him at the end of his journey through life: "For you, the world (is) made of images, for me of ideas."[8] This distinction further reinforces the difference between their patriarchal and matriarchal worlviews. Narcissus thinks biblically—in the beginning was the Word, and the Word was God. As Goldmund ponders Narcissus's view of reality, he arrives at the opposite end of such cosmogonic mythology—in the beginning was Eros, and Eros was one with the Goddess, whose boundless love created the universe. In this reversal of perspectives, Narcissus's blind faith in God the Father in heaven turns into Goldmund's blind love for the Mother Goddess on earth, who reveals herself visually in all her material abundance—and seeing is believing! In a matriarchal universe, caring for the earth and its wellbeing becomes increasingly central. In addition, the shift from Narcissus's "thought" to Goldmund's "image" anticipates the postmodern turn from the verbal to the visual, from the written word to the symbol.

Looking back at his many loves, Goldmund concludes: playfulness, love, contentment, "pleasure without thought—did not flourish among men, for that one needed women, wandering, freedom, and ever new impressions."[9] Recklessness, abandon, excess, nonconformity—these qualities characterize decadence and depravity, but strangely, also second half of life spirituality, though with different motivation and with vastly different results.

7. Hesse, *Narcissus and Goldmund*, 60.

8. Hesse, *Narcissus and Goldmund*, 279.

9. Hesse, *Narcissus and Goldmund*, 296–97.

DEEPER SPLENDOR

HERMAN HESSE'S MYSTIC SENSIBILITY (INTUITION) IN *SIDDHARTHA*

While the difference between artisans, poets, and thinkers are rather clear and distinct, what about mystics? For Hesse, mystics are "thinkers who cannot detach themselves from images, therefore not thinkers at all. They are secret artists: poets without verse, painters without brushes, musicians without sound. There are highly gifted, noble minds among them, but they are all without exception unhappy."[10]

Hesse's 1922 novel *Siddhartha* deals with the spiritual journey of self-discovery of a man named Siddhartha, who lived in India during the time of the Buddha. In the Sanskrit language, the word Siddhartha, the Buddha's own personal name, is a composite of two words together meaning "one who has found meaning in life." In the novel, Siddhartha leaves his home in search of spiritual enlightenment. Like the historical Buddha, Siddhartha becomes an ascetic wanderer, renouncing all personal possessions. Accompanied by his friend Govinda, Siddhartha meets the Buddha. While Govinda joins the Buddha's order, Siddhartha does not, for unlike the Buddha's followers, Siddhartha believes each individual must seek a unique meaning that cannot be derived from a single teacher or by joining a group. Thus, he resolves to pursue his quest alone.

In large part, Hesse wrote *Siddhartha* to overcome his anxiety and "sickness in life" by immersing himself in Indian philosophy such as expounded in the Upanishads and the Bhagavad Gita. In his attempt to find the wholeness he sought, Hesse lived as a virtual recluse. Following Hindu and Buddhist teaching, he structured his novel on the traditional three stages of life for Hindu males—student (chapters 1–4; focusing on the realm of the spirit), householder (chapters 5–8; focusing on the realm of the senses), and ascetic or homeless *sannyasin* (chapters 9–12; focusing on enlightenment)—as well as on the Buddha's Four Noble Truths (Part One) and the Eightfold Noble Path (Part Two), which together comprise the novel's twelve chapters.

As is true for many Indian seekers, the metaphor of the river is central to Siddhartha's self-understanding. As all water flows toward the ocean, and as water then evaporates into clouds and returns to earth as rain, so one's life experience—connected to *samsara* or transmigration—is likened to flowing water. As Hesse makes obvious, the image of the river is central

10. Hesse, *Narcissus and Goldmund*, 279.

to Siddhartha's spiritual growth and self-understanding, for it is said to embody not only nature but all reality (the Tao).

At one point in the story, Siddhartha comes to a broad river. In order to cross it, he needs the assistance of a ferryman, whom Siddhartha is unable to pay. The generous ferryman predicts that Siddhartha will return some day to compensate him in some way and transports him across free of charge. Reaching a city, Siddhartha is distracted by a beautiful woman named Kamala, who tells him that he must become wealthy to win her affections. Conflicted by her charms, Siddhartha sets aside his disdain for materialistic pursuits and becomes a successful businessperson. As a rich man, Siddhartha becomes Kamala's lover. In midlife, Siddhartha becomes disillusioned with his way of life, acknowledging that it lacks spiritual fulfillment. Renouncing his lifestyle, he returns to the river, committed to remain near its spiritually inspirational influences. While there, he reunites with Vasudeva, the generous ferryman, pursuing a non-materialistic way of life. Through Vasudeva he learns that the river has many voices and has much to teach those who are willing and able to listen. The ferryman is able to point Siddhartha in the right direction (showing him how to find enlightenment within himself), but it is the river that becomes Siddhartha's final instructor, providing knowledge without words.

Some years later, Kamala, now a Buddhist convert, is traveling to see the Buddha with her reluctant young son, when a venomous snake near Siddhartha's river bites her. Upon seeing her, Siddhartha recognizes her and discovers that the boy is his son. After Kamala dies, Siddhartha attempts to befriend the boy, who one day flees altogether. Desperate to find the boy, Siddhartha eventually heeds Vasudeva's advice to let the boy find his own path in life, much as Siddhartha had done in his youth.

Listening to the river with Vasudeva, Siddhartha realizes that all of his experiences, including his own pain and suffering, are part of an interconnected whole in the cycle of nature. After Siddhartha's moment of illumination, Vasudeva retreats into the forest, leaving Siddhartha fulfilled but alone once again. This time, Siddhartha is the ferryman, guiding others toward enlightenment.

Toward the end of his life, Govinda hears about an enlightened ferryman and travels to Siddhartha, not initially recognizing him as his old childhood friend. Govinda asks the now elderly Siddhartha to relate his wisdom and Siddhartha replies that all beliefs are faulty because they only account for part of truth; for every true statement there is an opposite one that is also true, and together they account for the fullness of truth. Siddhartha urges Govinda to identify and love the world in its completeness By way of response, Govinda kisses his friend's forehead, and when he does, Govinda too experiences the enlightened vision of timelessness that Siddhartha had experienced with Vasudeva

In writing *Siddhartha*, Hesse came to the realization that we honor our spiritual mentors—be they the Buddha, Muhammad, Moses, or Jesus Christ—not through devotion to their dogma but by following their example. This teaching is central to the Buddhist Theravada tradition, which holds that the path to enlightenment is a solitary one, and that no person can lead another to self-understanding. Creeds and dogmas can be helpful guides, but each person's spiritual path is unknowable up front. Thus, it is up to each person to discover the way, intuitively and indirectly, from small clues experience provides along the way. When, at the book's end, Govinda asks Siddhartha, "Do you have a doctrine? Is there a belief or some knowledge that guides you, that helps you to live and do what is right?" Siddhartha replies, "I have had thoughts, yes, and insights, now and again . . . Here is one of the thoughts I have found: Wisdom cannot be passed on. Wisdom that a wise man attempts to pass on always sounds like foolishness."[11]

Siddhartha ultimately understands that the essence of enlightenment already exists within each person, and that it is present in the world at all times. Prescriptive paths simply lead people further from themselves and from the wisdom they seek. An indirect approach is more likely to take into account therapeutic resources in the world and is therefore better able to provide the necessary distance from which to apprehend the unity of the world. On his journey, Siddhartha finds that wholeness comes not from mastery of either material or spiritual reality but from finding the common ground between these polarities of existence. The river, with its opposing banks, represents the polarities, and the river itself represents their ideal union. Siddhartha achieves transcendence when he can accept that all is false and true at the same time, that all is simultaneously living and dead, and that all possibilities are present in the universe, ready to reveal themselves to us when we are willing and able to receive them.

As Hesse discovered in the Buddhist Theravada tradition, enlightenment is achieved, not by worshipping the Buddha or the Christ as a god, but rather through yielding, detachment, nonaction, and letting go. As

11. Hesse, *Siddhartha*, 118–19.

Jesus also taught, while the way to blessedness and contentment is through compassion and love, ultimately, bliss is experienced not by knowing or doing but simply by being. In Hesse's novel, an individual's experience—the totality of conscious events of a human life, including sensing, intuiting, thinking, and feeling—is the best way to approach understanding of reality and to attain enlightenment. Such understanding is attained neither through intellectual methods (knowing) nor through physical pleasure (doing), but rather by the entirety of life's experiences—mentally, emotionally, physically, and spiritually. Individually, events are meaningless in themselves, but taken together, they can lead to understanding.

HERMAN HESSE'S INTELLECTUAL SENSIBILITY (THINKING) IN *STEPPENWOLF*

Originally published in Germany in 1927, Hesse's *Steppenwolf* and its protagonist, like *Demian* and *Siddhartha*, reflect the profound crisis in the author's spiritual world during the late 1910s and the 1920s. The novel consists of three different, but overlapping, narrative texts. The book is presented as a manuscript written by the protagonist, a middle-aged man named Harry Haller. The novel opens with a brief statement by an unnamed narrator, the nephew of Haller's landlady, who decides to publish the manuscript under the title, *Harry Haller's Records (For Madmen Only)*.

The narrative begins by introducing Harry, the "Steppenwolf" of the novel's title, a man ill-suited for the world of everyday people. Harry feels himself a fractured self, part respectable human being and part instinctual wolf. He is a critical intellectual, but he despises most other intellectuals; he is a pacifist who is troubled by the rising tide of violence in the world around him. He loves the domestic security of the bourgeois world, yet feels that his own divided personality precludes him from identifying with it. Severely conflicted, he regularly contemplates committing suicide. However, he has the potential to be great, to be one of the "Immortals."

One evening, in his aimless wanderings about the city, he sees, or thinks he sees, a doorway with a sign above it that reads, "Magic Theater—Entrance Not for Everybody." Additional letters reflected on the street spell out "For Madmen Only." Harry cannot open the door, but a sign-bearer advertising the Magic Theater gives Harry a booklet entitled "Treatise on the Steppenwolf." This booklet, cited in full in the novel's text as Harry reads it, addresses Harry by name and strikes him as describing himself precisely.

It speaks of a person who is half man and half wolf who hates the bourgeois lifestyle but who is also at the same time incapable of surrendering himself to the pleasure of the senses.

One evening, Harry accepts a dinner invitation from a professor with whom he is acquainted, but appalled by his host's philistinism and nationalism, he leaves in fury. In a pub he meets a young prostitute, Hermine, who quickly recognizes his desperation. She helps him to enjoy pleasures that previously he had hardly known. Grateful that she has broken through his isolation, he agrees to obey all her commands. Hermine informs Harry that eventually she will make him fall in love with her, after which she will ask him to kill her.

She reconciles him to jazz music by teaching him to dance, and then arranges for him to be introduced to the pleasures of sex by Maria. He also meets, through Hermine, a mysterious saxophonist named Pablo. After attending a lavish masquerade ball, Pablo brings Harry to his metaphorical "magic theater," where he discovers facets of his personality that had long been hidden. Pablo explains to Harry that the goal of the theater is the dissolution of the personality, a goal that can be accomplished only through laughter.

Once inside this theater, Harry goes down a corridor lined with dozens of strange doors, some of which he enters. Each door opens on a new, surreal world. Harry runs from one world, in which men and machines are engrossed in a bloody war, to another, where all the women he has ever wanted are available for him to enjoy. At the climax of the Magic Theater sequence Harry enters a room where he finds Hermine and Pablo's love-spent, naked bodies lying on the floor. Believing that the moment has come to fulfill his promise to kill Hermine, Harry stabs her with a knife that has magically appeared in his pocket.

The classical composer Mozart appears and tells Harry that he has abused the Magic Theater with excessively serious behavior. Mozart explains that life is full of conflict, and that the task Harry must face is to greet these aspects with laughter. Harry's account ends on a note of failure, but also with the realization that he is not, as he thought, composed of two selves, but rather, as he discovered in the Magic Theater, that he consists of multiple identities. According to Hesse, this is true not only in Harry's case but is an inherent condition of all humans. Behind one of the theater's doors, a man closely resembling Pablo teaches Harry that the individual is comprised of innumerable selves that may be reconfigured in varying ways, like chess pieces.

Drawing upon the Eastern ideas of reincarnation and transmigration of the soul, as well as upon the psychoanalytic theories of Carl Jung, in *Steppenwolf* Hesse articulates a highly personal hypothesis of the multifaceted nature of the soul. As he notes in the novel, Haller's "sickness of the soul . . . is not the eccentricity of a single individual, but the sickness of [Hesse's society], the neurosis of that generation to which Haller belongs, a sickness, it seems that by no means attacks the weak and worthless only, but, rather precisely those who are strongest in spirit and richest in gifts."[12] Haller belongs to those who are caught "between two ages, two modes of life, with the consequence that it loses all power to understand itself and has no standard. . . . He belongs to those whose fate it is to live the whole riddle of human destiny heightened to the pitch of a personal torture, a personal hell."[13] This book, as Hesse stated in his 1961 preface, "is not a book of a man despairing, but of a man believing."

Harry registers the instability of human selfhood in terms of a dualism, one that pits two selves against each other. His task, as human, is to discover that what calls itself selfhood is, in the final analysis, a multiplicity of potential and actual personalities. In the Magic Theater, he learns to discover the many possibilities that slumber unacknowledged within him: the austere pacifist can take delight in technological warfare, the ascetic intellectual discovers that he can desire many women. The theater itself owes its magic to the fact that it is a place of irony, of knowing detachment, of experiencing not authentically but in the make-believe of fiction. This, it seems, is the lesson he learns from the Immortals (who consist not only of distinguished past artists such as Mozart and Goethe, but also of Pablo the saxophonist), though he is not yet ready to accept it.

Since the 1960s, when Hesse became a cult figure in America and *Steppenwolf* became a virtual Bible for that era's counterculture, the name "Steppenwolf" has become associated in popular culture with various organizations and establishments, including several Magic Theatre companies and by the American band *Steppenwolf*, whose iconic song, "Born to be Wild," was notably featured in the 1969 film *Easy Rider*. While the drug-induced hallucinations of the Magic Theater proved so attractive to the hippie generation of the late 1960s and early 1970s, unveiling the

12. Hesse, *Steppenwolf*, 22.
13. Hesse, *Steppenwolf*, 22–23.

kaleidoscopic richness of which the human psyche, once liberated from social constraints, is capable, in Hesse's novel we also hear Jungian aspirations toward wholeness, toward a re-integration of the intriguing, mysterious, and multi-faceted human personality. Hermine is a case in point. As a figure, she represents the clash of old and new values. Experientially, she oscillates between being the experienced prostitute who on the one hand knows how to deal with a client who is a frustrated, aging intellectual, and on the other represents a voice from the spiritual universe of the Immortals.

HERMAN HESSE'S *THE GLASS BEAD GAME*

The Glass Bead Game, Hesse's last full-length novel, also published under the title *Magister Ludi* (Latin for "Master of the Game"), was begun in 1931 but published in Switzerland in 1943, after being rejected for publication in Germany due to the author's anti-Fascist views. In 1946, when honoring Hesse in its Award Ceremony Speech, the Swedish Academy acknowledged this novel to be a key to Hesse's winning the Nobel Prize in Literature.

The novel takes place at an unspecified date centuries in the future. The setting is a fictional province of central Europe called Castalia, a region reserved by political decision for the life of the mind. Castalia is home to an austere order of intellectuals with a twofold mission: to run boarding schools, and to cultivate and play the Glass Bead Game, whose exact nature remains elusive. Playing the game requires years of hard study of music, mathematics, and cultural history. The game is essentially an abstract synthesis of all arts and sciences.

The novel follows the life of Joseph Knecht, whose surname means "servant," and is a cognate with the English word "knight." The plot chronicles Knecht's education as a youth, his decision to join the order, his mastery of the Game, and his advancement in the order's hierarchy to eventually become Magister Ludi, the executive officer of the Castalian Order's game administrators. As the narrative progresses, Knecht begins to question his loyalty to the order, gradually coming to doubt that the intellectually gifted have a right to withdraw from life's big problems. His struggle precipitates a personal crisis, which, according to his personal views regarding spiritual awakening, leads him to resign as Magister Ludi and ask to leave the order, ostensibly to become of value and service to the larger culture.

The heads of the order deny his request, but Knecht departs Castalia anyway, initially taking a job as a tutor to his childhood friend Designori's energetic and strong-willed son, Tito. Only a few days later, the story ends abruptly with Knecht drowning in a mountain lake while attempting to follow Tito on a swim for which Knecht is unfit.

While the novel itself is worth reading, in my estimation its greatest value lies in the three stories labeled "Three Lives" that comprise the final section of the book. These are presented as earlier exercises by Knecht, when as a student in Castalia he was asked to imagine his life reincarnated at various places and times in past history. The first tells of a pagan rainmaker named Knecht who lived long ago, "when women ruled." Eventually Knecht's powers as shaman fail to summon rain, and he offers himself as a sacrifice for the good of the tribe. The second is based on the life of an early Christian hermit named Josephus, who acquires a reputation for piety but is inwardly troubled by self-contempt. He seeks a confessor, only to find that same confessor had been seeking him. The final story concerns the life of an Indian prince named Dasa, wrongfully displaced as heir to a kingdom by his half-brother. While working as a herdsman, Dasa encounters a yogi in meditation in the forest. He wishes to experience the same tranquility as the yogi, but is unable to stay. He later meets and marries a beautiful young woman, only to be cuckolded by his half-brother, now the Rajah. In cold fury, he kills his half-brother and finds himself once again in the forest with the old yogi, who guides him on the spiritual path and out of the world of illusion.

Hesse originally intended to write a book featuring several different lives of the same person as he is reincarnated. Instead, he focused on a story set in the future and placed the three shorter stories by Knecht at the end of the novel. Together, the three lives and the narrative of Knecht as Magister Ludi develop the four basic psychic functions of Jungian analytical psychology: sensation (rainmaker), intuition (Indian yogi), feeling (father confessor), and thinking (Magister Ludi).

While we might artificially categorize people as uniquely aesthetic, artistic, philosophic, and mystical—with overlap in most cases, since few people are one-dimensional—we must note that for Hesse, none is inherently higher spiritually than another. One can be deeply spiritual and spiritually fulfilled as artist, poet, thinker, or mystic. For this reason, the distinction frequently made between people in their spiritual first or second half of lives appears inadequate, since it seems evident that people can be fulfilled spiritually in first half of life spirituality (that is, living securely under rules and with clear boundary markers—ways of living and thinking described as precritical or as one's first naiveté) as authentically as in second half of life spirituality (that is, living maturely without rules or clear boundary markers—ways of living and thinking described as postcritical or as one's second naiveté). However, because second half of life seekers are willing to take risks and are more fully open to ambiguity and mystery, they tend to be less assertive, combative, dogmatic, and possessive and more open to change, qualities reflecting a higher and fuller dimension of spirituality.

QUESTIONS FOR DISCUSSION AND REFLECTION

In addition to the questions listed at the end of the preface, answer the following questions, writing your answers in a journal. If you are in a group study, be prepared to share your answers with those in the group.

1. Explain the value and use of the "lyrical novel" for analyzing the self and the meaning of personal identity.

2. After reading and reflecting on the segment on Hermann Hesse's biography, what did you learn about personality?

3. After reading and reflecting on the segment on *Narcissus and Goldmund*, what did you learn about the roles of *Geist* and *Seele* in healthy spirituality?

4. What role does *anima* play in Goldmund's search for psychic integration?

5. What role do dreams play in Golmund's search for psychic integration?

6. Explain the role of the "artist" as spiritual type in *Narcissus and Goldmund*.

7. Explain the role of the "mystic" as spiritual type in *Siddhartha*.

8. After reading and reflecting on the segment on *Siddhartha*, what did you learn about spiritual enlightenment?

9. Explain the role of the "intellectual" as spiritual type in *Steppenwolf*.

10. After reading and reflecting on the segment on *Steppenwolf*, what did you learn about the individual self?

11. After reading and reflecting on the segment on *The Glass Bead Game*, what did you learn about the spiritual journey?

Chapter 4

Fyodor Dostoevsky's
The Brothers Karamazov

THERE IS PROBABLY NO writer since the Renaissance who has made a deeper impression on contemporary imagination and creativity than Fyodor Dostoevsky (1821–1881), with the possible exception of his great contemporary, Leo Tolstoy. As I wrote in *Deep Splendor*, "Whenever the topic of spirituality (or religion) and modern literature arises, one of the first authors that comes to mind—perhaps the first—is the great Russian novelist Fyodor Dostoevsky. Unquestionably, the novel that best exhibits the connection between his literary artistry and his spiritual impulse is *The Brothers Karamazov*."[1] On that earlier occasion, however, I bypassed Dostoevsky's great novel, focusing instead on his earlier existentialist novella, *Notes from Underground*. Happily, in our study on spirituality, psychology, and modern literature, we turn our attention to *The Brothers Karamazov*, a work acclaimed as one of the supreme achievements in world literature. Dostoevsky's passionate philosophical novel, dealing with problems of faith, doubt, and reason, enters deeply into questions of God, free will, and morality. Like *Notes from Underground*, this novel is set in the context of a modernizing Russia but also against a backdrop of personal tragedy. While writing *The Brothers Karamazov*, Dostoevsky's three-year-old son Alyosha died of epilepsy, a condition inherited from his father. Hence, Dostoevsky named the book's hero Alyosha, imbuing him with qualities that he most admired.

---

1. Vande Kappelle, *Deep Splendor*, 150.

Dostoevsky's masterpiece, *The Brothers Karamazov* has influenced a wide variety of individuals since its publication in 1880. Admirers include scientists Albert Einstein and Sigmund Freud, philosophers Ludwig Wittgenstein, Martin Heidegger, and Jean-Paul Sartre, and writers Franz Kafka, Virginia Woolf, Albert Camus, Aldous Huxley, C. P. Snow, William Faulkner, W. Somerset Maugham, and Hermann Hesse.

Einstein praised the novel, finding it in 1919 to represent the summit of all literature. Agreeing with that assessment, Freud called it "the most magnificent novel ever written." Kafka likewise felt indebted to Dostoevsky and *The Brothers Karamazov* for their influence on his own work, particularly in the intergenerational father-son conflict. Nobel Prize laureate William Faulkner reread the book regularly, claiming it as his greatest literary inspiration next to Shakespeare and the Bible. He once wrote that he felt American literature had produced nothing comparable to Dostoevsky's novel. Nobel-Prize-winning author Hermann Hesse viewed Dostoevsky as not a "poet" but as a "prophet."

Dostoevsky lived in Russia in the mid-nineteenth century, a particularly tumultuous time in the country's long and chaotic history. The agitation, despair, and pride of the time worked their way into much of Dostoevsky's prose. Thus, understanding Dostoevsky's context and personal life is extremely valuable in interpreting his work. When Dostoevsky was born in 1821, Russia saw a bright future ahead. In 1812, Napoleon had tried to invade the massive country, but Russia had repelled the attack. Around the world, Napoleon was viewed as a tyrant, and Russia was admired and cheered for having halted such a dangerous force. Alexander I was called the "savior of Europe." During the Industrial Revolution, Russia was on the verge of Westernizing and becoming more technologically advanced, and its people were becoming increasingly progressive. It was truly an exciting time for Russian people, especially in the cities. In 1825, there was a revolt later named "The Decembrist Revolt," which was intended to install a constitutional monarchy (with more protections than before), but Nicholas I became more protective of his government. Instead of becoming more liberal, the country adopted the slogan "Autocracy, Orthodoxy, Nationality." Russia slid back into its traditions and moved away from Westernization. In rural areas, however, many remained sympathetic to revolutionary influences, including anarchy and nihilism.

In the 1860s, nihilists rose to prominence. After being stymied when they appealed to the government for reform, they decided to take a grassroots approach and go straight to the people. The "Narodnik Movement," as it was called, was not harmless. The nihilists in the Narodnik Movement committed acts of terrorism and even assassination. Most famously, they carried out the assassination of Alexander II in 1881, the year Dostoevsky died.

Russia's battles during the nineteenth century were not restricted to its internal affairs. Russia fought several wars during this time. In 1853, Turkey declared war on Russia, beginning the Crimean War. In 1875, Russia clashed with the Ottoman empire because Russia wanted to extradite the Balkan Christians from their Ottoman rulers. In 1877, just four years before Dostoevsky's death, the Ottoman empire and Russia went to war. This was the second time during the nineteenth century that Christian Russia had gone to war with a nation (or empire) of a different faith. It is no wonder, then, that Russians took their religion as seriously as their nationalism.

Russia's political turmoil, its religious battles, and its constantly shifting world status kept its citizens from gaining a sense of stability. Its material strife and its ideological crises meant that no aspect of life was safe from constant challenges. It is this Russia about which Dostoevsky wrote, and Russia's struggles were his struggles. His works reflect how individuals can survive and comprehend life in a troubled nation. *The Brothers Karamazov*, a long and complex novel, engages with his contemporary Russian experience even while it speaks beyond his time and place.

Raised in a pious Russian orthodox family, Dostoevsky remained a religious thinker throughout his life. Educated as an engineer but in love with French and Russian literature, in 1844 Dostoevsky submitted his novel, *Poor Folk*, for publication in a prestigious journal. The editor gave it to the famous critic Belinsky for review. Reluctantly agreeing to read the literary work of an engineer, Belinsky became engrossed in its artistry, going to Dostoevsky's apartment at 4:00 a.m. to awaken the young man with the declaration that he was the future genius of Russia.

Shortly after Dostoevsky's auspicious beginnings, Belinsky hurt the young man deeply by rejecting his next manuscript. Disillusioned, the author drifted into a revolutionary circle of liberal thinkers, temporarily setting aside his religious views and observances. His radical political views led to his arrest in April 1849. In December of that year he was led, together with his fellow liberals, to a firing squad, only to be granted a last minute stay of execution. In exchange, the young writer served four years in a Siberian prison camp, followed by four years in the army. It is hardly accidental that many of his future novels would describe the last hours of a person about to die.

During this time his faith in Christ was revived, and, like the Russian people, actually sustained and strengthened through long periods of suffering. In the following years, Dostoevsky worked as a journalist, publishing and editing several magazines. He began to travel around western Europe, intrigued by progressive European ideas. In spite of the occasional moments of tranquility and his ecstatic commitment to Christ, the picture we have of Dostoevsky as he returned to Russia at the close of the 1850s is that of a troubled, questing spirit, open to intense momentary mystical experiences, who became progressively convinced of the spiritual treasures in the soul of ordinary Russian people and of the damage done to the Russian spirit by Westernization.

In his later years, while accepting the need to take the best of Western civilization, he called for a return to Russian values. Europe, he believed, had long ago sold its soul to the principle of abstract rationalism, legalism, and individualism, which the Catholic Church had inherited from Rome and passed on to Protestantism and then to socialism, which inevitably became atheistic. Russian Orthodoxy, on the other hand, with its ideals of universality and reconciliation, and its abilities to unite diverse peoples in a grand synthesis, had preserved its sense of organic community in its conception of "*sobernost*" (spiritual oneness). There is no doubt that the development of a coherent worldview along these lines helped to stabilize Dostoevsky's intellectual and emotional life and to restore his respectability in Russian high society. In later years, he gained not only the admiration of Russia's political and religious leadership, but also of the general populace.

Dostoevsky spent nearly three years writing *The Brothers Karamazov*, which was published as a serial between 1879 and 1880. Dostoevsky died less than four months after its publication. His funeral in 1881, conducted at Alexander Nevsky Monastery in St. Petersburg, was attended by over thirty thousand people.

THE BROTHERS KARAMAZOV: PLOT AND RESPONSE

While it is natural to read *The Brothers Karamazov* as a philosophical or theological treatise, in reality it is neither. The book is a novel, consisting of a tense dramatic plot constructed around an enigmatic crime. Into this plot Dostoevsky inserted religious-philosophic materials. In *The Brothers*

Karamazov, Dostoevsky joins a religious mystery play with a crime novel to form one of the most captivating and popular works of Russian literature.

The Brothers Karamazov is a family tragedy centered on a father and his sons. Fyodor, the eldest Karamazov, has three sons: Dmitri, Ivan, and Alexey (Alyosha). Ivan and Alyosha have the same mother, but Dmitri, the oldest, has a different mother. Fyodor is a greedy landowner, a bawdy lecher, and a neglectful father. Hence, the Karamazov brothers end up growing into young men under the care of various other people. However, they all have returned home to visit their father, and it is the first time they all have been together for quite some time.

At the beginning of the novel, Dmitri, now a twenty-eight-year-old soldier, has a dispute with Fyodor over his inheritance, and twenty-year-old Alyosha, who is living in a monastery, suggests that they see Father Zossima, Alyosha's mentor. Alyosha believes that the wise old man can settle the dispute peacefully. Father Zossima is patient and kind, but Fyodor and Dmitri end up quarreling anyway. After Fyodor drives the men to frustration, they leave the monastery separately, and Alyosha worries about their family's future. Dmitri promised to marry a girl named Katerina, who lent him three thousand rubles, but instead of paying it back, he spent it on a beautiful young woman named Grushenka. He wants to run away with Grushenka, but he feels that he needs to pay Katerina back before he can do so. This explains why he is so interested in getting the money from Fyodor. Alyosha talks to Dmitri, who confesses his complicated situation with women and money. As Dmitri struggles with his own passion and lust, Alyosha sees the decent side of his brother, even as he sees his own weaknesses.

Many years earlier, Fyodor had fathered a fourth son with a retarded servant girl named Lizaveta Smerdyashchaya. The girl died as she gave birth to the baby, named Smerdyakov after his mother, an epileptic boy who was taken in by Grigory and Marfa, Fyodor's servants. Fyodor never treats the child, Smerdyakov, as a son, but rather as a servant, and Smerdyakov develops a strange and malicious personality. Despite the limitations of his upbringing, however, Smerdyakov is not stupid. He enjoys nothing more than listening to Ivan discuss philosophy, and in his own conversations, he frequently invokes many of Ivan's ideas—specifically that the soul is not immortal, and that therefore morality does not exist and the categories of good and evil are irrelevant to human experience.

After the humiliating scene in the monastery, Dmitri sends Alyosha as an emissary to break off Dmitri's engagement with Katerina. Alyosha then argues about religion with Ivan in front of their smirking father. Alyosha also witnesses another confrontation between Dmitri and Fyodor over Grushenka, in the course of which Dmitri throws his father to the ground and threatens to kill him. The next day, Alyosha visits Katerina. To his surprise, Ivan is with Katerina, and Alyosha immediately perceives that Ivan and Katerina are in love. Alyosha tries to convince them that they should act on their love for one another, but they are both too proud and cold to listen. Meanwhile, Alyosha meets Ivan at a restaurant, and Ivan explains to him the source of his religious doubt. In a chapter titled "Rebellion" (5.4), Ivan proclaims that he rejects the world that God has created because it is built on a foundation of suffering. Ivan cannot reconcile the idea of a loving God with the needless suffering of innocent people, particularly children. Any God that would allow such suffering, he says, does not love humanity.

In perhaps the most famous chapter in the novel, "The Grand Inquisitor" (5.5), Ivan recites a poem he has written called "The Grand Inquisitor," in which he accuses Christ of placing an intolerable burden upon humanity by guaranteeing that people have free will and the ability to choose whether to believe in God. Set in the time of the Spanish Inquisition, Jesus makes his return to earth. Having performed a number of acts that echo the gospel narrative, Jesus finds himself in the Inquisitor's cell, where the latter proceeds to justify his procedure at great length. "Why, then, art Thou come to hinder us? For Thou hast come to hinder us, and Thou knowest that. . . . We are not working with Thee but with him [Satan]. . . . We took from him what Thou didst reject with scorn, that last gift he offered Thee, showing Thee all the kingdoms of the earth. We took from him Rome and the sword of Caesar, and proclaimed ourselves sole rulers of the earth. . . . We shall triumph and shall be Caesars, and then we shall plan the universal happiness of man."[2] The Church, offering mystery, miracle, and authority, has replaced Christ, the Inquisitor declares. Christ has no right to come back and interfere. The Grand Inquisitor claims to know humankind far better than Christ knows us. The old man claims that human creatures are weak: the masses require and always worship those who dominate them. It is not hard to understand why Dostoevsky's book is considered prophetic for future centuries. Dostoevsky sensed, to a degree

---

2. Dostoyevsky, *Brothers Karamazov*, 259, 267.

virtually unparalleled among his peers, the threats of totalitarianism in later times.

In Dostoevsky's account, Christ makes no answer, but kisses the aged Inquisitor and is allowed to leave. Alyosha, after hearing the story, goes to Ivan and kisses him softly on the lips. Ivan shouts with delight, "Plagiarism!" The brothers part with mutual affection and respect. That evening, Alyosha returns to the monastery, where the frail Zossima is now on his deathbed. Alyosha arrives just in time to hear Zossima's final lesson, which emphasizes the importance of love and forgiveness in all human affairs. Zossima dies stretching his arms out before him, as though to embrace the world.

Many of the monks are optimistic that Zossima's death will be accompanied by a miracle, but no miracle takes place. If anything, Zossima's corpse begins to stink more quickly than might have been expected, which is taken by Zossima's critics to mean that he was corrupt and unreliable in life. Sickened by the injustice of seeing the wise and loving Zossima humiliated after his death, Alyosha allows his friend Rakitin to take him to see Grushenka. Although Rakitin and Grushenka hope to corrupt Alyosha, just the opposite happens, and a bond of sympathy and understanding springs up between Grushenka and Alyosha. Their friendship renews Alyosha's faith, and Alyosha helps Grushenka to begin her own spiritual redemption. That night, Alyosha has a dream in which Zossima tells him that he has done a good deed in helping Grushenka. This dream further strengthens Alyosha's love and resolve, and he goes outside to kiss the ground, showing his reverence for nature and natural goodness.

Meanwhile, Dmitri has spent two days unsuccessfully trying to raise the money to pay Katerina the three thousand rubles he owes her. No one will lend him the money, and he has nothing to sell. Eventually, he goes to Grushenka's house, and not finding her there, he becomes convinced that she has gone to be with Fyodor. He rushes to Fyodor's house, but Grushenka is not there. While on the premises, Dmitri strikes Fyodor's servant, Grigory, leaving him bloody and unconscious. Then he flees. He returns to Grushenka's house, and learns she has gone to rejoin a lover who abandoned her several years ago. Dmitri now decides that his only course of action is to kill himself. However, he decides to see Grushenka one last time before he does so.

A few minutes later, Dmitri strides into a shop with his shirt bloody and a large wad of cash in his hand. He buys food and wine, and goes to see Grushenka and her lover. When Grushenka sees the two men together, she realizes that she really loves Dmitri. Dmitri locks the other man in a closet, and Dmitri and Grushenka begin to plan their wedding. However, the police suddenly burst in and arrest Dmitri, accusing him of the murder of his father, who has been found dead. Due to incriminating evidence against Dmitri, including the money found in his possession, he is apprehended. Dmitri claims that the money was what he had left after spending half of the three thousand rubles he stole from Katerina, but no one believes him.

In the interim, Alyosha befriends some of the local schoolboys. He meets a dying boy named Ilyusha, and arranges for the other boys to come visit him every day. Alyosha helps Ilyusha's family as the young boy nears death, and Alyosha is universally adored by all the schoolchildren, who look to him for guidance.

When Ivan talks to Smerdyakov about Fyodor's death, Smerdyakov confesses that he, and not Dmitri, committed the murder. Nevertheless, Smerdyakov tells Ivan that he too is implicated in the crime because the philosophical lessons Smerdyakov learned from him regarding the impossibility of evil in a world without a God made Smerdyakov capable of committing murder. This statement consumes Ivan with guilt. After returning home, he suffers a nervous breakdown in which he envisions a devil relentlessly taunting him. However, the apparition vanishes when Alyosha arrives with the news that Smerdyakov has hung himself.

At the trial, Dmitri's case seems to be going well until Ivan is called upon to testify. Obsessed with remorse, Ivan madly asserts that he himself is guilty of the murder, throwing the courtroom into confusion. To clear Ivan's name, Katerina leaps up and shows a letter she received from Dmitri in which he wrote that he was afraid he might one day murder his father. Even after the letter is read, most of the people in the courtroom are convinced of Dmitri's innocence. However, the peasants on the jury find him guilty, and he is taken back to prison to await exile in Siberia.

After the trial, Katerina takes Ivan to her house, where she plans to nurse him through his illness. She and Dmitri forgive one another, and she arranges for Dmitri to escape from prison and flee to America with Grushenka. Meanwhile, Alyosha's friend Ilyusha dies, and Alyosha gives a speech to the pupils at his funeral. In plain language, he says that they must all remember the love they feel for one another and treasure their memories of one another. The students give Alyosha a rousing cheer.

EVOLUTION OF *THE BROTHERS KARAMAZOV*

In 1877, Dostoevsky informed his readers that he wanted to occupy himself with a new novel, an "artistic work" that evolved significantly in conception over the next three years. Initially, he had in mind a "children theme." As he wrote to V. V. Mikhailov in March 1878, "I have planned and soon will begin a large novel in which, among other things, children will play a large part."

Two profound thinkers entered Dostoevsky's life at this period, whose influence determined his religious conception. These were Vladimir Solovyov and Nikolai Fyodorov. Solovyov, proclaiming a doctrine of Sophia (Divine Wisdom), inspired Dostoevsky through his view regarding the mystical transfiguration of the world. Solovyov spoke of Mother Earth as a mystical agent that could bring about world harmony. Solovyov's teachings influence Dostoevsky's conception of Father Zossima. In 1877, Solovyov delivered an inspired speech to the Society of the Friends of Russian Literature in which he attacked Western civilization for culminating its development by affirming the "atheistic individual." He believed that Russia's historic mission, religious in nature, was to counter this trend through the principle of "God-manhood," understood as requiring both faith in God and in humanity. This teaching clearly inspired *The Brothers Karamazov*. In fact, a number of Solovyov's ideas inspired Dostoevsky's characterization of Ivan Karamazov, including the power of his formal logic and rational ethic, with its combination of social utopia and religious philosophy. In Dostoevsky's novel, it is Ivan who expounds the notion of theocracy, on which Solovyov was working at that time.

Another individual who influenced Dostoevsky was Nikolai Fyodorov, who spoke of eliminating political conflict and social enmity by creating a classless society. Only a united family—children joining parents, and conservatives supporting progressives—could accomplish Christ's work on earth. Christ, by his own resurrection, had shown the way, Fyodorov argued. If humans joined together in solidarity, using science and technology for the common good, then God's new heaven and new earth would emerge. According to Fyodorov, if humans could unite in love, the world would not end in destruction, as prophesized in the Bible, for there would be no need of a Final Judgment. Freed from disaster, society would be transformed into the kingdom of God on earth, the culmination of the "God-manhood" process.

Significantly, at the heart of *The Brothers Karamazov* stands a parricide: Fyodor Karamazov is despised and hated by his sons. The crime,
whose responsibility falls not only on Smerdyakov and Dmitri but indirectly on Ivan and Alyosha as well, becomes a symbol of humanity's disuni-
ty and fragmentation. Creating a narrative to the contrary, Dostoevsky
leads readers to affirm the religious significance of life: kinship of spirit
(Alyosha and Zossima) is stronger than kinship of blood; resurrection love
is greater than hatred and revenge. In Alyosha's life and ministry readers
see Fyodorov's "God-manhood" doctrine at work. Instead of becoming a
monk, Alyosha leaves the monastery for the world, laying the foundation
for future human solidarity in his speech at Ilyusha's grave. Like Fyodorov,
Dostoevsky believes in a literal, personal resurrection of individuals, not
solely in the afterlife, but here and now on earth. Under Fyodorov's influence, Dostoevsky developed the theme of parricide as the ultimate expression of social tragedy.

Dostoyevsky's work on the novel was interrupted by the tragic death
in 1878 of his three-year-old son Alyosha. In *The Brothers Karamazov*,
Dostoevsky gives the dead boy's name to the youngest of the Karamazov
brothers, transferring his hopes and dreams into the novel's young hero. At
the novel's outset, the narrator tells us that *The Brothers Karamazov* is only
preliminary to a greater story. This greater story is likely a book Dostoevsky
planned, called *The Life of a Great Sinner*, which was to trace Alyosha's path
through sin and despair to final redemption. The book was intended to
exhibit Dostoevsky's belief that only by passing through the dark night of
the soul and enduring suffering could individuals come into God's grace
and become fully human.

In 1881, the year after publishing *The Brothers Karamazov*, Dostoevsky
was full of far-reaching plans. These included writing the second part of
Karamazov. In it, the former characters would reappear, but now twenty
years later, almost in the contemporary period. The main hero would be
Alyosha. However, Dostoevsky's health, for some years diminished by
emphysema, took a turn for the worse. On January 26, suffering from internal bleeding, Dostoevsky lost consciousness. Two days later, having recov-
ered, he informed his wife that death was imminent. Unable to stop his
hemorrhaging, a doctor pronounced him dead later that night. Dostoevsky's
funeral turned into an historic event—thirty thousand people accompanied his coffin, seventy-two delegations carried wreaths, and fifteen choirs

took part in the ceremony. Dostoevsky's death was experienced by every Russian as a universal loss.

THE LEGEND OF THE GRAND INQUISITOR

As is well known, Dostoyevsky was both a philosopher and a philosopher's problem, for his principal characters do not necessarily represent Dostoyevsky's point of view. However, it would be going too far to suggest that Dostoevsky never gives us a hint of his own views. As he indicated, the words of Father Zossima in "The Russian Monk" (2.6) come very close to his own beliefs. In *The Brothers Karamazov*, Dostoevsky's response to Ivan's atheistic stance, as stated in the chapters entitled "Rebellion" (5.4) and "The Grand Inquisitor," is found not so much in the words of any character as in the actual events of the novel.

In his legend, Dostoevsky portrays the Inquisitor with supreme skill. He is not a vulgar atheist or a petty sadist. Rather he is a majestic and tragic figure, an old cardinal who has given up his life to austerity in the service of Christ and who suddenly, in his last years, has lost his faith. A wise old man, an ascetic and a philanthropist, he is conceived by Dostoevsky as one who speaks against Christ in the name of Christ. He presents himself as Christ's disciple, continuing Christ's work. Depicted as an antichrist, he is more a false Christ than an antichrist. Rejecting the commandment of love for God, he has become a fanatic of the precept of love of neighbor. However, he turns atheistic love into hatred. Having lost faith in God, the Inquisitor also loses faith in humanity, for these two faiths are indivisible. Rejecting the spiritual aspect of human nature, he is transformed into a pitiable, sadistic despot, bent on establishing universal happiness through punishment and fear.

Ivan declares that without faith in God and in immortality, it is impossible to love humanity. The Grand Inquisitor proves this true; he begins with compassion and love for others but ends by transforming humans into subservient creatures. In order to make humans happy, he removes from them faith, courage, and freedom, aspects essential to their humanity.

The "Legend of the Grand Inquisitor" contains a "proof by the contrary." The Inquisitor reproaches Christ for having imposed an intolerable burden upon humans, having given them freedom while holding them to impossible standards. According to the Inquisitor, it is he and not Christ who is the Savior: he has loved human beings and fed them, caring for their needs by enslaving them and turning them into a herd. In writing this legend, Dostoevsky's point is that only Christ can meet human needs, for only Christ understands the relation between spirituality and freedom. The true and ultimate love of humanity is not a human but God, who gave His Son for the salvation of the world. The Christ of Dostoevsky is not only the Savior and the Redeemer, but also the sole Emancipator of humanity.

In his segment on the Grand Inquisitor, Dostoevsky includes powerful and irrefutable arguments against the Christian faith: the first, that a God who permits severe human suffering is unworthy of worship; the second, that Christ fundamentally overestimated the spiritual resources of the human race and the ability of human beings to act as morally free agents. Dostoevsky was aware of the strength of these arguments, but as he relates later on, the source of the Christian life is not the atheist's abstract love for humanity, but rather the active love that comes to believers from beyond the natural world. For Dostoevsky, if humans view the world with agape love, they will come to love all things, and in so doing, comprehend the divine mystery more every day.

As Nicholas Berdyaev pointed out, it is noteworthy that Dostoevsky's powerful vindication of Christ should be placed into the mouth of the atheist Ivan Karamazov. In the theological chapters, while it is never clear which side the speaker is on and on which side the writer, Dostoevsky's approach is evident: readers must decide. Dostoevsky wrote in such a way that he expected his readers to interpret and understand for themselves. Valuing freedom, he treats ambiguously matters related to choice.

While writing *The Brothers Karamazov*, Dostoevsky had been reading the writings of the Protestant Reformer Martin Luther. In his segment on the Grand Inquisitor, Dostoevsky may have used the opposition between the Inquisitor and Jesus as a foil for two major interpretations of Christianity: the Roman Catholic interpretation (represented by the Inquisitor), and the Protestant interpretation (the view imputed to the silent figure of Christ). On this reading of Ivan's position, the Roman Catholic ideal is that of achieving happiness and well-being for all, whereas the Protestant ideal makes individual freedom and dignity its central aims. The highest aim of Catholics, according to Ivan's legend, is the goal of achieving peace and happiness for all in a universal (catholic) theocratic Christendom. Dostoevsky regarded French socialism, which had strongly influenced the 1840s reformers in Russia, as merely an extension of this old Catholic ideal.

At the same time, Christianity had always valued the ideal of human freedom and dignity. This ideal of autonomy, basically a Pauline doctrine, was made central to Protestantism through Luther's "religious individualism," with its emphasis on the inner condition of faith and on the role of personal conscience in reading and interpreting scripture. The glorification of freedom that the Grand Inquisitor attributes to Christ is in line with the Protestant emphasis on the individual. In the sixteenth century, Luther abolished the clerical priesthood and denied the existence of miracles in the contemporary world. As the Inquisitor notes, however, this demand for autonomy places an overwhelming burden on people. In Protestantism, individuals must find faith in the solitude of their own hearts, without any worldly intermediaries or supports. Since only a small elect can live without external aid, the harsh demands of Protestantism mean that only an elect will achieve salvation.

When reading Dostoevsky's Grand Inquisitor story, it is important to keep in mind that this is Ivan's story, and that it presupposes Ivan's extreme polarized, "either-or" way of thinking. Both the Inquisitor and the figure of Christ in the story represent aspects of Ivan's ideals and aspirations. The Grand Inquisitor, like Ivan, is an atheist who claims to love humanity, and, like the 1860s radicals, dreams of achieving paradise on earth through a total reworking of human society on rational principles. However, as in the case with Ivan, the Inquisitor's claim to humanitarian love merely mask his deep contempt for the people.

The glorification of freedom and dignity attributed to Christ also reflects Ivan's deepest ideals. These aims, though imputed to Christ, in fact originate not so much from the gospels as from Luther's religious individualism. The picture of Christ in the story clearly reflects Ivan's Protestant-humanistic reading rather than Dostoevsky's own understanding of Christ. This should be clear from the fact that the words and deeds attributed to Christ are often wrong and at times blasphemous. It is claimed, for example, that Jesus rejected miracle, mystery, and authority, yet it was not Jesus but Luther who rejected miracle and authority. It should be clear, then, that the Grand Inquisitor story sets up an opposition not between Catholicism and Protestantism, or between secular reformism and traditional Christianity, but rather between two aspects of Ivan's anguished longings and ideals. For Ivan, it appears that the ideals of happiness and freedom are inconsistent with one another. Either we can follow the Catholic dream of happiness and peace for all in a vast authoritarian state, or we can accept the Protestant demand of individual freedom and responsibility without ecclesiastical assistance.

Ivan's story presents a harsh indictment of Christianity. As we might expect, Alyosha is unable to see through Ivan's dualism. Therefore he mimics Christ's kiss, not realizing how trivial that makes Christ look. However, on one point Alyosha's hunch is right. He correctly sees that Ivan has laid out only the tenets of the Western form of Christianity. "That's not the idea of the Orthodox Church," he exclaims. "That's Rome."[3] In "The Russian Monk," Dostoevsky tries to respond to Ivan's dilemma by working out an alternative understanding of the significance of Christianity—that of the Eastern Orthodox Church.

The Brothers Karamazov, Dostoevsky once wrote, is an answer to atheism. His book resulted from what he called "the crucible of doubt," for his own faith derived its strength from having passed through atheism and having come out a believer. Philosophically, Dostoevsky was not content simply to say what was wrong with Ivan's stance—indeed, he thought that, within Ivan's rationalist worldview, his views were "irrefutable." Instead, Dostoevsky demonstrated the inadequacy of Ivan's stance by describing its destructive existential implications in the actions and interactions of the characters throughout the novel as a whole.

PERSONALITY AND SPIRITUALITY IN *THE BROTHERS KARAMAZOV*

In *The Brothers Karamazov*, Dostoevsky created the Karamazov family, whose lives, passions, ideas, and personalities vividly embodied the creative imagination not only of the nineteenth century but also of centuries to come. As we noted in Hermann Hesse's characterization, it is possible to divide people practically into four ways of functioning, with talents and inclinations typical of artisans, poets, thinkers, and mystics. In his principal novels, Hesse's characters are artists (Demian and Narcissus) mystics (Siddhartha), intellectuals (Steppenwolf and Goldmund), and feelers (Joseph Knecht), living in the liminalities of life, caught in the dichotomy of darkness and light, nature and supernature.

Though Dostoevsky predated Hesse by over a half century, like Hesse's characters, the three legitimate Karamazov brothers uncannily reflect the basic psychic functions of Jungian analytical psychology—sensation

3. Dostoyevsky, *Brothers Karamazov*, 270.

(Dmitri is like his father: coarse, passionate, and intemperate); feeling (Alyosha, a sensate feeler, is kind, gentle, loving, and wise); and thinking (Ivan, an intuitive thinker, is acutely logical and demands a rational explanation for everything that happens; as a result, he is plagued by religious doubt and oscillates between outright atheism and belief in a malevolent God). The fourth son, Smerdyakov, half-brother to the other three, is malicious and mean-tempered.

As I suggested earlier, perhaps the best explanation for the psychological similarities in characterization between Dostoevsky and Hesse and their correspondence with Jungian analytical psychology is the familiarity of all three with typological theories based on the classic Greek theory of the four temperaments: Sanguine (sensual or artistic type), Melancholic (compassionate feeling type), Phlegmatic (intellectual or philosophic type), and Choleric (mystical intuitive type).

While we might categorize people as uniquely sensual, intuitive, intellectual, or compassionate, few people are one-dimensional. Despite their psychic differences, the four brothers are all Karamazovs. The father is a man of many passions and weaknesses, and like their fathers biologically, they all suffer from various splits in their personalities. Alyosha, cast in the mold of sainthood, is childlike, naïve, and temperamentally complex. Dmitri is impulsive and can be as chaotic as his father, but he functions, generally, on a higher level than his parent. While Ivan represents the intellectual element in the family, in many respects he too is a divided man. An atheist compelled to admit the existence of God, or at least of a God of his own making, he wavers between intellectual honesty and moral nihilism. Smerdyakov, the illegitimate degenerate, kills his father in the final tragedy.

On a spiritual and psychological level, *The Brothers Karamazov* is a story about the struggle between good and evil. Dostoevsky believed that the capacities for both good and evil are fundamental to human existence. He had little patience with utopian reformers who thought that humans are fundamentally good and that it is only their upbringing or socialization that causes evil. In contrast, Dostoevsky held that at the core of human nature is a deep-seated capacity for evil, which cannot be explained away in psychological or sociological terms. This resident or "primal evil" is a fundamental and irreducible part of our sensual nature, as much a part of who we are as our love of life and concern for others. Primal evil appears regularly, coming to us from around the world in daily reports of cruelty, torture, rape, and destruction we find so appalling. Dostoevsky kept a file of newspaper clippings dealing with cases of cruelty to children and animals, and in the chapter "Rebellion," he has Ivan recite a blood-chilling litany of such stories to Alyosha.

The recognition that there is a primal drive to evil within the human soul is not unique to Dostoevsky. What is striking about his view, however, is his understanding of what is necessary to subdue or tame this force. *The Brothers Karamazov* presents two unsatisfactory responses to primal evil. The first, found in Fyodor and to some extent in Dmitri, is the response of embracing this evil, taking pleasure in one's degradation and self-debasement. The second response, found in Ivan, starts with a reaction of revulsion toward the primal evil in oneself. Dostoevsky's claim is that this second response to evil—the fastidious perfectionism that tries to excise all dark drives and capacities—instead of purifying us, actually drives us into a deeper form of evil, a "second-order evil" that issues from egoism.

In *The Brothers Karamazov*, the attempt to rise above one's sensual nature through self-denial is called "laceration." Lacerated individuals are torn apart, both within themselves and in their relations to others. Trying to make themselves look good by making others look bad, lacerated individuals become caught up in manipulative power plays that tear them away from others and ultimately from themselves.

While laceration seems to originate from an idealistic impulse—a desire to free oneself from the sensual (and potentially evil) dimensions of human existence—it is in fact motivated by vanity and pride (the desire to be more than human, to be "like God"; see Gen 3:5). Generally, it results not in atonement but in vicious forms of second-order evil. Bent on being recognized as superior beings, lacerated individuals swing between dominating others and enacting the part of wounded victims. This struggle for self-affirmation, far from making one better, alienates others, and in the end breeds feelings of emptiness and worthlessness that lead to greater forms of cruelty and destructiveness. Historically, this form of idealism spawns self-serving moral nihilism—as is vividly illustrated in the failure of the Enlightenment project and more recently in the sad history of the Soviet Union.

For Dostoevsky, as for Hesse and Jung, humans consist of conflicting dimensions or conflicting sets of needs. On the one hand, there is the earthy, sensual side of the self, the dark "Karamazov" dimension. This raw, "primitive force" of the Karamazovs is evident primarily in Dmitri, who, in his sensuality, is very much like his father. However, unlike his father,

Dmitri also feels the need to rise above his sheer animal nature and achieve something higher. Dostoevsky sees that, unlike lower animals, humans are seldom content with simply satisfying basic needs and being able to survive. Humans typically feel a need to realize higher, more spiritual ideals. They seek to achieve a better, nobler life than that of merely getting by, doing so in ways we characterize as courageous, loving, or honest.

Dmitry is intensely aware that he is torn between sensuality and idealism: "I can't endure the thought that a man of lofty mind and heart begins with the ideal of the Madonna and ends with the ideal of Sodom. What's still more awful is that a man with the ideal of Sodom in his soul does not renounce the ideal of the Madonna, and in his heart may be on fire with that ideal, genuinely on fire, just as in his days of youth and innocence" (3.3).[4] This shattering paradox, able to love both Sodom and the Madonna (the Virgin Mary), as he puts it, defines not just Dmitri Karamazov, but humans in general. Dmitri's struggle between idealism and sensuality reflects the central question posed by *The Brothers Karamazov*: Is there any way to reconcile the tension within the self in order to achieve peace and fulfillment in this life? As becomes clear, this is also the question for the future prospects not only of Russia, but also of the human race.

Dostoevsky portrays the brothers as a spiritual unity, as an organically collective personality in its various manifestations. The principle of reason is represented by Ivan, the principle of feeling by Dmitry, and the principle of will, realizing itself in active love as the ideal, is represented by Alyosha. However, all human personalities bear in themselves a fatal dichotomy: the legitimate Karamazov brothers have an illegitimate brother Smerdyakov; he is their embodied temptation and personified sin. Thus, in the novel's artistic symbols, the author expounds his own teaching about personality.

The main hero of the novel, then, is not one brother but three brothers in their spiritual unity. While on a literary plane, Dostoevsky develops three personal themes through parallel characters, on the spiritual plane, the three parallel lines converge, for the brothers, each in his own way, experience a single tragedy, sharing a common guilt and a common redemption. Not only Ivan, with his idea "everything is permitted," and not only Dmitri, through the impetuosity of his passions, but also the kind, loving Alyosha—all are responsible for their father's murder. All consciously or unconsciously desire his death, and their desire compels Smerdyakov to the crime—he is merely their instrument. The brothers'

---

4. Dostoyevsky, *The Brothers Karamazov*, 111.

common crime also involves a common punishment: Dmitry atones for his guilt by exile to penal servitude; Ivan, by the dissolution of his personality through a nervous breakdown; and Alyosha by his conflicted spiritual crisis. Furthermore, all are purified through suffering and attain a new life.

Dostoevsky's novel unveils its author's spiritual biography and artistic confession. However, having transferred his hopes and concerns into a work of art, the story of Dostoevsky's (or Russia's) personality becomes the history of the human personality in general. As the accidental and individual disappears, what is ecumenical and universal prevails. In the fate of the brothers Karamazov, each of us recognizes his or her own fate.

QUESTIONS FOR DISCUSSION AND REFLECTION

In addition to the questions listed at the end of the preface, answer the following questions, writing your answers in a journal. If you are in a group study, be prepared to share your answers with those in the group.

1. After reading and reflecting on the segment on Dostoevsky's biography, what did you learn about personality?

2. After reading and reflecting on the segment on Dostoevsky's biography, what did you learn about spirituality?

3. After reading and reflecting on the segment on *The Brothers Karamazov*, what did you learn about paternal influence?

4. After reading and reflecting on the segment on *The Brothers Karamazov*, what did you learn about personality?

5. In your estimation, what was Dostoevsky's motivation for writing *The Brothers Karamazov*? Explain your answer.

6. In your estimation, what is the primary insight to be gained from *The Brothers Karamazov*? Explain your answer.

7. Explain the role Alyosha plays in *The Brothers Karamazov*.

8. In your estimation, what is the primary insight gained in the segment on "The Grand Inquisitor"?

9. If Dostoevsky was a theist, why, in your estimation, did he include such powerful and irrefutable arguments against the Christian faith in his segment on the Grand Inquisitor?

10. Explain the role of the Russian (Eastern) Orthodox Church in *The Brothers Karamazov*.

11. Explain how Dostoevsky's characters in *The Brothers Karamazov*, like Hesse's major characters, reflect the basic psychic functions of Jungian analytical psychology.

12. Explain why self-laceration, inimical to healthy spirituality, typifies many deeply spiritual individuals.

13. In your estimation, who was responsible for the death of Fyodor Karamazov? Explain your answer.

Chapter 5

Jane Austen's *Sense and Sensibility* and Charlotte Brontë's *Jane Eyre*

KNOWN PRIMARILY FOR HER six major novels, which describe and comment upon the British landed gentry at the end of the eighteenth century, Jane Austen (1775–1817) is the first major woman novelist to write in the English language. Credited with making important advances in narrative technique and demonstrating acute insight into morality, her use of biting irony, along with her realism, humor, and social commentary, have long earned her acclaim among critics, scholars, and popular audiences alike.

Despite their popularity, or perhaps to question her popularity, critics have criticized Austen's plots for being narrow and one-dimensional, focusing on the dependence of women on marriage in the pursuit of favorable social standing and economic security. However, if we consider Austen's novels in the context of eighteenth-century feminist ideas, we can see that her subject matter is the central focus of Enlightenment feminism, and that her views on the moral nature and status of women, marriage, authority, and the family is strikingly similar to that shown by the feminist writer Mary Wollstonecraft in *A Vindication of the Rights of Woman* (1792), an attack on the chauvinistic conventions of the time. If we miss Austen's engagement with fiction and morals as distinctly feminist, we find it difficult to give a coherent account of the uniqueness of her art.

Austen did have predecessors. There were women novelists of the eighteenth century whom she read and appreciated, including Fanny Burney, to whom Jane Austen's father compared his daughter when trying to pitch one of her novels. There was also Ann Radcliffe, who wrote what we call "gothic novels" (the classic gothic situation, focusing on horror, excitement, and sensation, features a young girl alone in a mysterious castle, abbey, or haunted house), and Maria Edgeworth, a contemporary of Austen whose novels are now being read thanks to Austen's status in the Western canon.

Prior to the eighteenth century, the literary field had been a challenge to women, but the invention of the novel made it a genre attractive to female authors. It would take a while, however, for the novel to make it into the ranks of literary respectability. Thought to be written by mavericks and social outsiders, the novel had a shaky footing even with the English, who pioneered the genre, though in the mid to late eighteenth century, Samuel Johnson, arguably the most distinguished man of letters in British history, came to its defense by pointing out its accuracy and honesty in portraying the human condition. Later, the distinguished twentieth-century English writer and critic C. S. Lewis would label Austen a literary daughter of Johnson, arguing that she had inherited his common sense, morality, and much of his style. Rather than delving deeply into the psyche of her characters, an approach Romantic and Modernist authors favored, Austen imbued them with wit and humor, following Johnson's advice to write "a representation of life as may excite mirth."

Written to criticize the sentimental novels of the second half of the eighteenth century, Austen's novels are generally viewed as transitional to nineteenth-century literary realism. Early English novelists such as Samuel Richardson and Henry Fielding, famous for writing epistolary novels—that is, novels told through journals, letters, and other documents—were followed by the school of sentimentalists, sensationalists, and Romantics such as Charles Dickens, George Eliot, and Sir Walter Scott, whose style and genre Austen rejected, returning to the tradition of Richardson and Fielding, using and exceeding their tradition of irony, realism, and satire.

Because Austen's novels did not conform to Romantic and Victorian expectations that powerful emotion be displayed conspicuously, nineteenth-century critics and audiences preferred the works of Dickens, Eliot, and Scott. Though the Romantic Scott was positive, Austen's work did not match the prevailing aesthetic values of the Romantic mindset. Although her six full-length novels have rarely been out of print, they brought her little fame during her lifetime. In the 1830s, however, her reputation was enhanced when her novels were republished and sold as an illustrated set. They gradually gained wider acclaim and popular readership, leading to their translation into many languages.

With the publication of *Sense and Sensibility* (1811), *Pride and Prejudice* (1813), *Mansfield Park* (1814) and *Emma* (1816), Austen achieved moderate success as a published writer. Nevertheless, she published all these novels anonymously, including two other novels, *Northanger Abbey* and *Persuasion*, both published posthumously in 1818. The publication in 1939 of Mary Lascelles's *Jane Austen and Her Art* led to the academic study of Austen. In addition to inspiring many critical essays and literary anthologies, Austen's novels have inspired numerous film and television adaptations. Today, she is one of the most beloved and widely read authors in the English language.

Despite her popularity and importance as a writer, we know very little about her actual life, for biographical information is limited and largely dependent on family records. During her lifetime, she wrote as many as three thousand letters, but only a small number survived. Many of her letters were written to her older sister Cassandra, who in 1843 destroyed most of them or cut pieces out, ostensibly to prevent their falling into the hands of relatives and ensuring that younger nieces did not read any of her often acerbic or critical comments on family members or friends.

Jane Austen was born in the small village of Steventon, England, the seventh child in a family of eight. For much of her life, her father, George Austen, served as the rector of Anglican parishes. He came from an old, respected, and wealthy family whose wealth was divided as each generation of eldest sons received inheritances. In George's time, his branch of the family fell into poverty. He and his two sisters were orphaned as children and had to be taken in by relatives. Attending Oxford on a fellowship, he eventually met and married Cassandra Leigh, a member of a prominent family. According to eyewitnesses, the atmosphere of the Austen home was open, amused, and intellectual, where the ideas of those with whom the Austens might disagree politically or socially were considered and discussed. Her father being a rector, Austen was surrounded by books and by intellectual and cultural conversation. During this period of her life, Austen attended church regularly, socializing with friends and neighbors and reading novels—often of her own composition—aloud to her family in the evenings. By 1801, her father had accumulated a library of approximately five hundred volumes, to which his children had access. Her favorite moral writers were Samuel Johnson in prose and William Cowper in verse. In addition to reading, a family passion was theatrical performance. The rectory barn became a small theater during the summers, as well as a place of dancing and card playing. According to her brother Henry, "Jane was fond of dancing, and excelled in it."

Jane Austen appears to have written from a young age. From 1787, when she was eleven, until 1793, she wrote sketches and over twenty pieces, many of them parodies of her reading. There is evidence that Jayne's family at this time took her writing seriously. Her father purchased a writing desk, which she probably used for the writing in 1795 of *Elinor and Marianne*, her first full-length projected novel, which eventually became *Sense and Sensibility*.

When Austen was twenty, she met Tom Lefroy, who had just finished a university degree and was moving to London for training as a barrister. She was quite taken by him, and the relationship progressed quickly, though by the time he had left the area to resume his legal studies, the relationship ended. Subsequently, none of her other suitors measured up to him, and from then on, she remained single. Around this time she wrote *First Impressions* (published in 1813 as *Pride and Prejudice* and arguably her most enduringly successful novel). In 1797, her father made the first attempt to publish her novels, sending *First Impressions* to an established publisher in London, who promptly returned the document (Austen may not have known of her father's efforts). Following the completion of *First Impressions*, Austen returned to *Elinor and Marianne*. She eliminated the epistolary format in favor of third-person narration and produced something close to *Sense and Sensibility*. Shortly thereafter she began writing a third novel, a satire on the Gothic novel entitled *Northanger Abbey*.

In 1811 the publisher Thomas Egerton agreed to publish *Sense and Sensibility*, which, like all of Austen's novels except *Pride and Prejudice*, was published "on commission," that is, at the author's financial risk. If a novel did not recover its costs through sales, the author was responsible for them. The alternative to selling via commission was by selling the copyright, where an author received a one-time payment from the publisher for the manuscript, which occurred with *Pride and Prejudice*.

Like many women authors at the time, Austen published her books anonymously. At the time, the ideal roles for a woman were as wife and mother, and a woman who wished to be a full-time writer was felt to degrade her femininity. When *Sense and Sensibility* appeared in 1811, the title page attributed authorship to "By a Lady." Significantly, the author wished her sex to be known. Had she adopted a pseudonym such as Sophia or Eugenia, female authorship would not have been so plainly asserted, for men, especially in satirical works, often adopted female pseudonyms. "By a Lady" was the best means of declaring a female viewpoint, while remaining anonymous. Austen made a profit from her work, which provided her with some financial and psychological independence. After the success of *Sense and Sensibility*, all of her subsequent novels were billed as written "By the author of *Sense and Sensibility*," though Austen's name never appeared on her books during her lifetime.

By early 1816, Austen felt sick, but ignored the warning signs. Her decline was unmistakable, and she began a slow deterioration likely due to Hodgkin's lymphoma. As her illness progressed, she experienced difficulty walking and lacked energy. By mid-April, she was confined to bed, and she died in July at the age of 41. Through her brother's clerical connections, arrangements were made for Austen to be buried in the nave of Winchester Cathedral. In the months after her death, family members arranged for the publication of *Persuasion* and *Northanger Abbey* as a set. Henry Austen contributed a "Biographical Note" in December 1817, which for the first time identified his sister as the author of the novels.

SENSE AND SENSIBILITY: PLOT AND RESPONSE

Henry Dashwood, his second wife, and their three daughters live for many years with Henry's wealthy bachelor uncle at Norland Park, a large country estate in Sussex. That uncle decides, in late life, to will the use and income of his property first to Henry, then to Henry's first son (by his first marriage) John Dashwood, so that the property should pass intact to John's four-year-old son Harry. The uncle dies, but Henry lives just a year after that and he is unable in such short time to save enough money for the future security of his wife Mrs. Dashwood and their daughters, Elinor, Marianne, and Margaret, who are left only a small income. On his deathbed, Henry Dashwood extracts a promise from his son John to take care of his half-sisters. But before Henry is long in the grave, John's greedy wife, Fanny, persuades her husband to renege on the promise, appealing to his concerns about diminishing his own son Harry's inheritance, despite the fact that John is already independently wealthy thanks to both his inheritance from his mother and his wife's dowry. Henry Dashwood's love for his second family is also used by Fanny to arouse her husband's jealousy, and persuade him not to help his sisters financially.

As soon as Henry Dashwood is buried, John and Fanny move in as the new owners of Norland, treating the Dashwood women as unwelcome guests, forcing Mrs. Dashwood to seek somewhere else to live. In the meantime, Fanny's brother, Edward Ferrars, visits Norland and is attracted to Elinor. Fanny disapproves of their budding romance, and offends Mrs. Dashwood by implying that Elinor must be motivated by his expectations of coming into money.

Mrs. Dashwood moves her family to Barton Cottage in Devonshire, near the home of her cousin, Sir John Middleton. Their new home is modest, but they are warmly received by Sir John and welcomed into local society, meeting his wife, Lady Middleton, his mother-in-law, Mrs. Jennings, and his friend, Colonel Brandon. Colonel Brandon is attracted to Marianne, but she is unmoved, for she considers the thirty-five-year-old Colonel Brandon an old bachelor, incapable of falling in love or inspiring love in anyone.

While out for a walk, Marianne gets caught in the rain, slips, and sprains her ankle. The dashing John Willoughby sees the accident and assists her, picking her up and carrying her back to her home. After this, Marianne quickly comes to admire his good looks and his similar tastes in poetry, music, art, and love. Willoughby openly courts Marianne, and together they flaunt their attachment to one another. His attentions, and Marianne's behavior, lead Elinor and Mrs. Dashwood to suspect that the couple are secretly engaged. Elinor cautions Marianne against her unguarded conduct, but Marianne refuses to check her emotions. Willoughby engages in several intimate activities with Marianne, including taking her to see the home he expects to inherit one day and obtaining a lock of her hair. When the announcement of marriage seems imminent, Willoughby informs the Dashwoods that his aunt, upon whom he is financially dependent due to his debts, is sending him to London on business, indefinitely, leaving Marianne distraught.

Edward Ferrars pays a short visit to Barton Cottage, but seems distracted. Elinor fears that he no longer has feelings for her, but she will not show her heartache. After Edward departs, sisters Anne and Lucy Steele, cousins of Mrs. Jennings, come to stay at Barton Park. Lucy informs Elinor in confidence of her secret four-year engagement to Edward Ferrars that started when he was studying with her uncle, and she displays proof of their intimacy. Elinor realizes that Lucy's visit and revelations are the result of her jealousy, and it helps Elinor to understand Edward's recent sadness and behavior towards her. She acquits Edward of blame and admires him for being held to a loveless engagement to Lucy by his sense of honor.

Elinor and Marianne accompany Mrs. Jennings to London. On arriving, Marianne rashly writes several personal letters to Willoughby, which go unanswered. When they meet by chance at a dance, Willoughby is with another woman. He greets Marianne reluctantly and coldly, to her distress. Soon Marianne receives a letter denying that he ever had feelings for her. Willoughby is revealed to be engaged to Miss Grey, a wealthy heiress. After Elinor reads the letter, Marianne admits to Elinor that she and Willoughby were never engaged. She behaved as if they were because she knew she loved him and thought that he loved her.

As Marianne grieves, Colonel Brandon visits and reveals to Elinor evidence of Willoughby's history of callousness and infidelity, informing her that Willoughby's aunt subsequently disinherited him, forcing him to marry Miss Grey for her money. Meanwhile, the Steele sisters have come to London, where they are asked to stay at John and Fanny Dashwood's London house. Lucy sees the invitation as a personal compliment, rather than what it is: a slight to Elinor and Marianne who, being family, should have received such an invitation first. Inadvertently, Lucy's older sister reveals the news of Lucy's secret engagement to Edward Ferrars. Edward's mother is outraged at the information and disinherits him, promising his fortune instead to his brother Robert. Meanwhile, the Dashwood sisters visit family friends on their way home from London. While there, Marianne develops a severe cold and falls deathly ill. Upon hearing of her illness, Willoughby comes to visit, attempting to explain his misconduct and seek forgiveness. Elinor pities him and shares his story with Marianne, who finally realizes that she behaved imprudently with Willoughby and could never have been happy with him. She values Elinor's more restrained conduct with Edward and resolves to model herself after her courage and good sense. Mrs. Dashwood and Colonel Brandon also arrive and are relieved to learn that Marianne has begun to recover.

When the Dashwoods return to Barton, they learn from their servant that Lucy Steele and Mr. Ferrars are engaged. They assume that he means Edward Ferrars, but Edward himself soon arrives and corrects their misconception: it was Robert, not himself, whom Lucy ultimately decided to marry. Thus, Edward is finally free to propose to his beloved Elinor, and not long after, Marianne and Colonel Brandon become engaged as well.

The couples live together in Delaford and remain in close touch with their mother and younger sister at Barton Cottage.

PERSONALITY AND SPIRITUALITY IN
SENSE AND SENSIBILITY

Despite containing tragic circumstances and anguishing situations, Jane Austen's novels are comedies, not tragedies. As Austen's other novels, *Sense and Sensibility* is a comedy that ends in marriages, which traditionally affirms the connections between sexes and families, and between desire and public ritual or social convention. However, as Austen makes abundantly clear in *Sense and Sensibility*, a common theme in her novels is the vulnerability of women in a society where they are dependent upon men for protection and financial security. In a patriarchal society, men seek security through employment, but in the case of landed gentry, through wills and the lines of inheritance, a system fixated on priority of male birth. Feminist critics have long engaged in conversation about the topics of wealth, inheritance, and earning in Austen's novels, contending that *Sense and Sensibility* shows marriage as the only practical solution against the insecurity of women remaining unmarried. Furthermore, in *Sense and Sensibility*, young women like Marianne and Elinor discover that in order to find male protectors and achieve happiness in life, they must submit to powerful conventions of society. In patriarchal societies, women such as Mrs. Ferrars and Lucy Steele demonstrate how women can become agents of repression. In order to protect themselves and their interests, they too must participate in the same patriarchal system that oppresses them.

While earlier reviews of *Sense and Sensibility* focused on the novel as a dramatized book of conduct that valued "female prudence" (associated with Elinor's sense) over "female impetuosity" (associated with Marianne's sensibility), recent feminist readings find *Sense and Sensibility* critical of social conventions such as property, marriage, and family. Thus, in her book *Jane Austen: Women, Politics, and the Novel*, Claudia Johnson finds that rather than writing pleasurable, happy-ending novels, Austen critically examines the codes of propriety and their enforcement by depicting the unfair marginalization of women resulting from the absence of male protectors.

According to this view, in *Sense and Sensibility*, Austen depicts male characters unfavorably. Johnson calls them "uncommitted sorts," flawed individuals who live irresponsibly. In this regard, Johnson compares Edward Farrars to Willoughby, claiming that the differences between them as individuals do not hide the fact that their failures are identical; Johnson calls both males "weak, duplicitous, and selfish," lacking the honesty and forthrightness of exemplary men such as Colonel Brandon.

Despite the gender stereotypes of her era, Austen's protagonists deviate from predominant views to reveal her own progressive thinking. While acknowledging the differences between genders, Austen considers men and women to be equals. For example, Elinor exemplifies a heroine unique to her time—an intellectual. Thus, in constructing Elinor's character, Austen opposes the patriarchally imposed concept of genteel feminine gender, focusing not on Elinor's sentimentality but rather on the rationality of her passions.

A further strand in Austen's reconstruction of gender in this novel appears in Marianne, a character typically viewed as quintessentially "feminine" because she is perceived to be ruled by sentimental passion. However, Marianne strikingly breaks the gender mold in her courtship behavior. Once Willoughby shows sexual interest in her—and he is a demonstrative lover—his behavior and hers are nearly indistinguishable. Marianne recognizes no need to wait until Willoughby has "declared himself" before displaying public and private expressions of her affection for him. She has little interest in perception by others, and believes that authenticity in a woman entails showing her loving feelings for a man as freely as he shows his for her. Marianne rejects many of the rules society prescribes for women in favor of what she believes to be within an individual woman's power: to define for herself the decorum suited to her gender.

Lest we exceed Austen's vision, we must note that despite Marianne's willingness to cross gender boundaries, at the end of the novel, Marianne conforms to patriarchy's conception of a young woman's way. In her characterization, Austen both renounces and affirms sexual stereotypes, leaving ambiguous her ability or desire to reshape gender. A possible solution to Austen's inconsistency is Moreland Perkins's suggestion that she presented Marianne to her audience as exhibit B in her fictional case for feminine gender reform, and Elinor as exhibit A.[1] Marianne's behavior is socially reformist but not revolutionary in nature: she courts disapproval but she is reluctant to cross the line that separates the respectable young woman from the outcast. As she tells her sister regarding her behavior with Willoughby,

1. Perkins, *Reshaping the Sexes*, 177.

"if there had been any real impropriety in what I did, I should have been sensible of it at the time, for we always know when we are acting wrong, and with such a conviction I could have no pleasure" (1.13).[2]

By changing the title from *Elinor and Marianne* to *Sense and Sensibility*, Austen added psychological, philosophical, and spiritual depth to what began as a sketch of two characters, for the dichotomy between "sense" and "sensibility" is the lens through which this novel is most commonly analyzed. According to this understanding, Elinor, the older sister, represents qualities of "sense" (reason, restraint, social responsibility, and a clear-headed concern for the welfare of others). In contrast, Marianne, her younger sister, represents qualities of "sensibility" (emotion, spontaneity, impulsiveness, and rapturous devotion). Whereas Elinor conceals her regard for Edward Ferrars, Marianne openly and unashamedly proclaims her passion for John Willoughby. Their different attitudes toward the men they love, and how to express that love, reflect their opposite temperaments.

However, in this novel, Austen presents characters that are more complex than in staple sentimental fiction. Elinor, representing sense, does not lack passion, and Marianne, representing sensibility, is not always foolish and headstrong. Furthermore, *Sense and Sensibility* cannot simply be understood as a straightforward study in personality contrast. As the novel progresses, Marianne and Elinor each begin to take on the rounded character of a single, central heroine. Austen may have started with the intention of using the notion of contrasting heroines—one representing female good sense and prudence and the other impulsiveness and excess—but she discovered that plan's inadequacies as her characters became more representative of human nature in all its complexity.

Although Austen is famous for satirizing the "cult of sensibility," in *Sense and Sensibility* she seems to argue not for the dismissal of sensibility but for the creation of a balance between reason and passion; too little feeling is as dangerous as too much. In fact, the sisters are more alike than different: Elinor is capable of romantic passion and Marianne of good sense. Austen's characterization, filled with foibles and human inconsistencies, does not allow the adequate representation of a single heroine with a good head and a sound heart. Life is not that simple, and neither are humans.

Both Elinor and Marianne achieve happiness at the end of the novel, but they do so by learning from one another, together discovering how to feel and express sentiments fully while also retaining dignity and

2. Austen, *Sense and Sensibility*, 68.

self-control. *Sense and Sensibility's* success is not a result of the triumph of sense over sensibility or of their division; rather, it is about the need for women to have strong heads as well as good hearts. *Sense and Sensibility* endures for its conjunction of temperamental and spiritual qualities. While the differences between the Dashwood sisters are significant, their differences are antithetical to healthy spirituality, which emphasizes balance, harmony, integration, and wholeness.

As individuals possess distinct personalities, so also historical eras. While *Sense and Sensibility* can be read as a contrast between Elinor's sense and Marianne's sensibility, this dichotomy between sense and sensibility has cultural and historical resonances as well. Austen wrote this novel around the turn of the eighteenth century, on the convergence of two cultural movements: Classicism and Romanticism. Elinor represents the characteristics associated with eighteenth-century neo-classicism, including rationality, insight, judgment, moderation, and balance. She never loses sight of propriety, economic practicalities, or perspective. It was during the Classical period and its accompanying cultural Enlightenment that the novel first developed as a literary genre. Thus, with the character of Elinor, Austen gestures toward her predecessors and acknowledges the influence of their legacy on her generation. In contrast, Marianne represents the qualities associated with the emerging era of sensibility, embracing romance, imagination, idealism, excess, and a dedication to the beauty of nature: Austen's characterization of Marianne reminds us that she was the contemporary of Wordsworth, Coleridge, and Walter Scott, the luminaries of the English Romantic literary scene. In this regard, Austen's depiction of Elinor and Marianne can be said to reflect the changing literary landscape that served as a backdrop for her life as a writer.

CHARLOTTE BRONTË

In creating groundbreaking and beloved novels, three women's names in particular stand out in nineteenth-century literature: Jane Austen, Emily Brontë, and Charlotte Brontë. Born the year before Austen's death, Charlotte Brontë (1816–1855) was the eldest of the three Brontë sisters who survived into adulthood and whose novels became classics of English literature. As with Jane Austen and Emily Brontë, we must ask how women in their late teenage and early adult years, who had seen little of the world and had been largely educated at home, produced novels of towering genius. Since all died at relatively early ages—Emily at the age of 29, Charlotte at 38, and Jane at 41—what might they have produced had they lived longer?

To understand Charlotte Brontë's legacy, we must understand that her fiction is deeply rooted in two settings: her family background and the region of England in which she grew up. Charlotte's family name was originally Prunty, derived from the name of a village in Northern Ireland, Pronteaigh. Charlotte's father, Patrick, was born into a poor farming family, but he showed remarkable intellectual abilities and, in 1802, began attending Cambridge University. After a bloody uprising in Ireland in 1798, the English viewed the Irish with mistrust, so Patrick changed his name to Brontë to distance himself from his Ulster origins. The unusual name he chose, Brontë, is an Anglicization of the Greek word for "thunder"; furthermore, the name was also associated with Lord Nelson, Britain's famous naval heroes, one of whose titles was Duke of Bronte. The Brontë children were all consciously or unconsciously influenced by their father's and their own name change.

The name change succeeded, for in 1820, Patrick was appointed rector of an Anglican parish in the village of Haworth in Yorkshire, a wild region of barren moors and savage winds. The following year Patrick's wife Maria died of cancer, leaving five daughters and a son. Their father had a good library, and during their childhood, they composed length sagas around heroes such as Nelson, Wellington, Byron, and Napoleon. Both Rochester from *Jane Eyre* and Heathcliff from *Wuthering Heights* can be traced back to the strong men favored in these fantasies. In 1824 the Brontë sisters were enrolled at the Clergy Daughters' School in nearby Cowan Bridge. According to Charlotte, the school's living conditions and disciplinary regiment were deplorable, permanently affecting her health and physical development, conditions she depicted in the schooling of Jane Eyre at Lowood. (In *Jane Eyre*, Charlotte describes a typhus epidemic that spread across the school due to its insalubrious conditions.) After the deaths of his two oldest daughters, who both died of tuberculosis due to their school's poor conditions, Patrick removed Charlotte and Emily from the school.

At home, the three surviving Brontë sisters wrote poems (Charlotte wrote more than two hundred poems in the course of her life), which they published privately under gender-neutral names such as Currer Bell (Charlotte), Ellis Bell (Emily), and Acton Bell (Anne). They also wrote realistic fiction with powerful romantic themes. In 1847, Charlotte, still writing as Currer Bell, had her novel *Jane Eyre* published by George Smith, one of the best publishers in London. The novel was a huge success; Charlotte was suddenly famous, and remained so for the rest of her short life. Her sister Emily's first and only novel, *Wuthering Heights*, was published the same year, but by one of the most disreputable publishers in London, Thomas Newby. Emily died a few months after publishing her novel, to few reviews.

What we know of Charlotte's life comes mainly from Elizabeth Gaskell's *The Life of Charlotte Brontë*, published in 1857. Between 1831 and 1832, Brontë continued her education at Roe Head in Mirfield, where she met her lifelong friends Ellen Nussey and Mary Taylor. She returned to Roe Head as a teacher from 1835 to 1838, where she was unhappy and lonely, emotions she expressed in poetry. In 1838, she took up the first of many positions as governess to families in Yorkshire, a career she pursued until 1841. She disliked her work as governess, noting her employers constantly humiliated her, treating her like a slave. In 1842, she and Emily traveled to Brussels to enroll at a boarding school run by Constantin Heger and his wife Claire. In return for board and tuition, Charlotte taught English and Emily taught music. Their stay was cut short when their aunt, Elizabeth Branwell, who had joined the family to look after the children following their mother's death, died abruptly in 1842. Charlotte returned alone the following year to take up a teaching post at the school. While there, she fell hopelessly in love with Constantin, who, as far as we know, did not reciprocate her feelings. Her unrequited love inspired the longing relationships at the center of many of her novels, particularly Jane Eyre's mad love for her employer, Rochester.

When she returned to England in the mid-1840s, Charlotte and her sisters produced a vanity publication of their poems, which sold only two copies. In 1848, fatal illness swept through their family, taking the lives of Branwell as well as Emily and Anne. Only Charlotte would live to see the name Brontë become famous. Charlotte continued to live at Haworth, writing a string of successful novels; she also had her sister's *Wuthering Heights* published by a reputable firm. In 1854, she married Arthur Bell Nicholls, her father's curate, and a few months later, at the age of thirty-eight, she became pregnant. Her health declined rapidly soon thereafter, and she and her unborn child died in 1855.

JANE EYRE: PLOT AND RESPONSE

Mid-Victorian novelists, including Charles Dickens, George Eliot, and Charlotte Brontë, were fascinated by a form of narrative known as the *Bildungsroman*. This word translates into English as "portrait novel," or more precisely, the life-story of a protagonist from childhood through a series of trials to maturity. Like Dickens in *David Copperfield*, Brontë used first-person narration. While this form of narration limits the point of view to one consciousness, it has what Brontë sought—dynamism and urgency.

As noted above, *Jane Eyre* presents itself as a recollection of the heroine's early life, from childhood to marriage, set in the north of England. The novel progresses through five distinct stages; Jane's childhood at Gateshead Hall, where she is emotionally and physically abused by her aunt and cousins; her education at Lowood School, where she gains friends and role models but suffers privations and oppression; her time as governess at Thornfield Hall, where she falls in love with her mysterious employer, Edward Fairfax Rochester; her time in the Moor House, during which her earnest but cold clergyman cousin, St. John Rivers, proposes to her; and ultimately her reunion with, and marriage to, her beloved Rochester. Throughout these sections, Brontë provides perspectives on a number of important social issues and ideas, many of which are critical of the status quo.

Jane Eyre is a young orphan being raised by Mrs. Reed, her cruel, wealthy aunt. A servant named Bessie provides Jane with some of the few kindnesses she receives, telling her stories and singing songs to her. One day, as punishment for fighting with her bullying cousin John Reed, Jane's aunt imprisons Jane in the red-room, the room in which Jane's Uncle Reed died. While locked in, Jane, believing that she sees her uncle's ghost, screams and faints. She wakes to find herself in the care of Bessie and the kindly apothecary Mr. Lloyd, who suggests to Mrs. Reed that Jane be sent away to school. To Jane's delight, Mrs. Reed agrees.

At Lowood School, Jane finds that her life is far from idyllic. The school's headmaster is Mr. Brocklehurst, a cruel, hypocritical, and abusive man. He preaches a doctrine of poverty and privation to his students while using the school's funds to provide a wealthy and opulent lifestyle for his own family. At Lowood, Jane befriends a young girl named Helen Burns, who dies of consumption when a massive typhus epidemic sweeps Lowood. The epidemic also results in the departure of Mr. Brocklehurst by attracting attention to the insalubrious conditions at Lowood. After a group of more sympathetic tutors takes Brocklehurst's place, Jane's life improves dramatically. She spends eight more years at Lowood, six as a student and two as a teacher.

After teaching for two years, Jane yearns for new experiences. She accepts a governess position at a manor called Thornfield, run by a housekeeper named Mrs. Fairfax, where she teaches a lively French girl named Adèle. Jane's employer at Thornfield is an impassioned man named Rochester, with whom Jane finds herself falling secretly in love. She saves Rochester from a fire one night, which he claims was started by a drunken servant named Grace Poole. But because Grace Poole continues to work at Thornfield, Jane concludes that she has not been told the entire story. Jane sinks into despondency when Rochester brings home a beautiful but vicious woman named Blanche Ingram. Jane expects Rochester to propose to Blanche, but Rochester instead proposes to Jane, who accepts almost disbelievingly.

The wedding day arrives, and as Jane and Mr. Rochester prepare to exchange their vows, the voice of Mr. Mason cries out that Rochester already has a wife. Mason introduces himself as the brother of that wife—a woman named Bertha. Mr. Mason testifies that Bertha, whom Rochester married when he was a young man in Jamaica, is still alive. Rochester does not deny Mason's claims, but he explains that Bertha has gone mad. He takes the wedding party back to Thornfield, where they witness the insane Bertha Mason scurrying around on all fours and growling like an animal. Rochester keeps Bertha hidden on the third story of Thornfield and pays Grace Poole to keep his wife under control. Bertha was the real cause of the mysterious fire earlier in the story. Rochester then asks Jane to be his mistress, but her virtue will not permit such an arrangement. She flees Thornfield in a state of near breakdown.

Penniless and hungry, Jane is forced to sleep outdoors and beg for food. By coincidence, Jane collapses on the doorstep of an unknown relative, St. John Rivers, a clergyman, and his sisters. They take her in, and she discovers that she is not an orphan after all but an heiress, kept in ignorance by the villainous Reeds. Jane immediately decides to share her inheritance equally with her three newfound relatives.

St. John decides to travel to India as a missionary, and he urges Jane to accompany him as his wife. Jane agrees to go, but refuses to marry her cousin because she does not love him. St. John pressures her to reconsider, and she nearly gives in. However, she realizes that she cannot abandon forever the man she truly loves. One night she hears Rochester's voice calling her name over the moors. She hurries back to Thornfield, only to find that it has been burned to the ground by Bertha Mason, who lost her life in the fire. Rochester saved the servants but lost his eyesight and one of his hands. Jane travels to Rochester's new residence, Ferndean, where he lives with two servants. At Ferndean, Rochester and Jane rebuild their relationship and marry. At the end of her story, Jane writes that she has been married for ten blissful years and that she and Rochester enjoy perfect equality in their life together. She says that after two years of blindness, Rochester regained sight in one eye and was able to behold their first son at his birth.

PERSONALITY AND SPIRITUALITY IN *JANE EYRE*

There are two great spiritual mentors in life: great suffering and great love. Charlotte Brontë writes powerfully and poignantly because she experienced both. Originally published as *Jane Eyre: An Autobiography*, Brontë's novel revolutionized prose fiction by being the first to focus on its protagonist's moral and spiritual development through an intimate first-person narrative, where actions and events are colored by spiritual and psychological intensity. The book's style was innovative, combining romanticism and naturalism with gothic melodrama. Brontë believed art was most convincing when based on personal experience. In parts of the novel, Jane describes events as she experienced them. However, at times she slips into the present tense, creating a jarring impression that reflects her agonized mental state. The reader can also interpret this switch as Brontë reliving traumatic events, emphasizing their lasting impact. In *Jayne Eyre*, she transformed experience into a novel with universal appeal.

Throughout the novel, Jane struggles to find the right balance between moral duty and earthly pleasure, between obligation to her spirit and attention to her body. She encounters three representative religious figures: Mr. Brocklehurst, Helen Burns, and St. John Rivers. Each represents a model of religion that Jane ultimately rejects as she forms her own ideas about faith and principle, and their practical consequences.

Mr. Brocklehurst illustrates the dangers and hypocrisies that Charlotte Brontë perceived in the nineteenth-century evangelical movement. Mr. Brocklehurst adopts the rhetoric of evangelicalism when he claims to be purging his students of pride, but his method of subjecting them to various privations and humiliations, like when he orders that the naturally curly hair of one of Jane's classmates be cut so as to lie straight, is entirely unchristian. Of course, Brocklehurst's proscriptions are difficult to follow, and his hypocritical support of his own luxuriously wealthy family at the expense of the Lowood students shows Brontë's wariness of hypocritical spirituality. On the other hand, Helen Burns's meek and forbearing mode of Christianity is too passive for Jane to adopt as her own, although she loves and admires Helen for it. St. John Rivers provides another model of Christian behavior. His is a Christianity of ambition, glory, and extreme self-importance. St. John urges Jane to sacrifice her emotional deeds for the fulfillment of her moral duty, offering her a way of life that would require her to be disloyal to her own self. Although Jane ends up rejecting all three models of religion, she never abandons morality, spirituality, or belief in God.

Jane ultimately finds a comfortable middle ground. Her spiritual understanding is not hateful and oppressive like Brocklehurst's, nor does it require retreat from the everyday world as Helen's and St. John's religions do. For Jane, religion helps curb immoderate passions, and it spurs one on to greater efforts and achievements. These achievements include self-knowledge and trust in God.

Jane Eyre is also the story of a quest for love, respect, and equality. Jane searches, not just for romantic love, but also for a sense of being valued, of belonging. Thus Jane says to Helen Burns in chapter 8: "to gain some real affection from you, or Miss Temple, or any other whom I truly love, I would willingly submit to have the bone of my arm broken, or to let a bull toss me, or to stand behind a kicking horse, and let it dash its hoof at my chest."[3] Yet, over the course of the book, Jane must learn how to gain love without sacrificing and harming herself in the process.

Her fear of losing her autonomy motivates her refusal of Rochester's marriage proposal. Jane believes that "marrying" Rochester while he remains legally tied to Bertha would mean rendering herself a mistress and sacrificing her own integrity for the sake of emotional gratification. On the other hand, her life at Moor House tests her in the opposite manner. There, she enjoys economic independence and engages in worthwhile and useful work, teaching the poor; yet she lacks emotional sustenance. Although St. John proposes marriage, offering her a partnership built around a common purpose, Jane knows their marriage would remain loveless.

3. Brontë, *Jane Eyre*, 64.

The idea of equality of men and women emerged in the Victorian period,[4] and *Jane Eyre* has been described as the first major feminist novel. Brontë came of age as a writer, as a feminist, and as a human being ready to explore herself when she insisted that it was morally desirable to establish her heroine on the same terms as the traditional hero—by virtue of her interiority: her qualities of mind, character, and personality. Paradoxically, in freeing Jane Eyre from the conventional trappings of femininity and granting her liberty to feel and express her feelings, to think and express her thoughts, in asserting her "humanness," Brontë created the first "anti-heroine": one who defied the conventions of both fiction and society.

Jane struggles continually to achieve equality and to overcome oppression. Orphaned, poor, and plain, faced with the pressures of making her own way in a world that measured the likelihood of a woman's success by the degree of her marriageability (her familial connections, economic status, and above all, her beauty), Jane tests the limits of social, moral, and psychological possibility, discovering the inner power that is and always has been available to women. While feminist rhetoric is not overt in the novel, Brontë's feminism is illustrated in chapter 23, when Jane responds to Rochester's callous and indirect proposal: "Do you think I am an automaton?—a machine without feelings? . . . Do you think, because I am poor, obscure, plain, and little, I am soulless and heartless? You think wrong!—I have as much soul as you,—and full of as much heart! . . I am not talking to you now through the medium of custom, conventionalities, nor even of mortal flesh:—it is my spirit that addresses your spirit; just as if both had passed through the grave, and we stood at God's feet, equal, as we are!"[5]

In addition to class hierarchy, Jane must fight against patriarchal domination—against those who believe women to be inferior to men and treat them as such. Three central male figures threaten her desire for equality and dignity: Mr. Brocklehurst, Edward Rochester, and St. John Rivers. All three are misogynistic on some level. Each tries to keep Jane in a submissive position, where she is unable to express her own thoughts and feelings. In her quest for independence and self-knowledge, Jane must escape Brocklehurst, reject St. John, and come to Rochester only after ensuring that they marry as equals. She will not depend solely on Rochester for love

4. The Victorian era is named for Queen Victoria, whose reign lasted from 1837 to 1901.

5. Brontë, *Jane Eyre*, 249–50.

and she can be financially independent. Furthermore, Rochester is blind at the novel's end and thus dependent upon Jane. The feminism at the heart of *Jane Eyre* is summed up in four words that are found at the novel's conclusion: "Reader, I married him." As the syntax makes clear, Jane is in charge.

Jane Eyre has survived and triumphed for nearly two centuries, not because it is good melodrama, or even because it is a great novel of womanhood—one that is both sympathetic to and critical of the age and society in which it was created—but because it features some of spirituality's greatest features: justice, courage, resilience, equality, and compassion.

QUESTIONS FOR DISCUSSION AND REFLECTION

In addition to the questions listed at the end of the preface, answer the following questions, writing your answers in a journal. If you are in a group study, be prepared to share your answers with those in the group.

1. In your estimation, was Jane Austen, in her characterization of the female principle, a feminist or a Victorian social conformist? Explain your answer.

2. Explain why the novel as genre became such an important venue for woman writers in the late eighteenth and nineteenth centuries.

3. Explain the role of comedy, humor, and wit in secular and religious literary interpretation.

4. Explain the change in reaction from Austen's initial lukewarm response in the eighteenth century to her wide acclaim and popular readership in the twentieth century and beyond.

5. After reading and reflecting on the segment on *Sense and Sensibility*, what did you learn about the role and financial status of women in Austen's society?

6. After reading and reflecting on the segment on *Sense and Sensibility*, what did you learn about the role and financial status of men in a patriarchal society?

7. In portraying male and female characters, how does Austen demonstrate gender equality?

8. Explain the depth, subtlety, and limitation in Austen's use of the categories of "sense" and "sensibility" in this novel.

9. Explain and assess the meaning of the author's statement, "*Sense and Sensibility* endures for its conjunction of temperamental and spiritual qualities."

10. Explain how Charlotte Brontë's life influenced her literary perspective in general and *Jane Eyre* in particular.

11. Explain the three models of religion depicted by Brontë in *Jane Eyre* and the personal form of spirituality she develops in their place.

12. Explain why *Jane Eyre* is described as "the first feminist novel."

Chapter 6

Nathaniel Hawthorne's *The Scarlet Letter* and Thomas Hardy's *Tess of the D'Urbervilles*

CONSIDERED ONE OF THE MOST important authors of American literature and the genre of Romanticism, Nathaniel Hawthorne (1804–1860) graduated from Bowdoin College in 1825 determined to become a writer. His classmates at Bowdoin included Franklin Pierce—who later became President of the United States—Horatio Bridge, and Henry Wadsworth Longfellow, all of whom helped advance his career. His dark outlook on humanity, revealed both in his short stories and in his 1850 novel *The Scarlet Letter*, ran counter to Ralph Waldo Emerson and Henry David Thoreau, his peers in the Transcendentalist movement, who believed that there were elements of the divine in human beings.

For more than a decade, he devoted himself to learning his craft, living at home, reading, writing, and destroying many of his productions, but sending some of his stories to magazines, such as "Young Goodman Brown" and "The Minister's Black Veil," where they were published anonymously, though none drew major attention. In 1837, Horatio Bridge offered to help cover the cost of collecting and publishing these stories under Hawthorne's name into the volume *Twice-Told Tales*, which made Hawthorne known locally. After some ventures in editing undertaken to support himself, and after a brief period of employment in the Boston Custom House and a short period in 1841 as a member of the experimental socialist community at Brook Farm, Hawthorne married, at the age of thirty-eight, the illustrator and transcendentalist Sophia Peabody. Several years living in the Old Manse in Concord (Emerson's ancestral home, which for three years,

Hawthorne rented from Emerson) brought him into contact with Emerson and Thoreau.

Like Sophia, Hawthorne was a reclusive person. Although he was strong and well built, his boyhood had been less active than most. On the death of his father in 1808, Hawthorne's mother retired into her room and became a semi-recluse for the remainder of her long life. The quiet home became unusually quiet when Hawthorne developed lameness playing ball that required three years to overcome. During this period, reading became a substitute for physical activity. After a year in Maine, where he deepened his habit of solitude, he returned to Salem to live in his mother's house. For the next twelve years (1825 to 1837), he chiefly read and wrote. During this period his style improved so markedly that he turned out tales that still remain some of the best in the language. By 1837, he had developed a style that was unique among American writers for its dignity and intensity.

A Democrat, Hawthorne obtained a political position as Surveyor at the Salem Custom House in 1846, a job he lost after the presidential election of 1848, when he was forced out of office by the new Whig administration of Zachary Taylor. Angered and yet eager to return to writing, he moved to Concord, Massachusetts, where he began *The Scarlet Letter* almost immediately and wrote so rapidly that the book was finished by 1850, followed soon after with *The House of the Seven Gables, The Blithedale Romance, A Wonder-Book for Girls and Boys*, and other works.

Hawthorne then settled in the Red House in Lenox, in the Berkshires of western Massachusetts, where he formed his most significant literary friendship when he became a neighbor of Herman Melville, then at work on *Moby-Dick*, which Melville dedicated to Hawthorne. At this time he also wrote a campaign biography of Franklin Pierce, which became particularly important for Hawthorne financially, since Pierce, after being elected president in 1852, appointed Hawthorne to the lucrative position of consul in Liverpool.

Hawthorne then spent seven years in England and in Italy, adding steadily to his notebooks but unable to complete any creative work until, at the end of his stay in Italy, he wrote *The Marble Faun*. Returning to Concord in 1860, he died after four unhappy years, during which, working against failing health and flagging creative energies, he tried to bring to satisfactory conclusions several late romances which he left unfinished at his death. Survived by Sophia and three children, he was buried in the Sleepy Hollow Cemetery in Concord.

HAWTHORNE'S *THE SCARLET LETTER*:
PLOT AND RESPONSE

When Hawthorne wrote *The Scarlet Letter*, his original plan was to write a novella to be included among the tales that he meant to call *Old-Time Legends*, but he was encouraged by the publisher James T. Fields to enlarge the story and publish it separately. When the work was completed, it included a preface that referred to his three-year tenure in the Salem Custom House. Apparently, "The Custom House" was originally intended to be the introduction for *Old-Time Legends*, for the essay was probably finished before Hawthorne began writing *The Scarlet Letter*. The reasons for its being included in the same volume as *The Scarlet Letter* are not altogether certain, though Hawthorne had made it clear to Fields that he was not sure that *The Scarlet Letter* by itself would make a saleable volume. In addition, "The Custom House" served as an admirable introduction to the longer work because it contained a backstory for how the book came to be written. The nameless narrator had been the surveyor of the customhouse in Salem. In his spare time, he had discovered a packet of documents, among them a manuscript that was bundled with a scarlet, gold-embroidered patch of cloth in the shape of an "A." When the narrator lost his customs post, he decided to write a fictional account of the events recorded in the manuscript. *The Scarlet Letter* is the final product.

Hawthorne (for whom the narrator serves as mask) had a right to feel bitter about being fired as Surveyor of the Salem Custom House. To be sure, he had been appointed to the position by President Polk, a Democrat. But when Taylor, a Whig, was elected in 1848, he announced that proscription for party reasons was to cease. Under these circumstances, Hawthorne, it seemed, had no reason to fear loss of his job. However, a group of Salem Whigs, wishing to see Hawthorne removed, charged him with "corruption, iniquity, and fraud," and finally succeeded in having him replaced. The charges, of course, were wholly false, and his dismissal became a much talked about event in New England. Long after, Hawthorne realized that being fired made his name known throughout the country as his tales never could have done. Moreover, the situation provided him much material for "The Custom House" and for eventual characters such as Judge Pyncheon in *The House of the Seven Gables*. But at the time, Hawthorne was angry and hurt. Hawthorne wrote Longfellow that he meant to revenge himself in print on his political enemies. In "The Custom House," Hawthorne made allusions to local politicians, who did not appreciate their portrayal. As he admitted to Horatio Bridge, "I probably expressed more of [my contempt] than I intended." According to current reviewers *The Scarlet Letter*'s prefatory chapter soon provoked "the greatest uproar that ever happened here since witch-times."

Set in Puritan Massachusetts Bay Colony during the years 1642 to 1649, *The Scarlet Letter* tells the story of Hester Prynne, who conceives a daughter through an affair and then struggles to create a life of dignity and repentance. Containing a number of religious and historic allusions, the book explores themes of legalism, sin, and guilt through a man and a woman, essentially a new Adam and Eve in the seeming Eden of the New World, who deceive themselves for a moment into believing that they can escape the consequences of sin. *The Scarlet Letter* tells a story about what happens to a strict, tight-knit community when one of its members violates a societal taboo, and how shame functions in both the public and private realms of life. In this society, Hawthorne places three characters who represent three possibilities for action in a flawed world. None of these three characters represents the head or heart exclusively; rather, each illustrates the two in conflict. In telling the story of the adulterous but virtuous Hester Prynne, her weak, tormented lover Arthur Dimmesdale, and her vengeance-minded husband, Roger Chillingworth, Hawthorne explores ideas about the individual versus society and the nature of sin. The first-person, introductory chapter, written two hundred years after the events of the novel, indicates that the story will explore attitudes and beliefs that have evolved since the original setting. While the experience of Hester and Dimmesdale recalls the story of Adam and Eve (there is even a snake, personified by Chillingworth), it results in knowledge—not only of sin and expulsion, but also of what it means to be human. For both Hester and Dimmesdale, their passion results in guilt and suffering but also in greater empathy and self-awareness. The Puritan elders, on the other hand, insist on seeing earthly experience as merely an obstacle on the path to heaven. Thus, they view sin as a threat to the community that must be punished and suppressed. Their answer to Hester's sin is to ostracize her. Yet, Puritan society is stagnant, while Hester and Dimmesdale's experience shows that a state of sinfulness can lead to personal growth, empathy, and understanding of others.

The story begins in seventeenth-century Boston, then a Puritan settlement. A young woman (Hester Prynne) is led from the town prison with her infant daughter, Pearl, in her arms and the scarlet letter "A" on her breast. Her sentence requires her to stand on the scaffold for three hours, exposed to public humiliation, and to wear the scarlet letter for the rest of her life. As Hester approaches the scaffold, many of the women in the crowd are angered by her beauty and quiet dignity.

A man in the crowd tells an elderly onlooker that Hester is being punished for adultery. Hester's husband, a small, misshapen man much older than she, had sent her ahead to America but only now had arrived in Boston, under a new name. The consensus is that he had been lost at sea. While waiting for her husband, Hester has apparently had an affair, as she has given birth to a child. She will not reveal her lover's identity, however, and the scarlet letter, along with her public shaming, is punishment for her sin and her secrecy.

After introducing Hester as the protagonist, Hawthorne brings Hester in direct contact with Chillingworth, whom she has betrayed by committing adultery. He and Hester have an open conversation regarding their marriage, admitting that they were both in the wrong. Chillingworth however, now a physician, demands to know the identity of her lover. Hester refuses to divulge such information and Chillingworth accepts this, stating that he will persevere until he learns her secret. To further his plan, he forces Hester to conceal that he is her husband. If she ever reveals him, he warns her, he will destroy Pearl's father. Vowing to discover the identity of Pearl's father, Chillingworth acts as a proxy for the reader, who at this point is equally curious. Dimmesdale, Hester, and Chillingworth all keep their relationships to one another secret, so all three characters exist in isolation within the community. This dramatic irony, in which the reader knows each character's secret motivations but the characters remain ignorant of each other's true feelings, amplifies the tension.

Following her release from prison, Hester settles in a cottage at the edge of town and earns a meager living with her needlework. She lives a quiet, somber life with her daughter, Pearl, and performs acts of charity for the poor. She is troubled by her daughter's unusual fascination with the scarlet "A." The shunning of Hester also extends to Pearl, who has no playmates or friends except her mother. As she grows older, Pearl becomes capricious and unruly. Her conduct starts rumors, and, not surprisingly, the church members suggest Pearl be taken away from Hester. Hearing rumors that she may lose Pearl, Hester goes to speak to Governor Bellingham, who grants her wish.

As time passes, the conflict escalates with the growing relationship between Chillingworth and Dimmesdale. Because Dimmesdale's health has begun to fail, the townspeople are happy to have Chillingworth, the newly arrived physician, take up lodgings with their beloved minister. Being in such close contact with Dimmesdale, Chillingworth begins to suspect that the minister's illness is the result of some unconfessed guilt. He applies psychological pressure to the minister because he suspects Dimmesdale is Pearl's father. One evening, pulling the sleeping Dimmesdale's vestment aside, Chillingworth sees a symbol that represents his shame on the minister's chest.

In a climactic scene, Dimmesdale, tormented by his guilty conscience, goes to the square where Hester was punished years earlier. Climbing the scaffold in the dead of night, he admits his guilt but cannot find the courage to do so publicly in the light of day. Hester, shocked by Dimmesdale's physical and emotional deterioration, realizes that Dimmesdale, though he has been able to remain a member of society, has possibly suffered more than she has. Unlike Hester, Dimmesdale has kept his sin a secret, and continues to wear one face in public and another in private. Hester sees how Chillingworth has added to Dimmesdale's torment, and questions whether she is at fault for having concealed Chillingworth's identity.

Several days later, Hester meets Dimmesdale in the forest and tells him of her husband and his desire for revenge. She convinces Dimmesdale to leave Boston in secret on a ship to Europe where they can start life anew. Inspired by this plan, the minister seems to gain new energy. On Election Day, Dimmesdale gives one of his most inspired sermons. However, as the procession leaves the church, Dimmesdale climbs upon the scaffold and confesses his sin, dying in Hester's arms. Later, some witnesses swear that they saw a stigma in the form of a scarlet "A" upon his chest.

Although in hounding Dimmesdale to death, Chillingworth has achieved his revenge, he is frustrated by Dimmesdale's public revelation: "Thou hast escaped me!" Chillingworth says, as Dimmesdale dies. "May God forgive thee!" Dimmesdale replies, "Thou, too, hast deeply sinned." This statement suggests that Chillingworth's cold-hearted pursuit of vengeance, and, by extension, the town's thirst to punish Hester, are equal if not greater sins to Hester and Dimmesdale's adultery.

Chillingworth, losing his will for revenge, dies shortly thereafter and leaves Pearl a substantial inheritance. After Dimmesdale's death, Hester leaves the community, but returns for unknown reasons and chooses to live out her life in quiet seclusion, wearing her scarlet "A" by choice and acting as a confessor to other women who have violated societal norms.

POINTS TO PONDER IN *THE SCARLET LETTER*

When *The Scarlet Letter* was published in 1850, it was one of the first mass produced books in America, selling out the first edition in ten days and earning Hawthorne much needed income. The book became a best seller in the United States, initiating Hawthorne's most lucrative period as a writer. Initial reviews varied; some critics objected to the book's "morbid intensity" and its dense psychological detail, while reviewers in religious periodicals regularly labeled it demoralizing if not downright immoral, finding it at odds with the Christian message of purity and peace and slanderous to their colonial antecedents. However, by 1879, no less a luminary than Henry James hailed *The Scarlet Letter* as "the finest piece of imaginative writing yet put forth in the country" and Hawthorne's "most substantial title to fame." James's praise reverberated through dozens of essays and critical studies over the next fifty years. By the turn of the twentieth century, Hawthorne had become the crown prince of American literature, praised as a literary genius by many, though none more effusively than D. H. Lawrence, who called *The Scarlet Letter* "a perfect work of the American imagination."

During the twentieth century, the meaning and significance of Hawthorne's romance[1] was hotly debated, ranging from focus on gender and sexuality to psychology, morality, theology, and spirituality. Over that period, *The Scarlet Letter* was also adapted regularly for film and television, notably from the 1926 silent film starring Lillian Gish to the highly praised 1979 PBS miniseries.

Few writers had been better prepared for composing *The Scarlet Letter*. For years, Hawthorne had studied the history of early New England, not only in its events but more importantly, in its customs, beliefs, and ideas. His notebooks and journals were filled with ideas and details for stories, and more importantly, he learned in his tales and sketches how to project his ideas through character and symbol. In "The Gentle Boy," for example, he

---

1. When, in the preface to *The House of the Seven Gables* (1851), Hawthorne made his now famous distinction between the novel and the romance, he was distinguishing between "fact" (the provenance of the novel) and "truth" (the provenance of the romance). Hawthorne called his major works "romances" because he believed that unlike novels, romances allowed him liberty to transform fact into *meaningful* fact, and thus granted him greater facility to portray the "truth of the human heart."

had dealt with the hostility of Puritan society to a Quaker child, in "Young Goodman Brown" with the ambiguity of sin, in "The Minister's Black Veil" with the effects of an outer symbol of inner guilt, in "Rappacinni's Daughter" with a man of intellect who is willing to sacrifice a loved one for the sake of learning, in "Ethan Brand" with "unforgivable" sin and various combinations of the relation between head and heart, and in "Endicott and the Red Cross" with religious persecution, even giving passing mention to the character who eventually became Hester Prynne.

The major theme of *The Scarlet Letter* is the conflict between the individual and society, the archetypal American theme that shaped American literature in the centuries ahead. We may well ask the question, "Why the Puritan setting?" The Puritans were viewed as America's "Founding Fathers," establishing colonies in the 1600s that concentrated on biblical teachings, enacting a mission to live providentially according to God's will. However, this mindset led to hypocrisy, inflexible standards, vindictive policies, and moralistic behavior.

In his writings, Hawthorne both condemned and admired Puritanism. For one thing, Hawthorne's personal background complicates any answer we might give. Born from old New England stock, one ancestor, William Hathorne, was a Puritan and the first of the family to emigrate from England. He became an important member of the Massachusetts Bay Colony and held many political positions, including magistrate and judge, becoming infamous for his harsh sentencing. In addition, William's son John Hathorne was one of the judges who oversaw the Salem witch trials. (Hawthorne probably added the "w" to his surname in an effort to dissociate himself from his notorious ancestors.)

While Hawthorne was never shy in expressing his gratitude to the Puritans for their early political struggle for liberty, particularly in demanding liberty of conscience and freedom in law from their British rulers, he always felt that the religious system of Puritanism was cold, hard, and confined. He seems to praise the attitude of individual believers, but not the system of belief. While personally affirming the doctrines of providence and original sin in his writings, he consistently deplored the sin of pride, in his mind a natural consequence of those who would exclude much of the human race in the same way that predestination arbitrarily elects some to salvation and others to damnation.

In the Puritan way of life, religion and law were closely related. The law itself was severe, and severely carried out, as Hawthorne made clear in *The Scarlet Letter*. He never questioned the need for civil law, but he clearly criticized the Puritan method of conferring it. New England had become the home for Calvinistic theology, and in his romance, Hawthorne singled out shaming and social stigmatizing, both opposed to his understanding of a just and moral society. Another theme in *The Scarlet Letter* is the extreme legalism of the Puritans and how Hester chose not to conform to their legalistic norms. Shunned by her society, even though she spent her life helping the sick and the poor, she spent her life mostly in solitude, retreating into her own mind and values. Her thoughts led her to question Puritan rules and beliefs, such as their understanding of sin and salvation. For example, she acknowledges her sin, but she feels that her compassion and benevolence will not keep her from heaven. Alienated from Puritan society, both physically and spiritually, she moves beyond conformity to social mores to establish her own moral standards and beliefs.

At the end, the outcast is depicted as better than the Puritan community that shunned and expelled her. Unfortunately, Dimmesdale never attains the truth Hester has learned: that individuality and strength are gained by quiet self-affirmation and by reconfiguring, not rejecting, one's assigned identity. Significantly, throughout the narrative, both Dimmesdale and Hester achieve greater compassion because they have suffered. As a result, they can sympathize with how good people might still make mistakes. This ability to show empathy makes Hester and Dimmesdale highly valued within the community: Dimmesdale gains a greater reputation as a minister, and by the end of the book Hester becomes the epitome of a wise woman. By connecting the experience of suffering to the growth of empathy, Hawthorne suggests that even tragic events can have meaning and value.

Associated with the conflict between the individual and society is the theme of nature versus society, exemplified through *The Scarlet Letter* by human passion and sexuality but also represented by a wild rosebush, a symbol for individual freedom, romantic relationships, and other qualities antithetical to Puritan society. Hawthorne introduces a wild rosebush very early in his story, growing naturally beside the prison door where Hester is incarcerated. Hawthorne further associates the rosebush with Ann Hutchinson, an antecedent of Hester's who had been banished for challenging Puritan beliefs and practices. As Hawthorne's story unfolds, he associates the wild rosebush with Pearl, who, on seeing a rosebush during her visit to Governor Bellingham, longs for a red rose and cannot be pacified.

Pearl's attraction to the rosebush is immediate and constant, for the rose-bush is a symbol for defiance. When the governor asks Pearl who made her, she responds that she has not been made at all but rather "had been plucked by her mother off the bush of wild roses, that grew by the prison-door."[2] The symbol of the wild rosebush lives on after Hester and Dimmesdale die, for their tombstone reads, "On a field, sable, the letter A, gules" (a reference to the scarlet letter's red on a black background, just as the wild rosebush had red roses on the black background of the prison door).

A climactic scene takes place in the forest, where Hester and Dimmesdale can speak openly with one another and even dare to imagine a future where they can break free from the strictures of society and find happiness together. In Hawthorne's depiction, nature is on the side of lovers. Likewise, Pearl is free to roam safely through the forest, viewed as a safe haven for children and lovers. Nature is *The Scarlet Letter*'s most powerful declaration of independence—physically, morally, and spiritually. However, while nature offers this unconventional family freedom, individually, each member is still subject to the laws of society and must live with the conse-quences of their actions and beliefs. Nevertheless, throughout Hawthorne's book, nature images contrast with the stark darkness of the Puritans and their confining social and religious systems.

In addition to Puritan influence on social values and group behav-ior, another point to ponder regards Hawthorne's protofeminist depiction of women. In *The Scarlet Letter*, Hawthorne explores the theme of female independence by introducing a strong and independent female protago-nist, a heroine who, living at the margins of society, is able to make her own decisions and care for herself. Because Hester is cast out of the community, she is liberated from the traditional expectation that a woman be docile and submissive. Critics often view Hawthorne's use of female characters such as Hester Prynne as foreshadowing the self-reliance and responsibility that led to women's suffrage and reproductive emancipation. Aside from Hester, the women of Hawthorne's other romances are more fully real-ized than his male characters. This observation is equally true of his short stories, in which lead female characters serve as allegorical figures, such as Rappaccini's daughter and Young Goodman Brown's wife Faith Brown. In *Drowne's Wooden Image*, it is a woman who "first created the artist who afterwards created her image."[3]

2. Hawthorne, *Scarlet Letter*, 82.
3. Hawthorne, *Tales and Sketches*, 942.

In this brief survey, one last point requires comment: Hawthorne's letter "A." In this, the most famous and potent hieroglyph in American literature, we recognize the obvious symbolism of adultery, but in his story, Hawthorne includes other meanings, such as "art," "able," and "angel," for through them all, Hawthorne reveals a culture that is strangely graphic, expressing itself in letters and codes that demand interpretation. In this study of secrecy and violation, we encounter Hawthorne's commentary on social and private knowledge, communication, and meaning. In Hester Prynne, Hawthorne creates a character struggling between feelings she neither controls nor fully understands. It is precisely because he is not afraid to explore beliefs and behaviors underlying patterns of compulsion that Hawthorne so ably plumbs the depths of our common nature.

THOMAS HARDY

Common themes drive Hawthorne's *Scarlet Letter* and Thomas Hardy's *Tess of the D'Urbervilles*, facilitating their merger in this chapter. Like Hester Prynne in *The Scarlet Letter*, Tess may be seen as a feminist rebel, a strong, sexual, rebellious, and anarchic woman. Furthermore, the theme of nature versus society, exemplified by Hester and Dimmesdale's forbidden passion and by Pearl, the product of that passion, is also central to Hardy's novel.

At his death, Thomas Hardy (1840–1928) was the reigning figure in English literature, towering over his British literary peers. He was both a great novelist and a great poet, his writing career falling neatly into two chronological segments. From the 1860s until the late 1890s, he mainly wrote fiction; from the turn of the century until his death, he was principally a poet. Though he wrote poetry throughout his life and regarded himself primarily as a poet, initially he gained fame as the author of novels such as *Far from the Madding Crowd* (1874), *The Return of the Native* (1886), *The Mayor of Casterbridge* (1886), *Tess of the D'Urbervilles* (1891), and *Jude the Obscure* (1895).

Like Austen's characters Elinor and Marianne, who symbolize the convergence of the Classical and Romantic eras, Hardy's literary work straddled two eras, his poetry typifying the Modern period and his novels, late Victorian Romanticism. A Victorian realist in the tradition of George Eliot, Hardy was highly critical of much in Victorian society, including religion, marriage, industrialization and urbanization (twin engines of Victorian progress), and sexual and social morality, finding that Victorian mores and beliefs limited people's lives and caused unhappiness and despair. Such unhappiness, and the suffering it brings, are central to Hardy's novels.

Hardy was born in the village of Upper Bockhampton, a hamlet in the county of Dorset in southwest England, where his father was a stonemason and local builder. In *Far from the Madding Crowd*, Hardy first introduced the idea of setting his novels in his native region, an area he formalized as Wessex. As a youth, he was sent to good schools, where he excelled. While his family was reasonably well off socially and financially, at the age of sixteen he was removed from school and apprenticed to a local architect. In 1862, at the age of twenty-one, he moved to London to become an assistant architect to Arthur Blomfield, a church designer and restorer, for whom he worked for five years. In his spare time, he wrote poetry and attended lectures at King's College.

During this time he became actively conscious of class division and his social inferiority. Interest in social reform led him to the works of John Stuart Mill, particularly to Mill's essay *On Liberty*. Other influences affecting his thought include Horace Moule, a religious scholar who introduced him to Darwinism and other progressive ideas that cast doubt on traditional religious beliefs and practices, including literal interpretations of the Bible and traditional Christian views of God.

In 1867, bored by architecture and concerned about his health, Hardy returned to Dorset, where he dedicated himself to writing. In 1870, he met Emma Gifford, whom he married in 1874. Hardy's first novel, *The Poor Man and the Lady*, finished in 1867, was a sweeping satire on Victorian and urban society. Failing to find a publisher, Hardy showed it to the novelist George Meredith, who advised him to set that work aside and write novels with more plot. Tapping into his rural background, Hardy found he could use idyllic country settings to achieve success, combining his critical perspective with a warmly ironic style.

Like many Victorian novelists, Hardy composed his novels for serial installment in magazines. Forced to yield to changes by editors who felt his fiction was too critical or grim, Hardy's sense of loneliness, alienation, and frustration grew, increasing his anger for Victorian hypocrisy. Later, when his works were published as complete novels, he carefully restored the original version. In the serialized version of *Tess*, for example the heroine is tricked into marriage, whereas in the novel form, she is raped. Also, in *The Return of the Native*, the editor who first serialized the story insisted that the novelist add to the narrative, which calls for a tragic conclusion, a conventional happy ending. By 1895, when Hardy published his last great novel, *Jude the Obscure*, it met with such a negative response from the Victorian public for its controversial treatment of marriage, sex, and religion (some booksellers sold the novel in brown paper bags, and one cleric is reputed to have burnt his copy) that it led to Hardy's farewell from fiction. The book's apparent attack on the institution of marriage also caused a strain on Hardy's marriage, for Emma became concerned that the novel would be read as autobiographical.

Despite negative reviews, Hardy's work was greatly admired by younger writers, including D. H. Lawrence and Virginia Woolf, both of whom wrote approvingly of his novels and poetry. In 1910, Hardy was appointed a Member of the Order of Merit and was nominated for the Nobel Prize in Literature, for which he was nominated again in 1921. At his death, his ashes were buried in the Poets' Corner of Westminster Abbey among England's great authors, although oddly, to honor his wishes, his heart was removed from his body prior to cremation and interred with Emma's body at Stinsford.

HARDY'S *TESS OF THE D'URBERVILLES*: PLOT AND RESPONSE

Hardy's novel is set in an impoverished rural England in fictional Wessex, during the Long Depression of the 1870s. Tess is the oldest child of John and Joan Durbeyfield, uneducated peasants. However, John is given the impression by Parson Tringham that he is the descendant of an ancient noble family, the d'Urbervilles, the surname of an extinct noble family. Knowledge of this immediately goes to John's head.

That same day, Tess, his eldest daughter, joins the other village girls in the May Day dance, where she exchanges glances with Angel Clare, youngest son of Reverend James Clare. Angel is on a walking tour with his two brothers, but stops to join the dance and partners several other girls. He notices Tess too late to dance with her. That night, Tess's father gets too drunk to drive a load of beehives to a neighboring town and so Tess undertakes the journey with a younger brother. However, she falls asleep at the reins and the family's only horse, Prince, is struck by a speeding wagon and fatally injured. Tess feels so guilty at Prince's death and the economic consequences for the family that she agrees, against her better judgement, to visit Mrs. d'Urberville, a rich widow in a rural mansion and "claim kin." She is unaware that in fact Mrs. d'Urberville's husband Simon Stoke adopted the surname and was unrelated to the real d'Urbervilles.

Tess fails to meet Mrs. d'Urberville, but chances on her libertine son, Alec, who takes a fancy to Tess and finds her a job as a poultry keeper on the estate. Although Tess tells her parents that she fears he may try to seduce her, they encourage her to take the job, secretly hoping Alec may marry her. Tess dislikes Alec, but endures his persistent unwanted attentions while earning enough to replace her family's horse. Despite his often cruel and manipulative behavior, the threat from Alec to Tess's virtue is obscured for Tess by her inexperience and almost daily, commonplace interactions with him.

Tess spends several months at this job, resisting Alec's attempts to seduce her. Finally, Alec takes advantage of her in the woods one night after a fair. Tess knows she does not love him, so she returns home to her family to give birth to Alec's child, whom she christens Sorrow. Sorrow dies soon after he is born, and Tess spends a miserable year at home before deciding to seek work elsewhere. She finally accepts a job as a milkmaid, where she enjoys a period of contentment. While there, she meets Angel Clare, the man from the May Day dance. Tess and Angel gradually fall in love, and Tess eventually accepts Angel's proposal of marriage. Still, she is troubled by pangs of conscience and feels she should tell Angel about her past. She writes him a confessional note and slips it under his door, but it slides under the carpet and Angel never sees it.

After their wedding, Angel and Tess both confess indiscretions: Angel tells Tess about an affair he had with an older woman in London, and Tess tells Angel about her history with Alec. Tess forgives Angel, but Angel cannot forgive Tess. He gives her some money and boards a ship bound for Brazil, where he thinks he might establish a farm. He tells Tess he will try to accept her past but warns her not to try to join him until he comes for her. In the meantime, Tess has a difficult time finding work and is forced to take a job at an unpleasant farm. At one point, she hears a wandering preacher speak, and is stunned to discover that he is Alec d'Urberville, who had been converted to Christianity by Angel's father. Alec and Tess are shaken by their encounter, and Alec implores Tess never to tempt him again. Soon after, however, he begs Tess to marry him, having turned his back on his religious ways.

Tess learns from her sister Liza-Lu that her mother is near death, and Tess is forced to return home to take care of her. Her mother recovers, but her father unexpectedly dies soon after. When the family is evicted from their home, Alec offers help, but Tess refuses to accept, knowing he only wants to obligate her to him again. At last, Angel decides to forgive his wife. He leaves Brazil, desperate to find her. Instead, he finds her mother, who tells him Tess has gone to the village of Sandbourne. There, he finds Tess in an expensive boardinghouse, where he tells her he has forgiven her and begs her to take him back. In one of the novel's most poignant moments, Tess tells Angel that he has come too late: she had gone back to Alec d'Urberville. Angel leaves in a daze, and, heartbroken to the point of madness, Tess goes upstairs and stabs her lover to death. When the landlady finds Alec's body, she raises an alarm, but Tess has already fled to find Angel.

Angel agrees to help Tess. They hide out in an empty mansion for a few days, then travel to Stonehenge, where Tess falls asleep. However, when morning breaks, a search party discovers them, arresting Tess and sending her to jail. Later, Angel and Liza-Lu watch as a black flag is raised over the prison, signaling Tess's execution.

POINTS TO PONDER IN *TESS OF THE D'URBERVILLES*

When I began writing *Deeper Splendor*, it seemed obvious to include Hawthorne and Hardy's novels in my study. Both had been required reading in high school, and both inspired my love for great literature. Far from home and alone at school, I was angered and appalled at how Hawthorne's Hester was treated by society at large, but I found myself bonding with Hardy's Tess, a pure woman victimized by flawed lovers and industrialized society. Unlike Tess, I was secure, well fed, and valued as a member of a small, select boarding school. Yet in my loneliness, coupled with a fertile imagination, I identified with Tess, and her story brought forth in me a deep desire for a just and equitable society.

At the center of Hardy's novel is Tess, whose resilience and steady growth in confidence shape her response to the problems caused not only by others but also by her emotions and self-image. The book gains its power through its concentration on her actions, her direct responses, and her refusal to be divided by the conflicting forces that beset her. Its subtitle, *A Pure Woman: Faithfully Presented*, tells us that Tess points beyond herself to a definite Victorian archetype, the innocent woman seduced and socially ruined. Though Hardy clearly meant to criticize Victorian notions of female purity, the double standard also made the heroine's tragedy possible and thus serves as a mechanism of Tess's broader fate. Hardy variously hinted that Tess must suffer either to atone for the misdeeds of her ancestors, or to provide temporary amusement for the gods, or because she possesses some lethal character flaw inherited from her ancestors.

When Hardy first submitted *Tess* to the publisher, it was refused publication on the grounds of its sympathetic portrayal of a "fallen woman" and hence as an affront to Victorian society. Hardy depicts Angel and Alec as figures of Victorian society hovering around Tess but misunderstanding her, unworthy of her, and unable to match her strength and spontaneity. Both represent the principal character types of the Victorian middle class— Alec, the cruel bourgeois, and Angel, the disinherited intellectual. Without roots, both exhibit a split between thought and feeling, and both lack an adequate image of selfhood. Alec's conversion and later regression may be seen as improbable, but it reflects his vulnerability and his relationship to Angel. Angel's father as the agent of Alec's conversion serves as a comment on the relationship of dogma to self, but also on ideological systems of the day that distort feelings and repress individuality.

Within Tess is a deep distrust of dogmatism in general, all ways of thinking that give abstract ideals or principles—whether religious or social—priority over the actual needs of specific human situations. Thus, Angel's mistake, according to Hardy, has been that of "allowing himself to be influenced by general principles to the disregard of the particular instance."[4] That is why the role of nature is so pervasive in this book, for nature is the opposite of idea. Against the unsatisfactoriness of creeds and dogmas is posed "the appetite for joy" that pervades nature. Tess is "pure" because in the central quality of her life and feeling she is, in this sense, natural.

Despite the side stories and supporting cast, the source of the novel's unity and strength lies in Tess's responses to her experience and suffering. Her charm, innocence, and resilience all indicate openness to experience and the healthy habit of being true to her feelings. Hardy does not expect readers to judge her actions as right or wrong, but simply to see them as authentically hers. While many of Tess's qualities are admirable, some are questionable, even shocking. It is impossible to label her, however, for she is an embodiment of human creativity and wisdom that neither Angel nor Alec rightly understand. She is truly the genuine d'Urberville, with flashes of haughtiness and ancient magnificence, connected to the soil, primeval

4. Hardy, *Tess of the D'Urbervilles*, 365.

and pagan in her natural beliefs. In this respect, Tess is the face of the English past brought into the present.

One of the recurrent themes of Hardy's novel is the way in which men define and dominate women, exerting power over them due primarily to male privilege. Alec's act of rape, the most life-altering event that Tess experiences in the novel, is clearly the most serious instance of male domination over a female. However, there are other, less blatant examples of women's passivity toward dominant men, such as when, after Angel reveals that he prefers Tess, Tess's friend Retty attempts suicide and her friend Marian becomes an alcoholic. This makes their earlier schoolgirl crushes on Angel seem disturbing, for such devotion is not merely fanciful love, but unhealthy obsession. These girls appear utterly dominated by a desire for a man who, Hardy tells us explicitly, does not even realize that they are interested in him. This sort of unconscious male domination of women is perhaps even more unsettling than Alec's outward and self-conscious cruelty. Typically, abuse of males over women continues to this day, and helps explain recurring suffering and trauma in millions of lives.

Even Angel's love for Tess, pure and gentle in many ways, dominates her in an unhealthy way. Angel substitutes an idealized picture of Tess's country purity for the real-life woman that he continually refuses to get to know. When Angel calls Tess names like "Daughter of Nature" and "Artemis," we feel that he may be denying her true self in favor of a mental image that he prefers. Thus, her identity and experiences are suppressed, albeit unknowingly. This pattern of male domination is finally reversed with Tess's murder of Alec, in which, for the first time in the novel, a woman takes active steps against a man. Of course, this act only leads to even greater suppression of a woman by men, when the crowd of male police officers arrest Tess at Stonehenge. Nevertheless, for a moment, the accepted pattern of submissive women bowing to dominant men is interrupted by Tess's poignant declaration, "I am ready." Spoken quietly and serenely to Angel and the police who surround the sacrificial slab upon which she lies, Tess's act seems heroic.

Another theme Hardy explores in this novel is what he called the "ache of modernism," a form of suffering each character experiences. Angel's middle-class bias and scruples make him reject Tess, a woman whom Hardy presents as a sort of rural Eve, in harmony with the natural world. Much of the heartbreak and tragedy Hardy describes can be interpreted as negative results of humanity's separation from nature. Hardy believed that, at their most fulfilled, humans exist in an "intelligent relationship with nature." Increasingly, however, the heroines and heroes of his fiction are forced to immigrate to towns. Urbanization was one of the great engines of Victorian progress, but inevitably, the migration to cities entailed a terrible loss of identity and links to one's ancestry.

Tess may be seen as a personification of nature, an idea supported by her ties with animals throughout the novel. Tess's misfortunes begin when she falls asleep while driving Prince to market and causes the horse's death; then she becomes a poultry-keeper, and when she and Angel fall in love, it is amid cows in a fertile valley. Yet Tess emerges as a powerful character not through this symbolism alone but because Hardy's feelings for her were strong, perhaps stronger than for any of his other invented personages.

Because of the numerous pagan references made about her, Tess has been seen variously as an earth goddess or a sacrificial victim. For example, early in the novel, she takes part in a May Dance, a festival for the goddess of the harvest, and when she baptizes her dead child, performing the ceremony herself, she chooses a passage from Genesis, the book of creation, rather than more traditional New Testament verses. Also, when Tess and Angel come to Stonehenge, which was commonly believed in Hardy's time to be a pagan temple, she willingly lies on a stone supposedly associated with human sacrifice.

Throughout the novel, Hardy repeatedly evokes elements from the Genesis story of Adam and Eve in the Garden of Eden. Such references, found also in *The Scarlet Letter*, give these novels broader metaphysical and philosophical dimensions. Like Hester, Dimmsdale, and Chillingworth, the roles of Eve, Adam, and the serpent in paradise are clearly delineated in *Tess*: Angel is the noble Adam newly born, while Tess is the indecisive and troubled Eve. Alec, with his open avowal that he is bad to the bone, is the conniving Satan. He seduces Tess under a tree, giving her sexual knowledge in return for her lost innocence. The very name of the forest where this seduction occurs, the Chase, suggests how Eve will be chased from Eden for her sins. This guilt, which will never be erased, is known in Christian theology as the original sin that all humans are said to have inherited.

Like most of Hardy's novels, *Tess* is an immensely powerful novel. It raises a question that we can trace to Shakespeare and back to Aristotle: Why do we enjoy tragedy? One answer is that it is not the suffering that we admire but the artistry with which that suffering is depicted. And few portray the complexities, hazards, and miseries of modern life in a more masterly fashion than Hardy. Paradoxical as it seems, he creates beauty out of suffering. Another answer appears in one of Hardy's poems: "If way to the better there be, it exacts a full look at the worst." As we learn from Hardy, we must look at life as it really is if we are to live fully. Like all great writers, Hardy gives us a better sense of what we are and how we can live. That knowledge of what life is makes life, if not worth living, at least understandable.

QUESTIONS FOR DISCUSSION AND REFLECTION

In addition to the questions listed at the end of the preface, answer the following questions, writing your answers in a journal. If you are in a group study, be prepared to share your answers with those in the group.

1. Identify the chief religious themes in *The Scarlet Letter*, and discuss how shame functions in both the public and private realms of life.

2. Explain how Hawthorne explores ideas about the individual versus society, and how sin, as defined socially, affects Hester, Dimmesdale, and Chillingworth in the novel.

3. Explain how sin in one's life can result in knowledge and awareness, not only of guilt and of alienation, but also of what it means to be human.

4. Explain how Puritans viewed sin socially and how it is viewed today. Explain how dealing with personal sin can lead to greater self-awareness and increased spiritual growth.

5. Explain and assess the role of Puritanism in Hawthorne's life and thought.

6. Explain the chief virtues and the major weaknesses in Calvinist theology. What does Hester's example teach women in particular and dissidents in general about how to cope with prejudice, bias, and shame in patriarchal, elitist, and supremacist communities?

7. Explain and assess Hawthorne as a protofeminist writer.

8. Explain how progressive ideas influenced Hardy's class-consciousness and religious nonconformity.

9. Explain the centrality of nature in spirituality and its role in *The Scarlet Letter* and in *Tess of the D'Urbervilles*.

10. Compare and contrast Hester Prynne and Tess of the d'Urbervilles as personifications of the female archetype.

11. Explain and assess Tess's deep distrust of religious fundamentalism in particular and dogmatism in general.

12. Discuss the profound and lasting effects of childhood trauma and sexual abuse on male and female sexuality, mental health, and spirituality.

Chapter 7

Charles Dickens's *Bleak House* and William Thackeray's *Vanity Fair*

No STUDY OF SPIRITUALITY, personality, and social justice in modern literature can ignore the novels of Charles Dickens. His influence on the genre is immense, particularly in his development of plot, his unforgettable cast of characters, his social vision, and the power of his social protest. Recognized by scholars and critics as a literary genius, many also regard him as the greatest novelist of the Victorian era. His works enjoyed unprecedented popularity during his life and continue to be widely read in the present.

Charles Dickens (1812–1870) began his literary career as a journalist. He edited a weekly journal for twenty years, and during his lifetime wrote fifteen novels, five novellas, and hundreds of short stories and nonfiction articles. He also lectured, performed readings, and campaigned vigorously for children's rights, against poverty, and for other social reforms.

When we think of Dickens, the works that promptly come to mind are *The Pickwick Papers*, *Oliver Twist*, *David Copperfield*, *A Tale of Two Cities*, *Great Expectations*, and the Christmas novella known as *A Christmas Carol*, featuring Ebenezer Scrooge, Jacob Marley, and the spirits of Christmas Past, Present, and Yet to Come. Despite the popularity of these works, in this chapter we examine *Bleak House*, a masterful critique of Victorian society. Beloved by Dickens's reading public and acknowledged by modern critics as containing some of Dickens's best work, initially, *Bleak House* was disparaged by Victorian reviewers, who complained that this novel too often featured satire instead of humor, complexity instead of vividness, and artifice instead of spontaneity, and that Dickens's sentiments about the poor had been transformed from edifying sympathy to vindictive indignation. *Bleak House* seemingly lacked the warmth and innocence that Dickens's readers had associated with his name since the success of his first novel, *The Pickwick Papers*, sixteen years before.

Dickens had begun his writing career as a reporter, and the journalistic environment in which he wrote turned him to think in terms of the needs and interest of his readers. Nevertheless, he was also a self-expressive artist of strong romantic tendencies, whose ultimate sources of power lay deeply buried in his emotions. *Bleak House* contains many of the elements that had made Dickens popular: it had vivid narrative, comedy, swift action, and the detailed, affectionate treatment of character and setting that had always entertained his readers. However, it also contains the pathos, terror, violence, and sense of social injustice that had moved them.

Bleak House is less autobiographical than *David Copperfield* or *Great Expectations*, but through figures such as Jo, Charley, and Esther, varied renderings of the familiar Dickensian theme of the neglected child, the parallels with Dickens's life are evident. Dickens's father, an unsuccessful civil servant, was an erratic provider for his family. At age twelve, Dickens was forced to work in a factory that manufactured shoe-blacking, while his father languished in prison for debt. The specter of this humiliating experience, and the poverty of these years, haunted Dickens for the rest of his life. Dickens reported later that the shame and degradation of this period consigned him to a meaningless, drudging existence without the chance of an education. At the same time, his father was imprisoned, increasing the youngster's isolation and despondency as he was left to wander the streets and make the most of his small earnings. This short period of Dickens's life had a disproportionately profound effect on his writing.

When his father, after coming into a small inheritance, was released from prison, Dickens went to a conventional school for a couple of years, and then, at the age of sixteen, entered a lawyer's office as a clerk. This was the first of his many opportunities to observe the legal profession, a subject featured in *Bleak House*. He gathered impressions of the legal profession during a brief career as a court stenographer, and for two years he observed the behavior of barristers and their clients, recording the absurdity, pathos, and tedium of their cases. His work as a stenographer and then as a newspaper reporter brought him into contact with London street life. London, no longer simply a bewildering urban wilderness, now became a field for exploration and observation, and this period of Dicken's life had as much to do with his work as a novelist as any other. During this time, he frequented the theater, and created ambitions of becoming an actor. His work as a reporter sent him to various provincial towns to cover elections and record speeches; these trips gave him a wide knowledge of England.

Dickens's work as a novelist originated in journalism. While working as a shorthand reporter in the House of Commons, he began writing sketches and short stories, publishing them under the name of "Boz," a family nickname he employed as a pseudonym for several years. Soon, his *Sketches by Boz* gained the attention of newspaper publishers, one of whom engaged Dickens to undertake the project that became *The Pickwick Papers*, a comedic series of sketches of British life. Seizing the opportunity, Dickens hired "Phiz" to provide engravings for each installment. The serial publication of *The Pickwick Papers* was a publishing sensation, leading to numerous spin-offs and merchandise ranging from Pickwick cigars, playing cards, figurines, puzzles, and comic books. Within a few years, Dickens had become an international literary celebrity, famous for his humor, satire, and keen observation of character and society.

Dickens's novels, most of them published in monthly or weekly installments, pioneered the serial publication of narrative fiction, which became the dominant Victorian mode for novel publication. Cliffhanger endings in serial publications kept readers in suspense. The installment format allowed Dickens to evaluate his audience's reaction, and he often modified his plot and character development based on such feedback. At a time prior to universal education and lacking radio, television, or electronic social media, many illiterate poor paid a halfpenny to have monthly episodes read to them, inspiring a new class of readers.

In 1836, Dickens married Catherine Hogarth, the daughter of George Hogarth, editor of the *Evening Chronicle*. Before *Pickwick* had completed its run of monthly issues, Dickens found himself writing two novels simultaneously, editing a newly founded magazine, and committing himself to write further novels. Having captured his public, Dickens, still under twenty-five years of age, embarked on a mission inspired by the Scottish philosopher Thomas Carlyle, who saw England as a society fractured by urbanization, the Industrial Revolution, and widespread meanness and cruelty. Dickens resolved to use the novel as an instrument of political and social reform, using a two-pronged approach. First, he needed to cast light on current abuses and the hardheartedness he believed originated with lawmakers in Parliament. Second, he resolved to focus on changing hearts by creating greater empathy. For Dickens, the novel could make readers aware of the pain and need of others, a malaise rampant in England's lower classes. The significance of Boz, as his readers also called him, was that he could penetrate the minds of his readers and change them. His readers left his novels different people from who they had been when they entered them.

Dickens set off on his mission with his second full-length novel, *Oliver Twist* (1836), written in part to counteract the 1834 Poor Law Reform Amendment Act, which was based on the thinking of Jeremy Bentham, the father of utilitarianism. The essence of Benthamism was that human beings organize their lives around the pursuit of pleasure and the avoidance of pain. Make the necessity to live on public charity sufficiently painful, Bentham argued, and human beings would choose the less painful option of work and economic independence. Dickens saw this line of rational social policy for what it was: cruel and heartless, and he would use fiction to oppose it. Recall the scene in *A Christmas Carol* (1834) in which two men visit Ebenezer Scrooge in the hopes of getting a charitable donation from him. Scrooge proved to be a Benthamite to the core, and, as Scrooge's heart is softened in the story by the spirits of Christmas, so Dickens believed he could change hard hearts to sympathetic ones.

The old social welfare system was based on the "parish system," which presumed that the needs of the poor and destitute would be met by communal philanthropy. The parish system presumed a stable local population, but with the Industrial Revolution, the British population lost its moral roots. In *Oliver Twist*, Dickens made his argument with a daring innovation, making the hero of his novel a child. In that novel, the young hero's restless movement from place to place is symbolic of the migratory shifts of population taking place in England in the first half of the nineteenth century. London alone doubled in population every ten years.

During the fifteen years after *Pickwick* and *Oliver*, Dickens not only wrote the series of great novels leading up to *Bleak House* (1853), but he carried on extensive editorial work and undertook hugely popular and remunerative reading trips to the United States and Italy. Additional novels followed, including *A Tale of Two Cities* (1859) and *Great Expectations* (1861), which were resounding successes. Set in London and Paris, *A Tale of Two Cities* became his best-known work of historical fiction and one of the best-selling novels of all time.

Between 1868 and 1869, Dickens gave a series of "farewell readings" in England, Scotland, and Ireland. Delivering seventy-five readings in the provinces and a further twelve in London, he suffered fits of paralysis, followed by a stroke, leading to the cancellation of further public appearances. After he regained sufficient strength, he arranged for an additional series of readings. He made his last public appearance at a Royal Academy Banquet in the presence of the Prince and Princess of Wales. On June 8, 1870, he suffered another stroke at his home and never regained consciousness. Contrary to his wish to be buried privately, he was laid to rest in the Poets' Corner of Westminster Abbey.

DICKENS'S *BLEAK HOUSE*: PLOT AND RESPONSE

Bleak House is the story of the Jarndyce family, who wait in vain to inherit money from a disputed fortune in the settlement of the extremely long-running lawsuit of Jarndyce and Jarndyce. The novel is pointedly critical of England's Court of Chancery,[1] in which cases could drag on through decades of convoluted legal maneuvering. Dickens's story begins in the High Court of Chancery, where the case of Jarndyce and Jarndyce has gone on for generations and has "become so complicated that no man alive knows what it means." The current issue concerns two young wards of the court, Ada Clare and Richard Carstone, who are seeking permission to take up residence with a distant cousin, Mr. John Jarndyce. Later, the lawyer Mr. Tulkinghorn stops by the London home of Sir Leicester Dedlock and Lady Honoria Dedlock. Lady Dedlock is also connected with the suit, and, as the lawyer goes over affidavits with her, she takes a sudden interest in the handwriting on one of the documents.

At this point, Esther Summerson is introduced. She had been raised by her unfeeling godmother, who died when Esther was thirteen years old. Esther then learned that her godmother was actually her aunt and that Mr. Jarndyce was now her guardian. He had paid for her education in a boarding school and then engaged her to be a companion to Ada. The three young people arrive at Jarndyce's home, Bleak House, to a warm welcome. As the novel goes on, Richard and Ada fall in love, and Richard tries and

---

1. Unlike law courts, which are based upon pre-defined causes of action, the Chancery Courts, presided over by Lord Chancellors on behalf of the monarch, provide a more flexible and pragmatic approach to the resolution of disputes. Approaching each case on its own merits, the Court of Chancery provides remedies to deserving parties, which the strict letter of the law is not intended to accomplish.

rejects several vocational options in the belief that he will inherit a substantial sum when the lawsuit is settled.

Later, Tulkinghorn learns that the handwriting Lady Dedlock asked about belongs to a copyist named Nemo, who had recently died of an opium overdose. The lawyer also meets Jo, a street urchin who knows Nemo and declares him a kind person. Tulkinghorn subsequently relays this information to Lady Dedlock, and, after disguising herself as her maid, Hortense, Lady Dedlock seeks out Jo and asks him to show her places connected with Nemo. Tulkinghorn then has a police detective, Inspector Bucket, seek Jo's help in identifying the woman who was interested in Nemo. Jo recognizes Hortense's clothing but not Hortense, who has been fired by Lady Dedlock. However, Tulkinghorn promises to help Hortense find employment in return for her cooperation. Tulkinghorn begins searching for a sample of handwriting from a Captain Hawdon.

Tulkinhorn's clerk, Mr. William Guppy, tells Lady Dedlock that he has learned that Esther's name is actually Esther Hawdon and that Nemo's last name was Hawdon. Lady Dedlock realizes that Esther is her daughter from an affair with Captain Hawdon and that her sister, who had told her that the baby died, had taken Esther and secretly raised her. One day Lady Dedlock encounters Esther and reveals to her that she is her mother. During this time Tulkinghorn succeeds in acquiring a sample of Hawdon's handwriting. Tulkinghorn subsequently reveals to Lady Dedlock that he has learned her secret but promises not to tell Sir Leicester without notice. Later, a furious Hortense confronts Tulkinghorn for not having gotten her a job, and she offers to help incriminate Lady Dedlock, but Tolkinghorn dismisses her.

Meanwhile, Esther tells Jarndyce the story of her parentage, and not long thereafter, Jarndyce proposes marriage to Esther, which she accepts. Tulkinghorn then decides that he will tell Sir Leicester the secret without consulting Lady Dedlock. That night, however, Tulkinghorn is fatally shot, and Bucket arrests George Rouncewell, an estranged son of the Dedlock family's housekeeper. Jarndyce and Esther ask Allan Woodcourt, a doctor who works among the poor, to look in on Richard, whose obsession with the lawsuit is taking a toll on his health. Ada reveals that she and Richard have married.

Bucket is not convinced that George is guilty of Tulkinghorn's murder and continues to investigate. Eventually, he tells Sir Leicester about Lady Dedlock's relationship with Hawdon and the resultant daughter. He then arrests Hortense for the murder, having discovered that she was trying to frame Lady Dedlock. Those attempts led Lady Dedlock to believe that she was suspected of the murder, and she is certain that her humiliating secret will soon be revealed. Before leaving home, she writes a letter to her husband denying her involvement in the murder but admitting her past.

When Sir Leicester, who has had a stroke from the shock of Bucket's revelations, reads the letter from his wife, he instructs Bucket to find her and tell her that he fully forgives her. Bucket enlists the aid of Esther, and, after an exhaustive search, they find Lady Dedlock at the gate of Hawdon's burial ground, dead. When Esther falls ill, Woodcourt tends to her, and one night he tells her that he is in love with her. Esther and Jarndyce then decide to set their wedding date for the following month.

Meanwhile, Bucket reports that a Jarndyce will has been found that is more recent than those involved in the lawsuit. Jarndyce then offers Woodcourt a house in London, also named Bleak House, and gives Esther his blessing to marry Woodcourt. The new will finally ends the Jarndyce and Jarndyce case in Richard's favor, but at this point it becomes clear that all the money in the estate has been eaten up in legal costs. The shock of this revelation is too much for Richard to take, and results in his death. However, in typical Dickensian fashion, the novel ends on a positive noted, for the remaining major characters enjoy happier fates.

POINTS TO PONDER IN *BLEAK HOUSE*

Like most sizeable works of fiction, *Bleak House* is built around several themes or motifs, that is, insights, concepts, attitudes, or explorations of certain aspects of human experience. A novel built around a clearly formulated and debatable or controversial theme is sometimes called a thesis or propaganda novel. While *Bleak House* has an obvious theme, it is not technically a thesis novel, or at least not a clear example of one. Foremost, *Bleak House* is a romance—affairs of the heart figure prominently—and it is a murder mystery as well (Inspector Bucket is one of the first detectives in British fiction). Nevertheless, in *Bleak House*, Dickens also comments more vigorously and incisively than before on some of the serious social questions of the day. The problem of poverty was, of course, one of the most persistent themes of Victorian social thought, and while Dickens was already famous as an eloquent advocate of the poor, *Bleak House* is one of his most powerful protests on the subject.

Bleak House has many themes, but the dominant ones are perhaps those brought forward by the two main lines of the plot: justice, and the meaning of the past. If the main theme concerns social justice, it is highlighted in the undeserved suffering created by the High Court of Chancery in general and by self-serving lawyers (like Tulkinghorn) in particular. Legal corruption permeates this novel like a disease, issuing in particular from the complicated lawsuit to which all the characters are connected. The excesses of the Court of Chancery, long a subject of Dickens's criticism, were particularly prominent in 1851, for Parliament was considering a Chancery reform bill through most of the year and actually passed such a measure just before Dickens began his work on *Bleak House*. The case of Jarndyce and Jarndyce is based on an actual suit, the famous Jennings case, which concerned a fortune left by a miser who had died in 1798 without leaving a will, and which was still unsettled in 1915. Dickens provides his customary witty dissection of the layers of Victorian society. Despite an outrageous cast of characters—from the wearyingly earnest to the brilliantly shallow, from the foolish to the foppish—in reality, it is the public sphere as a whole that Dickens satirizes in *Bleak House*. Everything resembles Chancery: Parliament, the provincial aristocracy, and even Christian philanthropy is caricatured as moribund and self-serving. In the novel, Dickens implicitly criticizes people who might be well intentioned but who neglect their homes and families in order to be (or try to be) charitable to distant people about whom they know little.

Tradition is a second leading theme in *Bleak House*. Like many Victorian novels, *Bleak House* can be viewed as the story of an effort to escape the moral impositions of a burdensome past, as a contest between the living and the dead. However, the book's criticism is directed not only against the past itself, but more specifically against the agencies society employs for interpreting it. The function of the Court of Chancery is precisely that of determining how the fruits of the past are apportioned. The Court is seen as dangerous because it regards itself as an instrument for imposing the will of the dead upon the living. To highlight tradition's negative influence on the present, Dickens introduces the symbol of fog. Like Chancery, fog is a central symbol. For Dickens, fog is a symbol of Chancery, but also of all similar institutions and operations. In other words, both Chancery and fog symbolize the "dead hand" of the past—of custom and tradition—that continues to kill in the present. Thus, law and fog symbolize the ponderous and murky forces of tradition that can suffocate creative energies and obstruct humanity's vision. Dickens's task is to write in such a way that the reader *feels* that some issue larger than that of corrupt lawyers and a local London court is at stake. That Dickens succeeds in making us feel (rather than merely reason out) the ultimate theme, the destructive heaviness of the dead hand, is proved by the fact that *Bleak House* is still a "living" book.

Though progressive-minded in various ways, we should not see Dickens as a past-hating revolutionary or social leveler. In attacking the dead hand of the past, Dickens was by no means rejecting *all* of the past or *all* of the British or Western tradition. We must remember that Dickens had plenty of traditional, or "conservative," bones in his body. He rejoiced in many aspects of tradition—that is, of the past living on into the present. He understood the necessity of legal codes and institutions, supported established religion, celebrated the British monarchy, and delighted in the British tradition of politeness and in many other "inherited" features of British (and Continental) civilization. Like Hawthorne, what he despises and rejects is the institutionalized selfishness and coldness that survive, not only within American or British culture, but within Western social and religious tradition as a whole.

In its apparent attempt to sum up a whole society—peerage, lawyers, industrialists, shopkeepers, preachers, philanthropists, brick makers, and crossing sweepers—*Bleak House* runs the risk of becoming a disorganized aggregation rather than a unified work of art. To unify the two major worlds of his novel, Dickens creates two narrators, an "anonymous" third person narrator and Esther. The major peculiarity of *Bleak House* is that its story is narrated by two distinct voices, only one of which belongs to a character in the novel. The general opinions of the two, however, are similar: both sympathize with the poor and helpless, oppose burdensome traditions, and favor personal benevolence over abstract humanitarianism as a means of solving social problems.

Having conceived of his main character as a modest, self-effacing girl who is painfully conscious of the unworthiness of her birth, yet capable of charity and generosity, Dickens provides her with narrative material that is appropriate to her and serves to characterize her. Her interests do not go beyond personal and domestic matters; she is concerned with love affairs and family life, and with the pathos and sentiment these subjects generate. She expresses herself earnestly and sincerely, but rarely comments on general questions and has no sense of large moral issues or social forces.

On the other hand, the objective narrator is only a narrative voice, and not a fictional figure, but this narrator displays nearly as much personal character as Esther does. He has a wide-ranging, energetic, and severely ironic sensibility. He is capable of vigorous satire about people and institutions, and can comment incisively on extensive fields such as the law, the poor, and the nobility. While Esther confronts experiences with sensibility, the objective narrator manipulates symbolic values rationally and sensibly.

In his *The Structure of the Novel*, Edwin Muir distinguishes between the novel of character and the dramatic novel. The first type focuses upon psychological or spiritual developments, while the second surveys the activities of fixed characters as they move from place to place. In *Bleak House*, Dickens has intuitively formalized the distinction between these narratives principles by assigning one of them to each of his voices. In Esther's story, relationships change, the people undergo spiritual transformations, and the issues with which she is occupied ultimately find their resolutions. The world seen through her eyes resembles Muir's dramatic novel.

By contrast, the objective narrator surveys a wide general scene inhabited by characters and forces that persist in unchanging form because they represent permanent situations or states of mind. The present tense of this narrative suggests that things do not change. The world seen through this narrator resembles Muir's character novel.

These technical differences are not arbitrary, but appropriate to the moral views of the two narratives. The values of the character novel are social, and the values of the dramatic novel are individual or universal. These two types are neither opposites, nor do they complement one another; they are rather two distinct modes of seeing life: personally and socially. Accordingly, Dickens's objective narrator is concerned with evils that originate in social arrangements and arise from general forces that transcend any one life and operate independently of any one will. Esther, however, is occupied with the minds and hearts of her domestic circle, and the rest of the world is meaningful to her only as a reflection of this narrow perspective. In her dramatic narrative, moral values are matters of personal responsibility, and people meet their destinies through spiritual development or decline.

Through narration, Dickens makes it clear that perspectives differ. This does not mean that one is right or the other wrong; they are simply different. The doubling of characters and narrators is part of Dickens's effort to gain a more complete view of the issues than a single approach could accomplish. In *Bleak House*, we find that virtue and vice are distinct from each other, spread through the world in clearly marked packets. Not until *Great Expectations*, written eight years later, does Dickens succeed in weaving strands of good and evil together into conflicts of genuine moral complexity.

In *Bleak House*'s art of counterparts, the differences count as heavily as the similarities, the parallels moving together while also pulling against each other. The profound and subtle oscillation introduced by the alternating narrative voices prevent *Bleak House* from formulating its moral problems in fixed images. Rather, they appear in ambiguous forms, as matters of social responsibility when seen through the eyes of the objective narrator and as matters of private conscience when seen through the eyes of Esther. At their most extreme divergence, the two points of view from which *Bleak House* is narrated—the sentimental and the satirical—appear incompatible, making *Bleak House* seem to be two novels: a melodramatic tale and a bitter social satire.

The contrasts between the two narrators are never made explicit, for each is limited to his or her own field of observation and shows no knowledge of the other. The differences between the two narratives are not limited to matters of judgment. In style and subject, they embody radically different modes of perception, which are not so much contradictory as foreign to each other. At the hands of a great artist, reality undergoes considerable transformation. Some artists, such as Jonathan Swift in *Gulliver's Travels*, achieve the metamorphosis by transporting us into a different world, fantastic in nature. Dickens's metamorphosis of reality is in the details of his world. Swift's world is a fantasy world made plausible; Dicken's world is the everyday world distorted and satirized.

The final unity of *Bleak House* is not so much one of plot or of point of view as of theme and satiric intention. In both Esther's and the author's narrative, nature has everywhere been distorted. Abstractly stated, the theme is nothing. However, in the totality of its concrete illustrations—treated comically, ironically, mysteriously, or portentously—it is magnificent, for the great instrument of the theme in *Bleak House* is the style. The style, more accurately, is the thorough penetration of every detail by the theme.

WILLIAM THACKERAY

Born in Calcutta (then British India), where his father was a senior offi-
cial in the East India Company, William Thackeray (1811–1863) became
fatherless in 1815 and was sent to England to study at public schools before
attending Charterhouse School and briefly Trinity College, Cambridge.
Uninterested in academic study, he traveled for a time on the Continent,
visiting Paris and Weimar, where he met Johann Wolfgang von Goethe.
He returned to England to study law, but soon gave that up. On reaching
the age of twenty-one, he came into his inheritance from his father, but
he squandered much of it on gambling and on funding two unsuccessful
newspapers, for which he had hoped to write.

Forced to consider a profession to support himself, he turned first to
art, and then to a career in writing, including fictional writing for the newly
created magazine *Punch*, in which he published *The Snobs of England*, later
collected as *The Book of Snobs* (1848). This work popularized the modern
meaning of the word "snob." After having written for some fifteen years,
in his middle years he wrote *The Luck of Barry Lyndon* (1844), followed
by his first major novel, *Vanity Fair* (1848). Hailed as the next Charles
Dickens, Thackeray remained popular for the rest of his life, during which
he produced several large novels, notably *Pendennis* (1850), *The History
of Henry Esmond* (1852), and *The Newcomes* (1855). He also gave lectures
in London on the English humorists of the eighteenth century, and twice
visited the United States on lecture tours during this period.

Tragedy struck his family in 1849 when his wife, Isabella, succumbed
to depression after the birth of their third child. She eventually went incur-
ably insane and spent time in different asylums and then under personal
care until her death in 1894. Thackeray's health, never strong, worsened
during the 1850s, matters complicated by excessive eating and drinking,
all of which contributed to his early death in 1863, at the age of fifty-two.

THACKERAY'S *VANITY FAIR*: PLOT AND RESPONSE

Vanity Fair follows two heroines whose lives are intertwined: Becky Sharp
and Amelia Sedley. Their career seesaw up and down, and as one goes
up, the other goes down. We follow them from schooldays to middle age,
amid their friends and families during and after the Napoleonic Wars. The
story, commencing in 1814 London, is framed by its preface and coda as a

puppet show taking place at a fair. The narrator, variously a show manager or writer, despite being "omniscient" or authorial, is somewhat unreliable, repeating a tale of gossip at second or third hand.

Rebecca Sharp ("Becky"), daughter of an art teacher and a French dancer, is a strong-willed, cunning, moneyless young woman determined to make her way in society. After leaving school, Becky stays with her friend Amelia Sedley ("Emmy"), who is a good-natured, simple-minded young girl, of a wealthy London family. In London, Becky meets the dashing and self-obsessed Captain George Osborne (Amelia's betrothed) and Amelia's brother Joseph ("Jos"), a clumsy and vainglorious but rich civil servant home from the East India Company. Hoping to marry Jos Sedley, the richest young man she has met, Becky entices him, but fails. George Osborne's friend Captain William Dobbin loves Amelia, but only wishes her happiness, which is centered on George.

Becky Sharp says farewell to the Sedley family and enters the service of the crude and profligate baronet Sir Pitt Crawley, who has engaged her as a governess to his daughters. Her behavior at Sir Pitt's house gains his favor, and after the premature death of his second wife, he proposes marriage to her. However, he finds that Becky has secretly married his second son, Captain Rawdon Crawley. Sir Pitt's elder half-sister, the spinster Miss Crawley, is very rich, having inherited her mother's fortune, and the whole Crawley family compete for her favor so she will bequeath them her wealth. Initially her favorite is Rawdon, but his marriage with Becky enrages her, and when she dies, she leaves her money to Sir Pitt's oldest son, also called Pitt.

News arrives that Napoleon has escaped from Elba, and as a result, the stock market becomes jittery, causing Amelia's stockbroker father, John Sedley, to become bankrupt. George's rich father forbids George to marry Amelia, who is now poor, but Dobbin persuades George to marry her, which results in George's disinheritance. Subsequently, George Osborne, William Dobbin, and Rawdon Crawley are deployed to Brussels, accompanied by Amelia, Becky, and Amelia's brother, Jos.

The newly wedded Osborne soon grows tired of Amelia, and he becomes increasingly attracted to Becky, which makes Amelia jealous. Osborne also begins losing money to Rawdon at cards and billiards. At a ball in Brussels, George gives Becky a note inviting her to run away with him. However, the army receives marching orders to the Battle of Waterloo, and George spends a romantic night with Amelia before leaving.

The noise of battle horrifies Amelia, but Becky is indifferent and makes plans for whatever the outcome (for example, if Napoleon wins, she would aim to become the mistress of one of his marshals). She also makes a profit selling her carriage and horses at inflated prices to Jos, who is seeking to flee Brussels. At the Battle of Waterloo, George Osborne is killed, while Dobbin and Rawdon survive. Amelia bears George a posthumous son, who carries the name George. She returns to live in genteel poverty with her parents, spending her life in memory of her husband and care of her son. Dobbin pays for a small annuity for Amelia and expresses his love for her by small kindnesses toward her and her son. Nevertheless, she is too much in love with her husband's memory to return Dobbin's love. Saddened, he goes with his regiment to India.

Meanwhile, Becky also gives birth to a son, named Rawdon after his father. Becky is a cold, distant mother, although Rawdon loves his son. Becky continues her social ascent, first in post-war Paris and then in London, where she is patronized by the rich and powerful Marquis of Steyne. She is eventually presented at court to the Prince Regent, and charms him further at a game of "acting charades," where she plays the roles of Clytemnestra and Philomela. The elderly Sir Pitt Crawley dies and is succeeded by his son Pitt, who had married Lady Jane Sheepshanks. Becky is on good terms with Pitt and Jane originally, but Jane is disgusted by Becky's attitude to her son and jealous of Becky's relationship with Pitt.

At the summit of his social success, Rawdon is arrested for debt, possibly at Becky's connivance. The financial success of the Crawleys had been a topic of gossip, for they lived on credit even when it ruined those who trusted them. The Marquis of Steyne had given Becky money, jewels, and other gifts, but Becky does not use them for expenses or to free her husband. Instead, Lady Jane pays the fee that had prompted Rawdon's imprisonment. Rawdon returns home to find Becky singing to Steyne and strikes him down on the assumption—despite her protestations of innocence—that they are having an affair. Steyne is indignant, having assumed the money he had just given Becky was part of an arrangement with her husband. Rawdon finds Becky's hidden bank records and leaves her, expecting Steyne to challenge him to a duel. Instead, Steyne arranges for Rawdon to be made Governor of Coventry Island, a remote and pest-ridden location. Becky, having lost both husband and credibility, leaves England and wanders the continent, leaving her son in the care of Pitt and Lady Jane.

As Amelia's adored son George grows up, his grandfather, Mr. Osborne, takes him from his impoverished mother, who knows the rich old man will give him a better start in life than she could manage. After twelve years abroad, Joseph Sedley and Dobbin return. Dobbin professes his unchanged love to Amelia, but Amelia, who is affectionate, cannot forget the memory of her dead husband. Dobbin mediates a reconciliation between Amelia and her father-in-law, who dies soon after. He had amended his will, bequeathing young George half his large fortune and Amelia a generous annuity.

After the death of Mr. Osborne, Amelia, Jos, George, and Dobbin go to Pumpernickel (Weimar in Germany), where they encounter the destitute Becky. Having fallen in life, Becky lives among cardsharps and con artists, drinking heavily and gambling. Becky enchants Jos Sedley once again, and Amelia agrees to let Becky join them, but Dobbin forbids it, reminding Amelia of her jealousy of Becky with her husband. Amelia feels that Dobbins's refusal dishonors the memory of her dead and revered husband, and this leads to her break with Dobbin. Dobbin leaves the group and rejoins his regiment, while Becky remains with the group.

However, Becky has decided that Amelia should marry Dobbin. She shows Amelia George's note, kept all this time from the eve of the Battle of Waterloo, and Amelia finally realizes that George was not the perfect man she always thought, and that she has rejected a better man, Dobbin. Amelia and Dobbin are reconciled and return to England. Becky and Jos stay in Europe, where he dies, suspiciously, after signing a portion of his money to Becky as life insurance, thereby setting her up with an income. Becky returns to England and manages a respectable life, although her previous friends disown her.

POINTS TO PONDER IN *VANITY FAIR*

In 1847 and 1848, Thackeray first published *Vanity Fair* as a nineteen-volume monthly serial. The work carried the subtitle *Pen and Pencil Sketches of English Society*, which reflects both its satirization of early nineteenth-century British society and the many illustrations drawn by Thackeray to accompany the text. It was published as a single volume in 1848 with the subtitle *A Novel without a Hero*, reflecting Thackeray's interest in deconstructing his era's conventions regarding literary heroism.

The book's title is taken from John Bunyan's *The Pilgrim's Progress*, where "vanity fair" refers to a stop along the pilgrim's route, a never-ending fair held in a town called Vanity, which represents humanity's sinful attachment to worldly things. For Bunyan, the name refers to London; for Thackeray, the title refers to all of England up to the 1840s. While Bunyan's narrative canvas is narrow, Thackeray's vision is vast, covering a period from the battle of Waterloo (1815) through to the Victorian 1840s.

Bunyan had taken the name of his town from Ecclesiastes: "Vanity of vanities, says the Teacher (Preacher), vanity of vanities! All is vanity" (Eccl 1:2). As a theme, vanity characterizes a society obsessed with appearance, social standing, and material concerns. Using humor, irony, and satire, Thackeray describes how pillars of society such as aristocrats, wealthy merchants, and members of Parliament are overvalued in his day. Exposing vain people for their superficial concern, Thackeray's narrative exposes the fraudulent lifestyle that places value on appearance and possessions rather than on love, honesty, and goodness. Through characters such as Becky Sharp, Sir Pitt Crawley, and his elderly half-sister Miss Crawley, Thackeray highlights how a Vanity Fair society is superficial and ultimately meaning-less. While desire for wealth and social standing permeates the lives of most characters in the novel, rivalry and ambition underscores their relations with each other. Amelia is one of the few characters who wishes to marry for love, and even this motivation turns out to be disastrously naïve, as she becomes a victim of the greed of others.

In *Vanity Fair*, *Vanitas Vanitatum* (vanity of vanities) is one of Thackeray's favorite phrases. The novel ends with the words: "Ah! *Vanitas Vanitatum*! Which of us is happy in this world? Which of us has his desire? or, having it, is satisfied? – Come, children, let us shut up- the box and the puppets, for our play is played out."[2]

In the novel, vanity's two shades of meaning—"vanity" as love of self and of the things of the world, and "vanity" as emptiness and world-weari-ness—are shown to be two sides of the same coin. As a novelist, Thackeray lacked the jaunty optimism of Dickens, whose work was buoyed by his genuine belief in the goodness of humanity and in the power of charity to reform the world. Thackeray, to the contrary, presents human society as Vanity Fair, "not a moral place certainly; nor a merry one, though very noisy."[3] As at the end, so throughout the novel, Thackeray informs his

2. Thackeray, *Vanity Fair*, 743.
3. Thackeray, "Before the Curtain," *Vanity Fair*, 1.

readers that he will walk with them through the Fair, and advises them that after their walk, they should all come home "and be perfectly miserable in private."[4] In this remark, we find not only Thackeray's self-inclusion in life's parade of vanities, but also the recognition of the gulf that stretches between people's outward levity and the lonely places within their soul.

In the frontispiece added for the book edition of 1848, Thackeray shows the Preacher of Ecclesiastes, metamorphosed. Here he is Tom Fool, a clown standing on a tub haranguing a congregation of fools, representing characters in the novel. All are wearing long-eared caps, as is the preacher. In the background, two monuments recently erected in London are visible: Nelson's Column and a statue of Wellington. In Thackeray's illustration, Nelson is standing on his head, and Wellington is riding a donkey. The absurdity of vanity may be seen in the crowd around the preacher, cheerful and inattentive. It is obvious that the preacher does not expect to have any effect.

In writing "a novel without a hero," Thackeray held stubbornly to the conviction that most people are not heroic and that it is the novelist's task to show people as they are, not as they should be. As a novel without a hero, it is telling that even the most favored character, Dobbin, is described as hypocritical. For Thackeray, hypocrisy is a social convention akin to politeness, a quality prevalent amongst the elite of society. By highlighting Dobbin's ability to be hypocritical, Thackeray invites us to consider how all the participants at the Fair are flawed in varying degrees.

Victorian critics frequently complained of Thackeray's cynicism, calling him "the apostle of mediocrity" for the absence of "noble" characters in *Vanity Fair*. His bad characters, they complained, were attractive, and the good ones were stupid and dreary. Not only was there no hero, but one of the heroines had no heart and the other no head. Thackeray's point was that in Vanity Fair, few individuals are blameless and not many are consistently wicked. Like all the great humorists from Cervantes to Fielding, Thackeray saw human beings as an inscrutable mixture of the heroic and the ridiculous, the noble and ignoble. An astute realist, he recognized the complexity of human nature, and felt its complexity needed to be accented rather than simplified for sensible readers.

In rejecting heroism, Thackeray meant to explode the idea of the hero as a romantic ideal, an ideal he saw as outmoded and deeply flawed as a model for conduct. For Thackeray, the alluring figure of the hero/heroine

4. Thackeray, *Vanity Fair*, 189.

must be replaced by the less attractive idea of the gentleman/lady. What it means to be a gentleman rather than a hero, a lady rather than a heroine, is a central theme of the novel.

As we might expect, the gentleman in *Vanity Fair* is not identified by breeding, wealth, polished manners, good looks, or elevated status. Rather, it is William Dobbin, lacking in social graces and physically unattractive, who models the true gentleman. However, despite his honesty, humility, and purity, his unalluring attributes could never be mistaken for a romantic hero. Likewise, Amelia, having neither "just thoughts" nor "fairly good" brains, is attractive to men though invisible to women. Her kindness and outmoded romanticism often get in the way of good judgement. She is a lady, but not a heroine, except at brief, tragic moments. Becky, her polar opposite, is certainly not a lady. She is self-seeking, hypocritical, hard-hearted, and likely a murderess. Nevertheless, she is a survivor, having a good nature and an irrepressible capacity to take life as it comes. Like Thackeray, she is able to take risks, a gambler who needs the stimulus of danger.

Thackeray is often criticized for the behavior of his characters, whose faults tend to compound over time. None of his characters are wholly evil, however, although Becky's manipulative, amoral tendencies maker her come close. Nevertheless, Thackeray regularly solicits the reader's sympathy for Becky, first by the account of her upbringing (she is the orphaned daughter of a poor artist and an opera dancer), and by her own self-awareness and self-deprecation. It is easy to admire her grit and moxie, for she always lands on her feet and can easily be mistaken for a hero. However, in a novel dedicated to the elimination of the heroic, to admire Becky is to fall into the trap of hero worship.

In portraying his characters, Thackeray, unlike Jane Austen, never allows readers to rest in a simple opposition of sense and sensibility. Do we admire Amelia, or despise her? Is Becky a victim of her circumstances, or an amoral opportunist? Is Dobbins a gentleman, or a donkey? There are no absolute answers in the intricate world of *Vanity Fair*. There are only questions that expand in the reader's mind, leading to other questions: an infinite regress through fiction to reality.

We must never forget that *Vanity Fair* is not a reforming novel; it contains no hope that social or political change or even greater piety and moral reform can improve the nature of society. Rather, *Vanity Fair* is a satire of society as a whole, characterized by hypocrisy and opportunism.

Possessing a strong vein of skepticism, Thackeray turned to irony as nature's best interpreter. It is Thackeray's pervasive ironic tone that marks his view of the Fair and its inhabitants—a sense of the irony of life, of the contrast between the real and the apparent. Perhaps this is why Thackeray was never as popular as Dickens. Victorians knew and liked satire and humorous hyperbole, preferring sharp contrasting tones to mediocre greys.

Unlike Dickens, his chief rival, Thackeray lacked an integrative social theory. In *Vanity Fair*, Thackeray's reflections, voiced by the narrator, are usually trite and pedestrian, for Thackeray had no original, revolutionary view of the world. Thackeray's morality is "correct," like that of the gentleman living by the golden mean, avoiding excess through admirable mediocrity. Unlike *Bleak House*, *Vanity Fair* is descriptive rather than prescriptive, its view of life is large and tolerant, world-weary rather than one that demands change. If Thackeray found favor with Victorians, it is because, like Qoheleth (the author/preacher of Ecclesiastes), he viewed reality through a moral lens. However, if Thackeray was a preacher, he was a non-revolutionary one, for if *Vanity Fair* were a sermon on Ecclesiastes, its themes—"unity at all costs" and "don't rock the social boat"—would be bland and uninspiring.

Thackeray's bleak portrait of the human condition continues through his own role as an "omniscient" narrator, for he is one of the writers best known for using this technique. In *Vanity Fair*, Thackeray continually offers asides about his characters and compares them to actors and puppets, but his impertinence extends to his readers, criticizing all who may be interested in such "Vanity Fairs" as either lazy, benevolent, or sarcastic.

Although Thackeray's authorial voice surrounds the characters and their story with narrative commentary, his approach contravenes the familiar process of storytelling, for instead of a single reliable narrative voice, we are presented with a bewildering array of possible narrators who, we come to realize, are as self-contradictory and unreliable as the characters they describe. Sometimes the narrator claims omniscience, other times he is an irresponsible, baffled spectator. Above all, he is the preacher—the moral commentator. In the prefatory "Before the Curtain," added after the serial publication was completed, Thackeray introduces several possible candidates for the part of the narrator. Is he "The Manager of the Performance," contemplating his play? Is he an outsider walking through the Fair, but not taking part in its antics? Or is he, as the cover illustration suggests, poor Tom Fool, tolerated as an entertainer but ignored as a preacher? These uncertainties, of course, are intended. The narrative voices of *Vanity Fair* constitute an unnamed but ever-present cast of characters who surround the "real" characters of the story. In a way that Victorians found more difficult and disturbing than postmodern readers do, Thackeray viewed fiction as contiguous with reality.

In *Vanity Fair*, Thackeray concentrates on complexity of character rather than on plot. The book is so saturated with the vanities of Vanity Fair—the duplicity of social climbers and the weakness of human nature—that it is impossible to separate idea from plot or plot from character. If the book appears to ramble, it never strays from focus on the foibles of human nature. Even if the setting could be changed to modern times, its observation—vanity is universal and ever-present—would continue to hold true.

Nevertheless, as Thackeray indicates, not everyone bows down to the idols of Vanity Fair. The winners at the end of the story are those who cherish human relationships first: Amelia, Dobbin, and Lady Jane. Thackeray's perspective, then, is that although one may live in Vanity Fair, one need not be a slave to its values, which in the final analysis turn into futility and emptiness. *Vanity Fair* leaves readers hopeful that the next generation can be better than previous ones.

QUESTIONS FOR DISCUSSION AND REFLECTION

In addition to the questions listed at the end of the preface, answer the following questions, writing your answers in a journal. If you are in a group study, be prepared to share your answers with those in the group.

1. Explain how Charles Dickens life influenced his social consciousness.

2. Explain and assess Dickens's portrayal of the courts of law and of the legal profession in *Bleak House*.

3. Explain Thomas Carlyle's critique of nineteenth century English society, and assess the short- and long-range effects of the Industrial Revolution on Western societies.

4. Explain the social effects of utilitarianism when its values and principles are applied and enforced by social institutions.

5. Is *Bleak House* a propaganda novel? If so, what is its thesis or central theme?

6. Explain and assess Dickens's critique of Christian philanthropy in *Bleak House.*

7. Explain and assess the role of tradition as the "dead hand" of the past in perpetuating harmful and self-serving social customs and laws.

8. Explain and assess the role of religious tradition as a deterrent to transformative spirituality.

9. Explain and assess the merits of Dickens's technique in creating two narrators in *Bleak House.*

10. Explain Thackeray's choice of the title "Vanity Fair" for his novel. If a Vanity Fair society is superficial and ultimately meaningless, how, in your estimation, does such a title apply to contemporary American society?

11. Explain the logic behind Thackeray's ultimate choice of "A Novel without a Hero" as his book's subtitle.

12. Explain and assess the meaning of the author's statement, "There are no absolute norms in the intricate world of *Vanity Fair.*"

13. Explain and assess Thackeray's role as "preacher" in *Vanity Fair.*

Chapter 8

George Eliot's *Middlemarch* and Virginia Woolf's *Orlando*

IN THE TWENTY YEARS between the publication of Dickens's *Bleak House* and Eliot's *Middlemarch*, the novel had come a long way. Dickens had called on melodrama and sentimentality to solicit from his reader certain kinds of emotional response. He also felt the need to tie all loose threads of his story together, elements George Eliot set aside in her fiction. Like Thackeray, George Eliot helped bring the novel beyond neatness and happy endings. For Eliot, fiction ccould be messy, because in many ways, so is life.

In contrast to chapter 7, which focused on male writers, this chapter focuses on two female writers, each progressive yet distinctive in significant ways, one a feminist (Woolf), the other a chauvinist (Eliot). While it might not be clear from the chapter heading, let us clarify: George Eliot, one of the leading writers of the Victorian era, was the pen name of Mary Ann Evans (1819–1880). Why did Evans, a female chauvinist, write behind the protection of a male mask? During her lifetime, female authors were publishing under their own names, but it was from such authors that Evans wished to dissociate. She wanted to write fiction of ideas, the ideas that were making and reshaping Victorian society and culture, thereby escaping the stereotype of women's writing being limited to lighthearted romance. Evans may also have been inspired in her choice of names by the great female French novelist George Sand and by Charlotte Brontë, who began her literary career as Currer Bell. She may also have wanted to have her fiction judged separately from her widely known work as a translator, editor, and critic. Another factor in her use of a pseudonym may have been a desire to shield her private life from public scrutiny, thus avoiding the scandal that would have arisen because of her relationship with the married George Henry Lewes. Given that she came from a provincial evangelical background, Evans may also have wanted to avoid embarrassing family members, who may have had suspicions about fiction.

Eliot's background was extraordinary and wholly un-Victorian. She was nonconformist to the core, a philosopher-novelist espousing what she called the "religion of humanity," a moral code that would fill the hole left by the late-Enlightenment lack of confidence in religious dogma. She believed religious doctrines and creeds were no longer adequate in the modern world. She also believed that novels, like religion, could make people better humans. For her, fiction had the power to dissolve egotism and make people more sympathetic to their fellow human beings. In her mind, fiction had a higher mission than mere entertainment; she wished to make her readers think and specifically, to engage in moral reflection.

Eliot was born and brought up in the environs of Coventry, a provincial English town in the region of West Midlands, the region described in *Middlemarch*. As a youngster, Evans was a voracious reader and obviously intelligent. Because she was not considered physically attractive and therefore not having much change of marriage, her father invested in an education not often afforded women. The nonconformist low Anglicanism of rural towns like Coventry was less prejudiced than urban society against education for women. During her lifetime, the Midlands was also an area with a growing number of religious dissenters, further exposing Evans to nonconformity. She idolized her father, but ultimately could not subscribe to his strict Christianity.

From ages five to sixteen, she attended select schools, but after this period, she had little formal education. In 1836, her mother died, and Evans (then sixteen) returned home to act as housekeeper. Her father's position as an estate manager gave her access to the library at Arbury Hall, which greatly aided her self-education and breadth of learning. Her frequent visits to the estate also allowed her to contrast the wealth in which local landowners lived with the lives of the much poorer people on the estate, and the portrayal of different lives lived in parallel often appeared in her novels. She taught herself classical and foreign languages and engaged with the theological disputes of her time, notably what was called "higher criticism," the view that the Bible was metaphorically rather than literally true.

When she was twenty-one, her brother married and took over the family home, so Evans and her father moved to Foleshill. Closeness to Coventry society brought new influences, most notably those of Charles and Cara Bray. Evans, who had been struggling with religious doubts for some time, became intimate friends with the free-thinking Brays, whose home was a haven for people who held and debated radical views. There she met such contemporary thinkers as Robert Owens, Herbert Spencer, and Ralph Waldo Emerson. Through this society, Evans was introduced to writers such as David Strauss and Ludwig Feuerbach, who cast doubt on the literal truth of biblical texts. In 1846, she translated Strauss's *Das Leben Jesu* (1835) into English as *The Life of Jesus, Critically Examined*. The book had caused a sensation in Germany by arguing that the miracles in the New Testament were mythical accounts with little basis in fact. Evans's translation had a similar effect in England.

On her father's death in 1849, when she was thirty, Evans moved to London, where she became a leading journalist. She stayed at the house of John Chapman, who had published her Strauss translation. Chapman had recently purchased the left-wing journal, *The Westminster Review*, and in 1851 Evans became its assistant editor, publishing writings in the journal that commented on society and the Victorian way of thinking. She was sympathetic to the lower classes and criticized organized religion. In writings of this period, Evans formulated her personal philosophy, which was strongly influenced by the pioneer of sociology, the French philosopher Auguste Comte. According to Comte, society progressed through stages from primitivism to scientific reorganization; the final stage would transcend religion, but it could be conditioned by morality, which would replace the religion that had been lost in earlier stages of evolution or development. Evans was a freethinker, but she remained a stern moralist. Her thinking on such matters was strongly influenced by the man whom she met in 1851 and chose to live with, the philosopher and critic George Henry Lewes. Like Evans, Lewes was a leading light in London's higher journalism; he was a popularizer of science, an editor, and a Comtean. He was also married, but true to his freethinking philosophy, allowed his wife to live with another man. Keep in mind that divorce in this period was practically impossible, for it required an act of Parliament.

In 1854, she and Lewes traveled to Weimar and Berlin together for the purpose of research. Before going to Germany, Evans had translated Feuerbach's *The Essence of Christianity*, and while abroad she wrote essays and worked on a translation of Baruch Spinoza's *Ethics*. Working as a trans-lator exposed Evans to German texts of religious, social, and moral philoso-phy. Elements from this tradition would show up in her later fiction, much of which was written with her trademark sense of agnostic humanism. The trip to Germany also served as a honeymoon, and from that point, Evans and Lewes considered themselves married. Evans began referring to Lewes as her husband, legally changing her name to Mary Ann Evans Lewes after his death in 1878. It was not so much the adultery, but her refusal to conceal the relationship, that Victorians felt breached the social convention of the time, and attracted so much disapproval.

By 1856, Evans resolved to become a novelist, and set out a mani-festo in one of her last essays for *The Westminster Review*, "Silly Novels by Lady Novelists." The essay criticized the trivial and ridiculous plots of contemporary fiction written by women. In other essays, she praised the realism of novels that were being written in Europe at the time, an emphasis on realistic storytelling confirmed in her own subsequent fiction. At this time, she also adopted the pen name George Eliot. In 1858, her *Scenes of Clerical Life* was published as the work of "George Eliot" and well received, and was widely believed to have been written by a country parson. Eliot's first complete novel, published in 1859, was *Adam Bede*. It was an instant success, and prompted greater curiosity as to the author's identity. Public interest subsequently led to Evans's acknowledgement that it was she who stood behind the pseudonym. The revelations about Eliot's private life shocked many readers, but it did not affect her popularity as a novelist. After the success of *Adam Bede*, Eliot continued to write novels for the next fifteen years, including *The Mill on the Floss* (1860), *Silas Marner* (1861), *Romola* (1863), *Felix Holt, the Radical* (1866), her most acclaimed novel *Middlemarch* (1872), and *Daniel Deronda* (1876). Eliot's social accep-tance was finally confirmed in 1877 when she and Lewes were introduced to Princess Louise, the daughter of Queen Victoria. As it turned out, the queen admired Eliot and was an avid reader of her novels.

After Lewes's death in 1878, Eliot spent two years editing Lewes's final work, *Life and Mind*, for publication. In 1880, she married John Walter Cross, twenty years her junior. Later that year, Eliot fell ill with a throat infection, and her illness, coupled with kidney disease, led to her death at the age of sixty-one. Because of her denial of the Christian faith and her adulterous affair with Lewes, she was denied burial in Westminster Abbey. Rather, she was buried in London's Highgate Cemetery, in an area reserved for political and religious dissenters, beside George Lewes and close to the graves of Karl Marx and Herbert Spencer.

Throughout her career, Eliot wrote with a politically astute pen. From *Adam Bede* to *The Mill on the Floss* and *Silas Marner*, Eliot presented the cases of social outsiders and small-town persecution. *Felix Holt* was a study of early trade unionism and proletarian revolt; *Romola*, a historical novel, was set in Florence, Italy at the time of the fierce moralist Savonarola; her final novel, *Daniel Deronda*, was a study of marriage, morality, and the question of Jews in England.

Eliot set *Middlemarch* in 1829 to 1832, the period leading to the 1832 Reform Act, which introduced major changes to the electoral system of England, giving the vote to small landowners, tenant farmers, shopkeepers, and eligible renters and householders. Only qualifying men were able to vote, however, for by definition, voters had to be a male. Reform was Eliot's great theme, and throughout *Middlemarch*, Eliot asks: "How can society be made better?" Her answer is, not through legislation or by allowing people to vote, but by making people better.

ELIOT'S *MIDDLEMARCH*: PLOT AND RESPONSE

Middlemarch, A Study of Provincial Life, first appeared in eight bimonthly volumes in 1871 and 1872. Set in Middlemarch, a fictional English Midland town, it follows intersecting stories of various individuals and their spouses: Dorothea, an intelligent, wealthy woman with great aspirations; Lydgate, an idealistic, talented, and relatively poor medical doctor; and Fred Vincy, a spendthrift who learns how to make good decisions and become a productive member of society. As Doctor Lydgate, Dorothea, and Fred are drawn into the lives and intrigues of Middlemarch, the seeds are sown for an epic tale of passion, disillusionment, and blackmail.

Middlemarch is a vast canvas, but its focus is on the thwarted idealism of its two principal characters, Dorothea and Lydgate, both of whom marry disastrously. In the provincial town of Middlemarch, the progressive Dorothea Brooke seeks intellectual fulfillment in a male-dominated society. She is a nineteen-year-old orphan, living with her younger sister, Celia, as a ward of her uncle, Mr. Brooks. A young idealist, her hobby involves the renovation of buildings belonging to tenant farmers. Dorothea is courted by James Chettam, a young man close to her own age, but she is oblivious to him. She dreams of being a helpmeet to genius, and is willing to subordinate herself while doing something important in life. Disastrously, she identifies Edward Casaubon as the man of genius to whom she will dedicate her life. Casaubon is a pompous scholar twice her age, whose great project is an unfinished book, *The Key to All Mythologies*. It is intended as a monument to Christian syncretism, but his research is outdated, as he cannot read German. Dorothea's requests to assist Causabon make it harder for him to conceal that his research is out of date. Dorothea sees herself as a modern Saint Theresa, a woman who will change the work, but on her honeymoon in Rome, she realizes she has thrown her life away. When Dorothea realizes her terrible mistake, she experiences a feeling of desolation and detachment, almost as if she has been traumatized by rape. The destruction of Dorothea's ardent idealism, however, is a necessary step to growth, rebirth, and eventually, after many trials and much suffering, to regeneration and fulfillment.

Faced with Casaubon's coldness, Dorothea becomes friends with his younger disinherited cousin, Will Ladislaw, whom Casaubon supports financially. When Casaubon returns from Rome, he suffers a heart attack. In poor health, he grows suspicion of Dorothea's friendship with Ladislaw. He tries to make Dorothea promise, if he should die, not to pursue her relationship with Ladislaw. She is hesitant to agree, and he dies before she can reply. Dorothea later discovers that Casaubon's will contains a provision that calls for her disinheritance if she marries Ladislaw. Afraid of scandal, Dorothea and Ladislaw initially stay apart. Only later, when Ladislaw decides to leave town and visits Dorothea to say his farewell, does Dorothea realize she is in love with him. She renounces Casaubon's fortune and shocks her family by announcing that she will marry Ladislaw. At the end of her life, Dorothea, happily remarried, realizes that she was never meant to be a Saint Theresa. Indeed, the nineteenth century has no room for saints; it is too crowded, bureaucratic, and complicated.

During this time, Lydgate's story unfolds. He is a progressive young doctor who is passionate about medicine, especially his research. Lydgate has modern ideas about medicine and sanitation and believes doctors should prescribe, but not themselves dispense medicines. This draws ire and criticism of many in the town. He allies himself with Bulstrode, a banker and developer who wants to build a hospital and clinic that follow Lydgate's philosophy, despite the misgivings of Lydgate's friend, Farebrother, about Bulstrode's integrity.

Soon after arriving in Middlemarch, Lydgate becomes involved with and later marries Rosamond Vincy, whom he finds to be "polished, refined, and docile," all qualities he wants in a wife. For her part, Rosamond believes that marriage to Lydgate, who she does not realize is poor, will improve her social standing. Lydgate initially views their relationship as flirtations, but eventually the two become engaged and marry. Lydgate's efforts to please Rosamond soon leave him deeply in debt, and he comes to realize that he has made a mistake in choosing Rosamond. She is shallow and uninterested in his work, and her expensive lifestyle forces Lydgate to the brink of financial ruin. He seeks a loan from Nicholas Bulstrode, a widely disliked banker, but is refused.

Bulstrode is not without his own problems. He is being blackmailed by John Raffles, who knows about Bulstrode's shady past. In his youth, Bulstrode engaged in questionable financial dealings; his fortune comes from his marriage to a wealthy, much older widow. The widow's daughter, who should have inherited her mother's fortune, had run away. Bulstrode located her but failed to disclose this to the widow, so that he inherited the fortune in lieu of her daughter. The widow's daughter had a son, who turns out to be Ladislaw.

When Raffles becomes ill, Bulstrode tends to him and sends for Lydgate. During one of the doctor's visits, Bulstrode offers to lend Lydgate the money he had previously refused, and Lydgate accepts. Bulstrode subsequently disregards Lydgate's medical instructions, causing Raffles to die. When the true story about Bulstrode and Raffles comes to light, questions arise over Lydgate's possible involvement in the latter's death. One of the few people who believes his innocence is Dorothea, and he is taken by her compassion and kindness. Lydgate and Rosamond are ultimately forced to leave Middlemarch, and they move to London, where Lydgate becomes wealthy but considers himself a failure.

A third marital relationship involves Fred Vincy. He and Rosamond are the eldest children of Middlemarch's town mayor. Having never finished university, Fred is widely seen as a failure and a profligate, who allows himself to coast because he is the presumed heir of his childless uncle Mr. Featherstone, a rich but unpleasant man. Featherstone keeps as a companion a niece, Mary Garth. Although she is considered plain, Fred has loved her from childhood. His family hopes he will advance socially by becoming a clergyman, but he knows Mary will not marry him if he does.

On his deathbed, Mr. Featherstone reveals that he has made two wills and tries to get Mary to help him destroy one. Unwilling to be involved in the business, she refuses, and Featherstone dies with both wills still intact. Featherstone's plan had been for Fred to receive a significant sum of cash, but his estate and fortune instead go to his illegitimate son, Joshua. As a result of the will and changed through his love for Mary, Fred finds by studying land management under Caleb Garth, Mary's father, a profession that gains Mary's respect and their eventual marriage.

The conclusion narrates the ultimate fortunes of the main characters. Fred and Mary marry and live contentedly with their three sons. Lydgate operates a successful practice in London and attains a good income, but never finds fulfillment and dies at the age of fifty, leaving Rosamond and four children. After Lydgate dies, Rosamond marries a wealthy physician. Ladislaw engages in public reform, and Dorothea is content as a wife and mother to their two children.

POINTS TO PONDER IN *MIDDLEMARCH*

Despite mixed reviews initially, *Middlemarch* is now seen widely as Eliot's best work and as one of the great English novels. Virginia Woolf famously declared it the first novel in English written for grown-up people. Of course, she did not mean what later generations would understand by the term "adult fiction." Rather, what she meant was that this was fiction for morally mature people. Issues include the status of women, the nature of marriage, idealism, self-interest, religion, hypocrisy, political reform, and education. In a letter, Emily Dickinson said of Eliot: "What do I think of 'Middlemarch?' What do I think of glory—except that in a few instances this 'mortal has already put on immortality.'" For Dickinson, Eliot was one of those immortals.

The twenty-first century continues to hold this novel in high regard. For example, novelists Martin Amis and Julian Barnes have both called it probably the greatest novel in the English language. In a 2015 BBC Culture poll of book critics outside the UK, the novel was ranked at number one in "The 100 greatest British novels." Due to its ongoing popularity with the public, *Middlemarch* has been adapted several times for television and the stage.

Middlemarch originated in two separate and unfinished pieces that Eliot worked on during 1869 and 1870: "Middlemarch," which focused on the character of Lydgate, and "Miss Brooke," which focused on the character of Dorothea. By March 1871, Eliot began incorporating material from "Middlemarch" into the story of "Miss Brooke," leading to the eventual union. However, by May 1871, the growing length of the novel became a concern, as it threatened to exceed the three-volume format that was the norm in publishing. The solution was to publish the novel in eight two-month parts, borrowing the method used for Victor Hugo's 1862 novel *Les Misérables*. This was an alternative to the monthly serialized issues that had been used for long works by Dickens and Thackeray, while avoiding Eliot's objections to the slicing of her novel into small parts. The result was transformative, for with the deaths of Thackeray and Dickens in 1863 and 1870 and with the novel's final publication, Eliot became recognized as the greatest living English novelist.

Middlemarch is a highly unusual novel. Although it is primarily a Victorian novel, it has many characteristics typical to modern novels. In the Victorian era, women writers were generally confined to writing conventional romance fiction, and Eliot was not that kind of writer. A common accusation leveled against Eliot was that she was too intellectual and too depressing. Not only did Eliot dislike the constraints imposed on women's writing, she disliked the stories they were expected to produce. Her disdain for the tropes of conventional romance is apparent in her treatment of marriage. Eliot goes to great lengths to depict the realities of marriage, particularly of ill-advised marriages between inherently incompatible people. *Middlemarch* offers a clear critique of the usual portrayal of marriage as romantic, idyllic, and unproblematic.

Two major life choices govern the narrative of *Middlemarch*. One is marriage, and the other is vocation. Eliot takes both choices seriously. Short, romantic courtships lead to trouble, because both parties entertain unrealistic ideals of each other. They marry without getting to know one another. Marriages based on compatibility work better. Moreover, marriages in which women have a greater say also work better, such as the marriage between Fred and Mary. She tells him she will not marry if he becomes a clergyman. Her condition saves Fred from an unhappy entrapment in an occupation he doesn't like. Dorothea and Casaubon struggle continually because Casaubon attempts to make her submit to his control. The same applies in the marriage between Lydgate and Rosamond.

The choice of an occupation is also an important element in the book. Eliot illustrates the consequences of making the wrong choice. She also details at great length the consequences of confining women to the domestic sphere alone. Dorothea's passionate ambition for social reform is never realized. She ends with a happy marriage, but there is some sense that her end as merely a wife and mother is a waste. Rosamond's shrewd capabilities degenerate into vanity and manipulation. She is restless within the domestic sphere, and her stifled ambitions only result in unhappiness for herself and her husband.

Eliot's refusal to conform to happy endings demonstrates the fact that *Middlemarch* is not meant to be entertainment. Eliot wants to deal with real-life issues, not the fantasy world to which women writers were often confined. Her ambition was to create a portrait of the complexity of ordinary human life: quiet tragedies, petty character failings, small triumphs, and quiet moments of dignity. The complexity of her portrait of provincial society is reflected in the enormity of her canvas and the range of her characters. Her realist work is a study of every class of society in the town of Middlemarch—from the landed gentry and clergy to the manufacturers and professional men, farmers, and laborers. The contradictions in the character of the individual person are evident in the shifting sympathies of the reader. One moment, we pity Casaubon, the next we judge him critically.

Middlemarch stubbornly refuses to behave like a typical novel. The novel is a collection of relationships between several major players in the drama, but no single one person occupies the center of the action. No one person can represent provincial life. It is necessary to include multiple people. Eliot's book is experimental for its time in form and content, particularly because she was a woman writer.

Like Dickens and Thackeray, Eliot was an outsider. If we list all the larger areas in the religious-social-political-economic-personal contract that makes up society, then *Middlemarch* takes its place with *Vanity Fair* and *Bleak House*. *Middlemarch* consistently pokes through to the disorder that lies at the heart of a seemingly orderly society. While it is not cynical as is *Vanity Fair*, or consciously subversive as is *Bleak House*, *Middlemarch* nevertheless rebels against both social and religious stereotypes, and it reinforces those elements that emphasize free choice and breaking away from expected forms. When she touches on political, religious, business, or professional life, Eliot is strongly condemnatory, to the extent she illustrates how corruption lies at the heart of all ostensible success. She views money, both its acquisition and its status as power, as a corrupting influence, and empowerment itself as a form of hypocrisy. Hers is a society not heading toward corruption, but already corrupted; and here she finds common ground with both Dickens and Thackeray. They were all redefining the ground on which Victorians founded their beliefs and held to them; in that respect, they were morally and ethically experimental.

Middlemarch represents George Eliot's most comprehensive and finely rendered view of human experience. It is a vast, inclusive "Study of Provincial Life," setting out her beliefs about how society works, how it supports and thwarts the individuals who compose it, and how an accommodation can be made between the two. It is, in effect, an answer to all questioners, sage and pedestrian, modern and traditional, religious and agnostic, who ask, "How then must I live?"

Eliot's conclusion leaves us unsatisfied; we want happy endings, but she refused to bow to that convention. Eliot will not give us that ending because she knows that life doesn't work that way. In this, she takes realism, the innovation introduced by Jane Austen, to its farthest extent. *Middlemarch* demands a great deal from the reader, but it gives so much back, if we read it as Eliot intended.

Eliot is firmly in what the British critic F. R. Leavis called the "great tradition" of the English novel, by which he meant the moral tradition. As Leavis mapped it, this tradition begins with Austen and moves through Eliot, Henry James, and Joseph Conrad, terminating with D. H. Lawrence.

VIRGINIA WOOLF

Virginia Woolf, another English writer who deals with the topics of family, marriage, and womanhood, is considered one of the most important modernist twentieth-century authors and a pioneer in the use of stream of consciousness as a narrative device. Of her nine novels, her best-known are *Mrs. Dalloway* (1925), *To the Lighthouse* (1927), *Orlando* (1928), and *The Waves* (1931). She is also known for her short stories and essays, including *A Room of One's Own* (1929). Woolf became one of the central subjects of the 1970s movement of feminist criticism and her works have garnered much attention and widespread commentary for inspiring feminism.[1] A

1. In 1838, Woolf wrote, "I have already said all I have to say in my book *Three Guineas*." While this book is generally interpreted as opposing war, it is also the clearest presentation of Woolf's feminism. It is about war because it is about the better, nonsexist, and therefore peaceful world that feminism envisages. The basic complaint Woolf made

large body of literature is dedicated to her life and work, and she has been the subject of numerous plays, novels, and films. Woolf's fiction is studied for its insight into many themes, including feminism, marriage, war, shell shock, witchcraft, the role of social class in contemporary society, and the complexity of human experience. In this segment we will examine *Orlando*, one of her most accessible works.

Virginia Woolf (1882–1941) was born into an affluent household in London, the seventh child of Leslie and Julia Stephen, both parents well known in British intellectual circles at the turn of the century. The household was blended and complex, for it included older and younger siblings (Julia and Leslie had four children), two half-brothers and a half-sister (the Duckworths, from her mother's first marriage), and another half-sister, Laura (a disabled daughter from her father's first marriage who lived with the family until she was institutionalized in 1891).

Leslie Stephen loved hiking in Cornwall, a peninsula on England's rugged southwestern tip, and in the spring of 1881 he came across a large white house in St. Ives called Talland House, and took out a lease in September. Although it had limited amenities, its main attraction was the view overlooking Porthminster Bay toward the Godrevy Lighthouse, which the young Virginia could see from the upper windows and was to be the central figure in her *To the Lighthouse*. Each year from 1882 to 1895, the Stephen family leased Talland House as a summer residence. The sudden death of Virginia's mother, Julia, in 1895, when Virginia was thirteen, led to the first of Virginia's several nervous breakdowns and left a wound that Woolf experienced all her life. Additionally, her father exerted an emotional stranglehold on Virginia, not only during his lifetime, but also after his death in 1904. In her diary, she wrote that had her father lived, she would have been unable to produce books. *To the Lighthouse* attempts to understand and deal with unresolved issues concerning her parents, and there are many similarities between the plot and her own life.

Leslie Stephen's eminence as an editor, critic, and biographer, and his connection to William Thackeray, meant that his children were raised in an environment filled with the influences of Victorian literary society. Supplementing these influences was the immense library at the Stephen's house, where Virginia was home schooled in the classics and English

---

against men is that they treat women as inferior beings, relegating them to roles assigned by males. What she advocated was equal opportunity for all, which, allied to liberty and justice, would secure for women the full enjoyment of social advantages and, at the same time, the chance to develop their individual personalities freely and fully.

literature. Unlike the girls in the family, the brothers were formally educated and sent to Cambridge, a difference that Virginia greatly resented. Between the ages of fifteen and nineteen, Virginia attended the Ladies' Department of King's College, London, where she studied classics and history and met early reformers of women's higher education and the women's rights movement.

Although Virginia expressed the opinion that her father was her favorite parent, she was profoundly influenced by her mother throughout her life. It was Virginia who famously stated, "we think back through our mothers if we are women," and invoked the image of her mother repeatedly throughout her life in her diaries, letters, and in a number of her autobiographical essays. However, the image of her parents evolved considerably between 1907 and 1940, in which the somewhat distant, yet revered figures of her mother and father became more nuanced. Several issues she had to deal with involved her father's depressions and his need for attention, which created resentment in his children. Another issue involved Leslie Stephen's temper, Virginia describing him as "the tyrant father." Eventually, she became deeply ambivalent about her father. He had given her his ring on her eighteenth birthday, which created a deep emotional attachment as his literary heir. Yet she also saw him as victimizer and tyrant.

The death of her father provoked her most alarming collapse, and she was briefly institutionalized. Modern scholars have suggested that her breakdowns and subsequent recurring depressive periods were also influenced by the sexual abuses to which she and her sister Vanessa were subjected by their half-brothers George and Gerald Duckworth and by their cousin, James Kenneth Stephen. Virginia stated that she first remembers being molested by Gerald Duckworth when she was six years old. Scholars have suggested that this led to a lifetime of sexual fear and resistance to masculine authority.

Throughout her life, Virginia struggled, without success, to find meaning in her mental illness. She was institutionalized several times and attempted suicide at least twice. According to one psychiatric report, her illness was characterized by symptoms that today would be diagnosed as bipolar disorder, for which there was no effective intervention during her lifetime. In 1941, at the age of fifty-nine, Virginia died by suicidal drowning. Her experience informed her work, such as the character of Septimus Warren Smith in *Mrs. Dalloway* (1925), a veteran who returned from World War I with shell shock (deep psychological scars produced by post-traumatic stress). Like Woolf, Smith is haunted by the dead, and ulti-mately takes his own life rather than be admitted to a sanatorium.

Encouraged by her father, Woolf began writing professionally in 1900. Following her father's death in 1904, the Stephen family moved from Kensington to the more bohemian Bloomsbury district of London, where, in conjunction with her brothers' Cambridge friends and her sister Vanessa, she formed the artistic and literary Bloomsbury group. The ideas of this group formed the basics of her thinking, from which emerged her political ideas and social convictions. Later, this intellectual circle of writers and artists would include the economist John Maynard Keynes, the paint-ers Duncan Grant, Vanessa Bell, and Roger Fry, the novelist E. M. Forster, the critic Clive Bell, the philosophers Bertrand Russell and G. E. Moore, the publishers Leonard Woolf and David Garnett, and the essayist Lytton Strachey.

In 1912, Virginia married Leonard Woolf, a Cambridge friend of Virginia's brother Thoby, and in 1917, the couple founded the Hogarth Press, which published much of their work. The press chose to publish books by writers that took unconventional points of view. Initially, the press concentrated on small experimental publications. In addition to Virginia's novels, the press subsequently published many modernist works, including books by T. S. Eliot, the novels of Laurens van der Post, and the English translations of Sigmund Freud, publishing 527 titles until it became a subsidiary of Chatto & Windus before its purchase by Random House. In 2012, Random House reactivated the Hogarth Press as a fiction publisher for new and contemporary talent.

The amoral ethos of the Bloomsbury group encouraged a liberal approach to sexuality. In 1922, Virginia met the writer Vita Sackville-West, wife of Harold Nicolson. At that time, Sackville-West was the more success-ful writer as both poet and novelist, and it was not until after Woolf's death that the latter became considered the better writer. Sackville-West worked tirelessly to lift Woolf's self-esteem, helping her develop a more positive self-image by encouraging her to engage in reading and writing to calm her nerves. Sackville-West also chose the financially struggling Hogarth Press as her publisher to assist the Woolfs financially. Her novels, though not typical of the Hogarth Press, saved Hogarth and kept it profitable.

Over time, Virginia and Vita's relationship became sexual and roman-tic, reaching its peak between 1925 and 1928 before evolving into more of a friendship through the 1930s, though both women acknowledged affairs with other women at this time. After their affair ended, the two women remained friends until Woolf's death in 1941. Their period of intimacy proved fruitful for both authors, especially for Woolf, who produced three successful novels between 1927 and 1931, in addition to numerous essays.

After completing the manuscript of her last novel, *Between the Acts*, Woolf fell into a depression similar to that which she had earlier experienced. The onset of World War II, the destruction of her London home during the Blitz, and the cool reception given to her biography of her late friend, the post-impressionist painter Roger Fry, all worsened her condition until she was unable to work. After World War II began, Woolf's diary indicates that she was obsessed with death, which figured more and more as her mood darkened. On March 28, 1941, Woolf drowned herself by filling her overcoat pockets with stones and walking into the River Ouse near her home. Her body was not found until April 18. Her husband buried her cremated remains beneath an elm tree in the garden of Monk's House, their home in Sussex.

WOOLF'S *ORLANDO*: PLOT AND RESPONSE

The story of *Orlando* spans over three hundred years (1588–1928). During this time, Orlando ages only thirty-six years, and changes gender from a man to a woman. The story opens with the protagonist, Orlando, a young noble boy, pretending to chop off the heads of Moors, just like his father and grandfather had done. He is too young to fight, but he longs to go on adventures around the world like his family. Young Orlando goes out into the woods to write poetry and he falls asleep. He is awakened by trumpets sounding that Queen Elizabeth has arrived. Orlando runs to his house to get ready. When the Queen sees him, she is impressed by his youth and innocence. Two years later, she sends for him to come to her court, where the handsome Orlando serves as a page and becomes her steward, treasurer, and lover.

After her death, Orlando frequents pubs and has his way with many young women. When he grows tired of this lifestyle, he heads back to the court, this time under King James I. He dates many women, and becomes engaged to a woman of high birth and connections. This is the winter of the Great Frost, and the government has turned the frozen river into a carnival scene. One night on the river, Orlando sees a figure skate past him. He is not sure whether it is a man or a woman, but he is incredibly attracted to it. It turns out to be the Russian princess, Sasha. They grow close, become lovers, and plan to run away together. They plan to leave London together one night, but Orlando waits for her and she never arrives. He goes to the river to find that the frost has broken, and watches her Russian ship depart.

Heartbroken, Orlando locks himself inside his house, concentrating his efforts on writing. He invites Nick Green, a famous poet, to his house, who proceeds to find fault with Orlando's writing. Orlando is once again heartbroken and he burns all his poems and dramas save one, a poem entitled "The Oak Tree." One afternoon, he sees a figure on horseback in his courtyard. It is an extremely tall woman, the Archduchess Harriet of Romania. Repulsed by her advances toward him, Orlando decides to leave England immediately.

Appointed by King Charles as an ambassador to Constantinople, he performs his duties so admirably that King Charles makes him a duke. One night, during a period of civil unrest and murderous riots, Lord Orlando falls asleep for several days. He awakens to find that he has metamorphosed into a woman—the same person, with the same personality and intellect, but in a woman's body. Unperturbed, Orlando accepts the change and from this point on, though his amorous inclinations change frequently, Orlando remains biologically female.

The now Lady Orlando covertly escapes Constantinople accompanied by Rustum, an old gypsy, and joins Rustum's tribe in the mountains of Turkey. There, she feels at one with nature, but the gypsies mistrust Orlando because she values strange things like houses, bedrooms, and nature. Orlando decides to leave and sail back to England. On the ship voyage back to England, Orlando becomes romantic with Nicholas, the ship's captain. Finally, with her constraining female clothes and after an incident in which a flash of her ankle nearly results in a sailor's falling to his death, she realizes the magnitude of being a woman, and she cannot decide which gender she prefers.

On returning to England, Orlando meets Archduchess Harriet again, but she finds out that he is really a man, Archduke Harry. He proposes to Orlando, but she finds him too slow and boring to marry. She goes on to switch gender roles, dressing alternately as a man and a woman. Orlando engages energetically with life in the eighteenth century, spending time with famous poets like Addison, Dryden, and Pope, but she soon tires of them. Critic Nick Greene, apparently also timeless, reappears and promotes Orlando's writing, promising to help her publish "The Oak Tree."

As Orlando looks above, she sees great clouds come over London; the eighteenth century is over and the nineteenth century has begun.

The Victorian era is gloomy; no sunlight gets in, and the vegetation is overgrown. Orlando feels pressure to yield to "the spirit of the age" and find a husband. She goes out and meets a sea captain Marmaduke Bonthrop Shelmerdine. Like Orlando, he is gender non-conforming, and within minutes, they know everything about each other and know they are meant to be together. Orlando cannot believe that Shel has all the good qualities of a woman, and Shel cannot believe that Orlando has all the good qualities of a man. However, Shel is a seaman, and when the wind changes, he must leave to do his duty on his ship. Before he goes, he marries Orlando in a hasty but romantic ceremony.

Orlando finally finishes her poem, "The Oak Tree," and she travels to London. There she meets Nick Greene, who is now an eminent Victorian literary critic. He reads her poem and is impressed by it; he promises to have it published with excellent reviews. It is now 1901, and as King Edward VII succeeds Queen Victoria on the throne, the world becomes much brighter, if more desperate. Suddenly a light becomes very bright, and Orlando is struck ten times on the head. It is 10 a.m. on Thursday, October 11, 1928, the day Woolf's novel was published. Orlando has been struck by the present. She goes to the store, smells a candle, and thinks it is Sasha. She realizes that everything is interconnected. On the drive home from the store, Orlando thinks about all the different selves that compose her. She tries to identify the real Orlando, only to realize that Orlando is all of them.

The present frightens Orlando. She looks out over her house, thinking how it now belongs to history as well as to herself. In the novel's ending, Orlando's husband, now an aviator, flies over her house in an airplane, which hovers above Orlando until Shelmerdine leaps to the ground. A stray bird flies over his head and Orlando exults, "It's the goose! The wild goose!" The clock strikes midnight, and it is the present.

POINTS TO PONDER IN *ORLANDO*

In its day, *Orlando* was a success, both critically and financially. Nowadays, the novel's title has come to stand for women's writing generally, as one of the most famous works by a woman author that directly treats the subject of gender. In 1928, Woolf presented Sackville-West with *Orlando*, a

fantastical biography in which the eponymous hero's life spans three centuries and both sexes. *Orlando* was published shortly after the two women
spent a week traveling together in France. The novel is a veiled portrait of
Woolf's lover, Vita Sackville-West. It satirizes British culture in the sense
that it allowed "inversion" (as lesbianism was then called), as long as it was
presented as a fantastical allegory that was only real in the sense that it was
about Sackville-West.[2] In her novel, Woolf also intended to console Vita for
needing to hide her sexuality, for the unhappy end of her relationship with
Violet Trefusis in 1920, and for the loss of Knole, her ancestral home that
went to a cousin and that she would have inherited had she been a man. In a
letter praising Woolf for compensating for her sense of loss, Sackville-West
declared, "I confess, I am in love with Orlando; this is a complication I had
not foreseen."

In the book, Orlando as a woman wins control of her family estate,
which bears a close resemblance to Knole. Likewise, Trefusis appears in
the novel as the Russian princess Sasha, whom Orlando sincerely loves but
whose love ended in failure. That it was in Constantinople that Orlando
becomes a women is also significant, in that Sackville-West had lived there
between 1912 and 1914 and loved the city, which she viewed as full of
diverse cultures and peoples.

The picture of Sackville-West that Woolf presents as her alter-ego
Orlando is not completely positive, however, as Woolf felt contempt for
Sackville-West's literary abilities, regarding her a mediocre writer. The
recurring image of the grey goose that Orlando chases but never captures
is an allegory for Sackville-West's desire to write a great novel but never
managed. Perhaps fortunately for herself, a bewildered Sackville-West
never understood what the goose symbolized. For Woolf, the book also
compensated her own sense of loss, for Woolf was often hurt by Sackville-
West's promiscuity and unfaithfulness.

Woolf focuses on gender as a main issue in her novel. Orlando doesn't
have a fixed gender, but rather shifts from male to female. In *Orlando* we
find something akin to what Carl Jung called *animus* and *anima*—the male
qualities in the female and the female qualities in the male. According to
Jung, the spiritual journey reveals the human longing for wholeness, which

---

2. Even though the book simultaneously celebrated Woolf's love for Sackville-West
while also disguising it, the two women were immune from being prosecuted by the
authorities (male homosexuality, but not lesbianism, was illegal in Britain until 1967).

helps individuals become more balanced and enables relationships between the sexes to deepen.

Virginia Woolf would have agreed with D. H. Lawrence that human beings have two ways of knowing: knowing in terms of apartness (which is rational and scientific), and knowing in terms of togetherness (which is religious and poetic). In *A Room of One's Own*, she suggests that every mind is potentially bisexual (something we nowadays might prefer to call "asexual" or "gender neutral"), though she finds that among writers, including her contemporaries, men are generally depicted as functioning analytically (that is, knowing in terms of apartness), and women generally depicted as functioning synthetically (that is, knowing in terms of togetherness). In her opinion, however, to be truly creative one must use the "whole" mind. Hence, the greatest writers are "androgynous": they use and harmonize the masculine and feminine approaches to truth. In Jungian terms, such writers have discovered the "self," a point midway between the conscious and the unconscious in which there is a reconciliation of opposites. Like Jung, Woolf felt that neither an individual nor an age can find its point of equilibrium without frankly confronting and understanding the exact nature of the opposing forces. Thus, her interest in what it means to be male or female was related to her quest for the self or the point of balance that would stabilize her personality and gives her the sense of wholeness that characterizes the androgynous writer.

Men and women are physically different, but are they essentially different? If so, how? Orlando's sex change scene is important for determining the answers to these questions. As Orlando wakes up a woman, she is not perturbed by her change in gender because she feels no different than she did before. At first, she acts no differently, either. When she lives in the gypsy camp in the hills of Turkey, away from society and civilization, Orlando's sexuality seems to play no role in her life. However, when she travels on board the English ship, in women's clothes, she immediately begins to feel the difference. The skirts she wears, and the way people react to her, make her feel and act differently. What Woolf is suggesting is that gender roles are not biological, but societal. Gender is a concept imposed on people who live in society. When Orlando goes out into the night, a woman dressed as a man, she finds herself taking on traditional male mannerisms.

Orlando notices how it is harder to be a female than to be a male because of the limitations imposed on females. However, being a male is not ideal either, because males, as Orlando describes them, are driven by the desire to climb the social ladder and are not able to openly show their emotions. The way the narrator describes the differences between the two genders is realistic, for Woolf doesn't favor one gender over another. The point is that when society allows the freedom of gender neutrality, people will be freer as individuals to act according to their nature and personality.

Conformity to society is also thematic in *Orlando*. As Orlando is introduced to new historical eras and new situations, he changes to fit the rules of those around him. In the sixteenth century, he wears fine clothes and serves as a courtier to his queen; in the seventeenth century, she learns the Turkish language and adapts to exotic customs; in the eighteenth century, she figures out how to fit in with London society; and in the nineteenth century, she dons petticoats and finds a husband. Orlando knows she must change with each new adventure in order to survive and become accepted. However, Orlando finds such conformity oppressive. She grows tired of changing herself to fit those around her. Ultimately, when she reaches maturity in the twentieth century, she rejects the idea of conformity, choosing to remain whoever she chooses to be. She realizes that though she has matured, as people do, she has always been the same person all along. As Orlando grows in independence, Woolf's choice to span such a vast period of English history allows the reader to compare not only the experiences of men and women in England but also the effect of different eras on the freedom and agency of women.

Over the course of the novel, Orlando ponders the merits and demerits of fame. As a young man, he desires fame greatly: he wants to make a mark on the world through his writing, and later through his decoration of his large family home. However, after being scorned publicly by Sasha and Nicholas Greene, she turns inward, deciding that she will not write for fame but rather for personal fulfillment. Even when Orlando takes home Alexander Pope, the great author, she is intrigued and attracted to him when the carriage is in the dark, but when it is in the light, she sees that he is as common and grotesque as any other person. She chides herself for getting caught up in vanity and celebrity, and she breaks off her friendship with him when she realizes that, for all his genius writing, he does not truly respect women.

In her writings, Woolf was often critical of British historiography, which at the time was largely concerned with political-military history while neglecting the lives of women, which, with the exception of leaders like Elizabeth I, Anne, and Victoria, were almost totally ignored. *Orlando* takes place over several ages of British history, namely, the Renaissance, the Restoration, the Enlightenment, the Romantic, the Victorian, and the present, and Woolf used the various ages to mock theories of history. Woolf's father, whom she both loved and hated, had identified various writers in his book *English Literature and Society in the Eighteenth Century*, all of them men, as the "key" figures of the age, whereas Woolf wanted historians to pay attention to women writers as well. Hence, the unflattering picture Woolf presents of Alexander Pope is a caricature of her father's theories (Stephen had identified Pope as the "key" writer of early Georgian England). Furthermore, Stephen praised Sir Walter Scott as representing the "spirit" of the Romantic age, while dismissing Charlotte Brontë as a writer because she was out of touch with the "spirit" of the Victorian age. In *Orlando*, Woolf satirizes her father's theories, as it is during the Victorian Age that Orlando marries and changes drastically the quality of her writings, in opposition to the "spirit" of the Victorian era.

That the nineteenth century begins with a heavy thunderstorm, and throughout the scenes set in the Victorian age it always seems to be raining, reflects Woolf's view of the Victorian era as a dark one in British history, as it was only with the Edwardian era that sunshine returns to *Orlando*. That it was in Constantinople that Orlando becomes a woman reflects the city's status in the seventeenth century as a melting pot of cultures and a mixed population; in short, as a place with no fixed identity. Likewise, this city, partly in Europe and partly in Asia—half East and half West, initially pagan religiously (Byzantium), then Christian (Constantinople), and finally Muslim (Istanbul)—serves as an apt metaphor for shifting identities, whether they be national, cultural, ethnic, sexual, gender, or religious, making it the perfect backdrop for Orlando's transformation.

QUESTIONS FOR DISCUSSION AND REFLECTION

In addition to the questions listed at the end of the preface, answer the following questions, writing your answers in a journal. If you are in a group study, be prepared to share your answers with those in the group.

1. If there were a difference between "chauvinism" and "feminism," what would it be?

2. Explain George Eliot's logic in using a masculine pen name for her novels.

3. Explain and assess Eliot's belief system as the "religion of humanity," and how this perspective influenced her literary approach.

4. Explain the effect of "higher criticism" on biblical interpretation and biblical authority.

5. If, as Eliot stated, the purpose of *Middlemarch* is to make people better, did she accomplish her goal? If so, how?

6. In your estimation, what is Eliot's chief advice regarding marriage in *Middlemarch*?

7. In your estimation, what is Eliot's chief advice regarding vocation in *Middlemarch*?

8. Explain the influence of Woolf's parents on her lifestyle, career, and literary technique.

9. What is your takeaway after reading the segment on Woolf's *Orlando*?

10. What did you learn in this chapter about spirituality and gender?

11. Assess the merits of Woolf's notion that human minds are essentially bisexual (or gender neutral), and that the greatest writers are androgynous.

12. What did you learn in this chapter about conformity and nonconformity?

13. In your estimation, which woman of the twentieth and/or twenty-first century lived the most significant life or left the most significant legacy? Explain your answer.

Chapter 9

E. M. Forster's *A Passage to India*

IN THE PREVIOUS CHAPTER we spoke of the Bloomsbury group, a set of writers, thinkers, artists, and political theorists who left an indelible stamp on twentieth-century literature, particularly throughout its best-known literary figures, the novelists Virginia Woolf and E. M. Forster. Known as the Bloomsberries, members espoused what we might call intellectual liberalism, a doctrine derived from John Stuart Mill via the Cambridge ethical philosopher G. E. Moore. The Bloomsbury code of liberalism was given its most concise expression in Forster's belief that it is more honorable to betray one's country than to betray one's friends.

As Woolf, a founder of the Bloomsberries, famously declared, human nature changed "in 1910, on or about December 10." That, she thought, was the day that Victorianism died and a new order arose. Speaking of the date of the post-impressionist exhibition by painter Roger Fry, a member of the Bloomsbury group, it was that event that led the Bloomsberries to look to Paris rather than London for inspiration, for globalism, not nationalism, modernism, not Victorianism, would guide progressive Western artists and thinkers.

Edward Morgan Forster (1879–1970) was born and raised in an upper-middle class environment. His father was an architect and his mother had a strong influence on his emerging character. Forster's intellectual character was formed at Cambridge, as was his connection with the Bloomsberries. In addition to short stories and essays, Forster had five novels published in his lifetime, for which he received numerous awards. Although he failed to receive the Nobel Prize in Literature, he was nominated on sixteen separate occasions. According to his friend Richard Marquand, Forster was critical of American foreign policy in his later years, which was one reason he refused offers to adapt his novels for the screen, as Forster felt such productions would involve American financing. Nevertheless, his major novels were all adapted as films after his death.

Many of his novels examine class difference and hypocrisy, including *A Room with a View* (1908), *Howards End* (1910), and his greatest success, *A Passage to India* (1924). The characters of Mrs. Wilcox in *Howards End* and of Mrs. Moore in *A Passage to India* have mystical links with the past and striking abilities to connect with people from beyond their own circles. Forster, together with Henry James and Somerset Maugham, was the earliest fiction writer to portray characters from diverse countries. By exploring cultural conflict, their work anticipates the concept of humans shedding national identities and becoming more tolerant and progressive.

Sexuality is another key theme in Forster's work. Forster was gay, and knew it early in life. However, he kept his private life strictly private, to avoid the fate of Irish poet and playwright Oscar Wilde, who was convicted of gross indecency for consensual homosexual acts, imprisoned, and died an early death at age forty-six. Forster's novel *Maurice* (1971), published posthumously, is a homosexual love story. The novel was controversial, given that Forster's homosexuality had not been known or widely acknowledged. Some critics have argued that a general shift from heterosexual to homosexual love can be observed through the course of his writing career. The foreword to *Maurice* describes his struggle with sexuality, as does the short story collection *The Life to Come*, also published after his death.

Forster traveled widely in the early years of the twentieth century with his mother. He visited India for long and life-changing periods before and after World War I. The vision of self-realization that he glimpsed there inspired him to write his last great novel, *A Passage to India*, for which he won the James Tait Black Memorial Prize for fiction. He never married, and lived with his mother from 1925 until her death in 1945. In the 1930s and 1940s, he was a broadcaster on BBC Radio, during which time he became publicly associated with the British Humanist Association. In addition to his broadcasting, he advocated individual liberty and penal reform and opposed censorship by writing articles, sitting on committees, and signing letters. He spent his final years at King's College, Cambridge, where he was elected an honorary fellow in 1946. He declined a knighthood in 1949, but in 1969 accepted membership in the Order of Merit for distinguished service in the field of literature. He died of a stroke in 1970 at the age of ninety-one.

Forster was acutely alive to European culture and civilization and the failure of those values to penetrate the lower classes of English life. This idea found expression in *Howards End*; the famous epigraph to this work is "Only connect." This ambitious "condition-of-England" novel depicts various groups among the Edwardian middle classes, represented by the Schlegels (progressive intellectuals), the Wilcoxes (self-serving industrialists), and the Basts (struggling lower-middle class aspirants). The novel tells the story of two sisters, Helen and Margaret Schlegel, based to some degree on Virginia Woolf and her sister Vanessa Stephen. Rich, highly cultured, and philanthropic, they espouse the cause of a self-improving clerk, Leonard Bast, but their high culture and his lack of culture stand in the way of any connection. Even less positive is the Schlegels' attempt to connect with the business world, represented by the Wilcox family in the novel. However, the connection proclaimed in the epigraph is initiated when Mrs. Wilcox, a strangely mystical mother figure, bequeaths the family home, Howards End, to Margaret Schlegel, though the Wilcox family temporarily suppresses the will, causing much suffering, including the murder of Leonard Bast. In the conclusion, the epigraph is achieved, for Margaret marries the widower Mr. Wilcox, and Helen bears the deceased Bast's illegitimate child. Forster's idealized connection between poetry and prose, culture and commerce, and England and Germany, would not last, for the war that split the world of the Germanic Schlegels and the Anglo-Saxon Wilcoxes was only four years away when the novel was published in 1910.

FORSTER'S *A PASSAGE TO INDIA*: PLOT AND RESPONSE

Set against the backdrop of the British Raj (the period of direct British rule over the Indian subcontinent from 1858 until the independence of India and Pakistan in 1947) and the Indian independence movement in the 1920s, the story revolves around four characters: Dr. Aziz, his British friend Mr. Cyril Fielding, Mrs. Moore, and Miss Adela Quested. During a trip to the fictitious Marabar Caves (a place of deep religious symbolism modeled on the Barabar Caves of Bihar), Adela thinks she finds herself alone with Dr. Aziz in one of the caves (when in fact he is in an entirely different cave), and subsequently panics and flees; it is assumed that Dr. Aziz has attempted to assault her. In the caves, Adela may or may not have been sexually assaulted; we never really know. Aziz's trial, and its run-up and aftermath, bring to a boil racial tensions and prejudices between Indians and the British during the colonial era.

The story begins when two Englishwomen, the young Adela Quested and the elderly Mrs. Moore, travel to India. Adela expects to become engaged to Mrs. Moore's son, Ronny Heaslop, a British civil magistrate in the fictional Indian city of Chandrapore. Adela and Mrs. Moore each hope to see the real India during their visit, rather than cultural institutions imported by the British. At the same time, Aziz, a young Muslim doctor in India, is increasingly frustrated by the poor treatment he receives at the hands of the English. Aziz is especially annoyed with Major Callendar, a civil surgeon who has a tendency to summon Aziz for frivolous reasons in the middle of dinner. Aziz and his educated friends hold lively conversation about whether or not Indians can be friends with the English in India. That night, Mrs. Moore and Aziz happen to run into each other while exploring a local mosque. Aziz is moved and surprised that an English person would treat him like a friend.

Mrs. Moore returns to the British club down the road and relates her experience at the mosque. Ronny Heaslop initially thinks she is talking about an Englishman and becomes indignant when he learns the facts. Adela, however, is intrigued. Because the newcomers had expressed a desire to see Indians, Mr. Turton, the city tax collector who governs Chandrapore, hosts a party so that Adela and Mrs. Moore may have the opportunity to meet some of the more prominent and wealthy Indians in the city. At the event, which proves to be rather awkward, Adela meets Cyril Fielding, the principal of the government college in Chandrapore. Fielding, impressed with Adela's open friendliness to the Indians, invites her and Mrs. Moore to tea with him and the Hindu professor Godbole. At Adela's request, Fielding invites Aziz to tea as well.

At Fielding's tea party, everyone has a good time conversing about India, and Fielding and Aziz become friends. Aziz promises to take Mrs. Moore and Adela to see the Marabar Caves, a distant cave complex. Ronny Heaslop arrives and rudely interrupts the party. Aziz mistakenly believes that the women are offended that he has not followed through on his promise and arranges an outing to the caves at great expense to himself. Fielding and Godbole are supposed to accompany the expedition, but they miss the train, so Aziz continues alone with the two women, Adela and Mrs. Moore.

Inside one of the caves, Mrs. Moore is overcome with claustrophobia. But worse than the claustrophobia is the echo. Unnerved by the uncanny sound, which seems to turn every sound she makes into a noisy "*ou-boum*," Mrs. Moore declines to continue exploring. Adela and Aziz, accompanied by a guide, climb to the higher caves while Mrs. Moore waits below. Adela, suddenly realizing that she does not love Ronny, asks Aziz whether he has more than one wife—a question he considers offensive. Disconcerted by the bluntness of her remark, he ducks into a cave to compose himself, and when he returns, Adela is gone. The guide tells him that Adela has gone into a cave by herself. Aziz looks for her in vain. Deciding she is lost, he strikes the guide, who runs away. Finding Adela's field-glasses lying broken on the ground, he picks them up and carries them with him. Aziz then looks down the hill and sees Adela speaking to another young Englishwoman, Miss Derek, who has arrived with Fielding in a car. Aziz runs down the hill and greets Fielding, but Miss Derek and Adela drive off without explanation. Apparently, Adela has injured herself while descending from the caves. Fielding, Mrs. Moore, and Aziz return to Chandrapore on the train. At the train station, Aziz is arrested and charged with sexually assaulting Adela in a cave, a charge based on Adela's claim that Aziz had followed her into the cave and tried to grab her, and that she had fended him off by swinging her field glasses at him. The only evidence the British have is the field glasses in the possession of Aziz.

Fielding, believing Aziz to be innocent, angers British India by joining the Indians in Aziz's defense. In the weeks before the trial, the racial tensions between the Indians and the English flare up. Mrs. Moore is distracted and miserable because of her memory of the echo in the cave and because of her impatience with the upcoming trial. Adela is emotional and ill, and she too seems to suffer from an echo in her mind. Ronny is unhappy with Mrs. Moore's lack of support for Adela, and they agree that Mrs. Moore will return to England prematurely, before she can testify at the trial. Mrs. Moore dies on the voyage back to England, but not before she realizes that there is no "real India," but rather many different Indias. Her absence from India becomes a major issue at the trial, where Aziz's defenders assert that her testimony would prove his innocence.

At Aziz's trial, Adela, under oath, is questioned about what happened in the caves. Shockingly, she declares that she has made a mistake: Aziz is not the person or thing that attacked her in the cave. Aziz is set free, and Fielding begins to respect Adela, recognizing her bravery in standing against her peers to pronounce Aziz innocent. Ronny breaks off his engagement to Adela, and she departs India, never to return.

Although he is vindicated, Aziz is angry that Fielding befriended Adela after she nearly ruined his life. The friendship between the two men suffers as a consequence, and Fielding departs for England. Believing Fielding is leaving to marry Adela and bitter at this friend's perceived betrayal, Aziz declares that he is done with the English and that he intends to move to a place where he will not have to encounter them. Aziz moves to the Hindu-ruled state of Mau, several hundred miles from Chandrapore, and begins a new life. Hearing that Fielding married Adela shortly after returning to England, Aziz vows never again to befriend a white person.

One day, walking through an old temple with his children, he encounters Fielding and is surprised to learn that Fielding married not Adela Quested, but Stella Moore, Mrs. Moore's daughter from her second marriage. The two men go for a final ride together before Fielding leaves, during which Aziz tells Fielding that once the English are out of India, the two will be able to be friends. Fielding asks why they cannot be friends now, and Aziz explains that he and Fielding cannot be friends until India becomes independent from British rule.

POINTS TO PONDER IN *A PASSAGE TO INDIA*

Although he published only five novels in his lifetime, the most recent, *A Passage to India*, appearing as long ago as 1924, E. M. Forster maintains a high rank among the writers of fiction in the twentieth century. *A Passage to India* is not only Forster's greatest novel, but also one of the outstanding literary accomplishments of the twentieth century.

Critical analysis of Forster's *Passage* typically focuses on the theme of cross-cultural friendship, particularly on the difficulty of English-Indian friendship and on the differences between Eastern and Western ways of life. Though the main characters in the novel are generally Christian or Muslim, Hinduism also plays a large thematic role. Additionally, Forster takes great care in this novel to strike a distinction between the ideas of "muddle" and "mystery." "Muddle" has connotations of disorder, whereas "mystery" suggests a mystical, orderly plan by transcendent spiritual forces. Fielding, who regularly speaks for Forster, admits that India is a muddle, whereas figures such as Mrs. Moore and Godbole view India as a mystery. In *Passage*, this muddled quality is mirrored in the makeup of India's native population, which is mixed due to different religious, ethnic, linguistic, and regional groups. The muddle of India disorients Adela the most; indeed, the events at the Marabar Caves that trouble her profoundly can be seen as a manifestation of this muddle.

Reading this book socio-politically—as an anticolonial work—or socio-religiously—as forbidden love between a Christian Englishwoman and a Muslim Indian doctor—or watching the film version for its entertainment value, is to miss its spiritual significance, conveyed through rich symbolism. Forster's plot, as his ending, is a version of the Hindu *neti, neti* approach to God: a negative approach meaning "not this, not that," but everything; "not now, not then," but always; "not here, not there," but everywhere. Forster's spirituality, depicted symbolically throughout the book, provides a poignant and unforgettable image of what Forster grappled with, at the highest artistic level, throughout his career—the need to connect. Such interconnectivity, he believed, needed to take place politically, culturally, socially, economically, and religiously, on both a personal and national level, practically and theoretically, psychologically and philosophically.

Forster's interest in both human and transcendent realities accounts for what his friend G. Lowes Dickinson termed Forster's "double vision," a sense of this world but also of a world or worlds above, behind, or within. Forster's "worlds behind" cannot be ignored or dismissed by critical readers, for in Forster the sense of the transcendent realm consistently influences the physical realm, a connection he depicts through characters in his novel. Nevertheless, the transcendent and physical realms remain distinct, and while some protagonists are closer to one realm or another, the Forsterian hero is incomplete, that incompleteness being the result of a dissociation between the character and the universe, between the individual living in a seemingly chaotic, temporal world while simultaneously also in the unifying, eternal reality.

Properly understood, *A Passage to India* serves as a tutorial on interconnectivity and hence, on global spirituality, for it is two novels simultaneously, a book about reason as well as about feeling: the latter, to help readers apprehend the transcendence within the temporal, and the former, subservient to feeling, to allow us to apprehend the temporal within the transcendent. Forster is not solely a novelist of ideas, nor is he solely a mystic, though he has been praised for, and accused of, being both. The voice we hear as we read him is not that of one who has pierced the heavens, nor that of one whose primary intent is to discuss the ideas needful for proper existence on earth. It is, rather, that of a mediator, neither divine nor human, who carries on from a midpoint between the two, knowing less than is possible for one, but sensing more than is possible for the other.

For Forster, India is more than a foreign land that the English may leave at their wish; it is the contemporary condition, the separation of humans from one another, from nature, and from God. Spirituality conditions key characters in *Passage*. Mrs. Moore, for example, is essentially intuitional and visionary, embodying the potentialities of the feminine spirit. As she tells her son, Ronnie Heaslop, God has put us on earth to love our neighbors, a belief she enacts with Aziz, for despite the brevity of their acquaintance, the two make immediate and lasting connection. However, in the Marabar cave, she undergoes a psychic experience in which she loses totally the sense of values that her mystical divination of unity had afforded her, losing interest in Aziz, in her own children, in God, and even in her own life. Nevertheless, she makes a lasting effect, and even after her death, her influence continues. The Hindus at the trial of Aziz invoke her name in the echoing chant—"Esmiss Esmoore"—for she has seemed like a goddess to them. She influences Adela toward realization that her accusation of Aziz has been false, and her presence is felt even after her death and helps weave the achieved unity—transitory though it may be—that we find throughout the final section of the novel.

The redemptive power that Mrs. Moore possesses after death merges with the elderly Hindu professor, Godbole. As the central figure in the last section of the novel and the one most responsible for whatever sense of hope appears there, he is the representative of Hinduism, while also serving as Forster's voice. His position is one of detachment, both from human reality and from the physical world, a detachment obtained by as complete a denial of individual consciousness as is possible, that denial and detachment bringing with them a sense of love and an awareness of unity. For Godbole, as for Foster, a full perception of the transcendent reality is impossible, as is a full awareness of the unity within the physical world. However, his achievement, though partial and won only by renunciation, is still a victory, and the only victory that humanity, apart from divine intervention, can achieve.

Forster's portrayal of Godbole is not to say that Forster was Hindu, or that he was propagating Hindu values in this novel. Nevertheless, Forster was making the point that Hinduism is more open to certain kinds of experience than are Christianity and Islam, and that Western monotheists in particular are impoverished by their repression of the irrational and the unseen. For Forster, the world of logic and common sense is important, but it is not enough. As he noted in 1914, after his first trip to India: Christianity is mainly concerned with conduct; it is an ethical code, a code with divine sanctions but applicable to daily life. Hindus, on the other hand, are not concerned with conduct but with vision; they are aware of the tangible world, but give priority to the intangible power behind it.[1]

In an important essay, "Art for Art's Sake," Forster commented on the apparent impossibility of humanity to achieve harmony with nature and between humans while constantly altering the natural order of things. For a better future to arise, he noted, the human race must experience "universal exhaustion," divesting control in order that new birth and new growth may be achieved. We see in his depiction of Mrs. Moore a concept similar to this. She, who always believed in harmony, must die through spiritual exhaustion, something she achieves in the Marabar cave and not in her actual death on the sea.

Hence, it is as a rebirth after exhaustion that we need to read the conclusion of *A Passage to India*. The book is interwoven with triads, from its basic structural level to its most metaphysical speculation. There are three cultures/races/religions: Anglo Christian, Muslim, and Hindu. The novel's three sections represent the three seasons of the Indian year; cold season, hot season, and rainy season. Contending for supremacy within these seasonal changes are animal, vegetable, and mineral elements. The concept of threeness occurs repeatedly in the narrative as well, such as when Aziz sees Mrs. Moore in the mosque and angrily shouts (before he learns that she has removed her shoes), "Madam! Madam! Madam!" Later, Mrs. Moore tells her son that what India needs is "Good will and more good will and more good will," and some pages later Aziz echoes that sentiment in the chant, "Kindness, more kindness, and even after that more kindness." The triads of the book suggest totality but also connection, both within the temporal realm and with the eternal reality.

From a natural or physical perspective, the three Indian seasons reflect the recurring cycle of birth, death, and rebirth. The book's first section, entitled "Mosque," deals with the vastness of space; in this immensity, God is discernible, despite increasing difficulty to perceive. In this section, the Mirabar Caves are an unknown quality, mysterious and faintly ominous. In the second section, entitled "Caves," the universe has become a cave,

1. Beer, *Passage to India: Essays in Interpretation*, 18–19.

one in which the God of love and goodness is missing. Evil is evident, and only as the section draws to a close does that evil begin to recede. The final section, entitled "Temple," is noisy, joyous, and confusing. Now, for the first time, Forster realizes that the two commitments of his "double vision"— the world of human reality and the midpoint between that reality and the transcendent reality beyond—cannot be brought fully and satisfactorily together, at least "not yet."

At the end, Fielding and Godbole—representing the worlds of reason and of feeling respectively—are separate and must remain so. In a world of spiritual disintegration, where humans are pilgrims and strangers, Fielding's clarity of reason, his acceptance of the physical world as "reality," and his desire to achieve universal brotherhood, while desirable and necessary qualities, cannot alone bring new integration, for by itself, rationality makes the earth no less hostile, and imparts no sense of connection with transcendent reality. Granting the contemporary condition as Forster describes it, the way of Godbole—love—is the only possible way, even though to exist it must maintain detachment from the physical world.

From a spiritual or metaphysical perspective, the threefold structure of *A Passage to India* represents the three Sanskrit terms that Hindus often use to describe "Brahman" (that is, God or ultimate reality): *sat*, *cit*, and *ananda*. *Sat* means "being," so Brahman is seen not as a being but rather as being itself; *cit* means "consciousness," so Brahman is seen as pure, eternal awareness; and Ananda means "bliss," so Brahman is seen as happiness, delight, and enjoyment. Thus, God is being-consciousness-bliss. To personalize God, Hindus approach the unseen metaphysical absolute through the triad of three deities: Brahma (the divine creator), Vishnu (the divine preserver), and Shiva (the divine destroyer).

To discover the spirituality inherent in *A Passage to India*, it is necessary to consider its most provocative image—the Marabar Caves—central to the novel both structurally and thematically. Mystery shrouds the caves throughout; that they are extraordinary we know from the first sentence of the novel, but as to what makes them so, we are never precisely told. Godbole, who knows their secret, won't reveal it. It is impossible to explain their unique nature, for, like God, they are infinite and empty. On a metaphysical level, the caves represent the Hindu Brahman— described as the empty absolute, devoid of attributes—or the Buddhist Nirvana—best described as "vast emptiness" or as "nothingness."

The Mirabar Caves are rich in mysteries, which exist not to be "solved" but to be wondered at, and characters in this novel are tested by whether they can or cannot deal with such mysteries. Not all characters enter the caves, but as becomes evident, some can enter and some cannot. Mrs. Moore and Adela both have traumatic experiences in the caves and are shattered by the mysteries they encounter there. Aziz, being Muslim and bored by most things Hindu, is a mere tourist to the caves and immune to their deeper significance. Fielding, being sensible, is curious about the caves, as he is curious about everything, but he is unable to understand them spiritually. Godbole alone, the devout detached Hindu, can enter the caves without fear and without evil consequences, for he is accustomed to wandering in such depths, and caves are central to Hindu worship.

As the novel unfolds, the implications of the Mirabar Caves gradually become clearer, not so much through specific description as through the efforts they produce on three of the major characters: Mrs. Moore, Adela, and Fielding. A voice, "very old and very small," speaks to Mrs. Moore in one of the caves and distorts her sense of values; she doesn't want to communicate with anyone, not even with God. In another cave, Adela undergoes the illusion that Aziz has attempted her seduction, an illusion strong enough to cause her severe shock and to send Aziz to trial. To Fielding, it is not the interior of the caves (he is unaffected there) but the distant view of them at sunset from the veranda of the club at Chandrapore that disturbs. The vastness of the hills and caves represents, for him, some kind of unifying reality, a reality that, as an agnostic, he cannot comprehend, for he lives wholly within the rational, phenomenal world, and his primary concern within that world is that of human relationships.

The vastness, so troubling to Fielding, is something that Mrs. Moore has always accepted; she is aware of the expanse beyond the phenomenal world and of a divine unity encompassing that expanse. Yet the effect made upon her within the cave is quite the reverse of that made upon Fielding as he views the hills from a distance. The reason Marabar produces dissimilar effects upon Fielding and Mrs. Moore is related to the difference in their intuitive powers. For certainly hers is much greater than his and is not so limited as is his by the reasoning faculty.

An echo produced by the emptiness and smallness of the caves is central to the effect the caves have on Adela and Mrs. Moore. What happens to Mrs. Moore in the cave? To put it simply, it is the case of her intuitive apparatus going blank, for there is nothing for it to receive. On a literal level, she hears a voice, but that voice is merely the echo produced by the striking of a match; on the metaphysical level, the voice is suggestive of the transcendent principle present at Marabar, a principle devoid of attributes and hence, unknowable. For Forster, the symbol of the lighting of a match is fascinating. When a visitor to the caves strikes a match, "immediately another flame rises in the depths of the rock and moves toward the surface like an imprisoned spirit . . . The two flames approach and strive to unite, but cannot, because one of them breathes air, the other stone."[2]

While this passage is capable of many interpretations, the match flame likely represents the individual soul (Atman), which, in the Hindu Upanishads, is one with Brahman. For Forster, the granite of the cave implies the matter of the phenomenal universe, and the reflection of the flame would be the Brahman that dwells in the stone, that is, in the universe. However, the phenomenal universe is but a mirror, and the existence of the identical flame in the wall is actually illusion. Union of Atman and Brahman can be achieved only by the extinction of consciousness, symbolized by the expiration of the match flame. We are once again at the moment of Nirvana (the word refers to the "blowing out" of the flame of life), when, according to Buddhist teaching, the individual soul (Atman) is released from consciousness and all illusion and merges with pure being.

According to Forster, the echo in a Marabar cave is "devoid of distinction. . . . And if several people talk at once, an overlapping howling noise begins."[3] Echoes, like the thousand manifestations of Brahman, spring from one source and can take on a cacophony of sounds, echoes generating echoes. For Mrs. Moore, the echo penetrates to the depths of her being and breaks up the neat compartments of her accustomed values.

At the conclusion of the novel, Forster brings his themes together in describing a single crack of thunder that has no accompanying echo: it is the suggestion of completed union. Although Mrs. Moore's vision in the cave is incomplete, the results produced upon her are similar to those produced at the moment of Nirvana. To Mrs. Moore, as in the moment of Nirvana, the physical world loses its significance, and all distinctions, moral as well as physical, are obliterated. Her response is initially one of "horror"; she feels she is becoming ill. That Forster intends the emptiness of the cave to represent Brahman and the echo to represent Mrs. Moore's incomplete awareness of that absolute is suggested also by the parallel that exists between

2. Forster, *Passage to India*, 125.
3. Forster, *Passage to India*, 147-48.

the "*ou-boum*" she hears and the divine Hindu sound "OM" (an audible symbol for Brahman, the cosmic Self). The nature of her experience causes her to lose interest in all reality, whether physical or transcendent.

It is worth noting that Mrs. Moore's attitude after the Marabar experience finds representation in one member of the Brahmanic triad. Brahma, Vishnu, and Siva represent creation, preservation, and dissolution. When activity prevails, Brahma is supreme; when goodness, Vishnu; and when apathy, Siva. It is Siva, certainly, who gains priority after Mrs. Moore's vision in the cave; a sense of evil, an absence of good, is the dominant note throughout most of the central section of the novel. Central to Hinduism's vision of Brahman is all-pervasiveness. An absolute reality, God encompasses and reconciles all realities, including all goodness and all evil, for in a nondual world, all qualities are on a continuum and are therefore interrelated. "Good and evil," Godbole tells Fielding, "are different, as their names imply. But, in my own humble opinion, they are both of them aspects of my Lord."[4] This is not to say there is no good or evil, better or worse, but only that, if we are to affirm unity, or even to grasp the idea of unity, we must trace life's echoes to their common source.

Unlike Godbole, Mrs. Moore requires a divine order perceptible to her reason. For her, God cannot encompass goodness *and* evil; God must be good only, and where goodness exists, God is present. However, India represents a world from which order has disappeared; it is a world in which good itself is no longer to be found. Mrs. Moore's love—representing the values of Western Christianity—is doomed. By contrast, Godbole's love—requiring none of the foundations upon which Mrs. Moore's love is built—is the only kind of love that can survive in the world that Forster depicts.

In Hindu mythology, the caves represent the "womb of the universe," from which emanate all the forms of created life. Through his cave symbology, Forster accomplishes an intricate, multiple functioning that binds the novel and life intuitively and holistically. In terms of plot, the caves provide the basis of Adela's accusation of Aziz; in terms of meaning, they suggest the impasse that Western civilization has reached in uniting the physical and spiritual dimensions of reality. For Forster, the caves point to a reality that exists beyond time and space, which human consciousness cannot fully reach, and to which that consciousness, even as it reaches out to apprehend ultimate reality, finally is a barrier.

---

4. Forster, *Passage to India*, 178.

To explain the caves and their echoes, it is helpful to go to psychology. If we seek a psychological explanation of the "womb of the universe" idea, we find a corollary in the psychological notion of the subconscious—or "unconscious," as Sigmund Freud termed it. While Freud viewed the unconscious as the depository of all that the conscious mind had repressed or forgotten, Swiss psychiatrist Carl Jung taught that the unconscious also contained transcendental qualities such as archetypes and other shared ancestral experiences he called the "collective unconscious." In this sense, the echoes of Forster's novel represent the unconscious breaking into the conscious mind, and for those unaccustomed to such visitation, it can seem—as it did to Adela—like a rape of the personality. For others, such as Mrs. Moore, such inbreaking can lead to a virtual abdication of the moral sense. For example, Mrs. Moore knew that Aziz was innocent, yet she did nothing to help him, a religion of "vision" having replaced her old religion of "conduct."

In *A Passage to India*, the caves represent the unconscious in two ways: the repressed elements in the individual life, and the survival in modern individuals of the prehistoric and the prehuman, those elements that Freud termed the id. The "*ou-boum*" echo, then, is something primal and prelingual, a sound emanating from the dark, distant, prehistoric past, prior to language and social morality. That is why the echo is so terrifying to Mrs. Moore. To yield to the primal forces of the subconscious is, to one trained in repression, nothing less than the abdication of culture and reason and a return to something like savagery. However, that is not how Godbole feels. Such returns, for him, are not frightening but renewing, for he knows those spiritual depths as places of vision and inspiration rather than as nightmare. Primal echoes, like radio waves emanating from our collective unconscious, come in an infinity of forms—through sight as well as sound, in seen and unseen form, as riddles, coincidences, and sometimes even as divine visitations. Ultimately, the echo of greatest significance is the idea of "nothing," for sometimes, when we think nothing is happening, is when we are most receptive to the divine.

In this postmodern period, when human beings, like their primal ancestors, are becoming increasingly aware of the interrelatedness of the natural and supernatural realms, we can read *A Passage to India* as a kind of bible of spiritual ecology. While it offers no solution to the human "muddle," it offers a vision of what is involved if we hope to mend our tragic divisions, including those that divide us from God and nature as well as those that divide us against each other and against ourselves.

QUESTIONS FOR DISCUSSION AND REFLECTION

In addition to the questions listed at the end of the preface, answer the following questions, writing your answers in a journal. If you are in a group study, be prepared to share your answers with those in the group.

1. Explain the Bloomsbury "code of liberalism."

2. In this chapter, what did you learn about class difference, social hypocrisy, or social elitism?

3. Explain the role or symbolism of Mrs. Moore in *A Passage to India*.

4. Discuss the deep religious symbolism of the Marabar Caves.

5. Explain Forster's distinction between "muddle" and "mystery."

6. Explain the meaning of the Hindu phrase "*neti, neti*."

7. Explain and assess Forster's "double vision" in *A Passage to India*, and how this novel serves as a tutorial on interconnectivity.

8. Discuss and assess Godbole's character and role in *A Passage to India*.

9. Explain the meaning of Forster's comment that to achieve a better world, the human race must first experience "universal exhaustion."

10. Explain the meaning behind Forster's use of triads in *A Passage to India*.

11. Explain the meaning of the symbol of the echo in the Mirabar Caves.

12. Explain the meaning of the lighting of a match in the Mirabar Caves.

13. Explain how goodness and evil are understood in nondual spirituality.

14. In your estimation, is Forster's perspective in *A Passage to India* essentially optimistic or pessimistic? Explain your answer.

Chapter 10

Ralph Ellison's *Invisible Man* and José Vasconcelos's *The Cosmic Race*

HAVING DEALT IN CHAPTER 9 with social and religious issues in India during the British Raj, this chapter focuses on issues of class, culture, and race in the Americas. The first segment of the chapter examines these issues primarily through an African-American lens, and the second segment, through an Ibero-American lens.

Ralph Waldo Ellison (1913–1994), named after Ralph Waldo Emerson, was born and raised in Oklahoma. His father, a small-business owner and a construction supervisor, died in 1916 from the effects of a work-related accident. The elder Ellison loved literature, and doted on his three children, one of whom died in infancy. In later life, Ralph discovered that his father had hoped he would grow up to be a poet. As a youngster, Ellison loved music, playing trumpet and alto saxophone with local musicians. Admitted to Tuskegee Institute, the prestigious Black university in Alabama founded by Booker T. Washington, he soon discovered that the institution was no less class-conscious than most white institutions. He spent his free time in the library reading modernist classics by James Joyce, Gertrude Stein, and T. S Eliot, and later cited Eliot's *The Waste Land* as a major literary influence. At Tuskegee, he also became familiar with Fyodor Dostoevsky's *Crime and Punishment* and *Notes from Underground*, together with Thomas Hardy's *Jude the Obscure*, identifying with the brilliant, tortured anti-heroes of these works.

Leaving Tuskegee before completing the requirements for a degree, he moved to New York City's Harlem district in 1936, then the culture capital of Black America. There he met Langston Hughes, who introduced him to the Black literary establishment, and the author Richard Wright, who encouraged him to write fiction as a career. From 1937 to 1944, Ellison had over twenty book reviews, as well as short stories and articles, published in literary magazines. Wright was then openly associated with the Communist Party, and Ellison also developed Communist sympathies. However, during World War II, both Wright and Ellison lost faith in Communism, feeling it had betrayed African Americans.

In 1946, Ellison married Fanny McConnell, a smart and accomplished person in her own right, a founder of the Negro People's Theater in Chicago and a newspaper writer. From 1947 to 1951, Fanny helped support Ellison financially while he wrote *Invisible Man*. Published in 1952, Ellison's masterpiece explores the theme of a person's search for identity and place in society, as seen from the perspective of the narrator, an unnamed African American man, first in the Deep South and then in the New York City of the 1930s. In contrast to contemporaries such as Richard Wright and James Baldwin, Ellison created characters that are dispassionate, educated, articulate, and self-aware. Through his protagonist, Ellison explores the contrasts between the Northern and Southern varieties of racism and their alienating effect. The narrator is "invisible" in this figurative sense, in that he is overlooked and unappreciated, which leads to a dissociative self-image.

Critically praised, the novel won the U. S. National Book Award for Fiction in 1953, making Ellison the first African American writer to win the award. More than a half century after its publication, *Invisible Man* is regarded by many as a milestone in American literature, even as a candidate for the greatest novel of the mid-twentieth century. In 1998, the Modern Library ranked *Invisible Man* 19th on its list of the "100 Best English-Language Novels of the 20th Century," and *Time* magazine called it "the quintessential American picaresque of the 20th century," rather than a "race novel" or even a *Bildungsroman*. Anthony Burgess, author of *A Clockwork Orange*, described *Invisible Man* as a "masterpiece," and *New York Times* critic Orville Prescott called it "the most impressive work of fiction by an American Negro which I have ever read."

In 1964, Ellison published *Shadow and Act*, a collection of essays, and began to teach at Bard College, Rutgers University, and Yale University. Writing essays about both the Black experience and his love for jazz music, Ellison continued to receive major awards for his work. In 1969, he received the Presidential Medal of Freedom; the following year, he was made a *Chevalier of the Ordre des Arts et des Lettres* by France and became a member of the faculty at New York University from 1970 to 1980.

In 1967, Ellison experienced a major house fire at his summer home in Massachusetts, in which he claimed more than three hundred pages of a second novel, *Juneteenth*, were lost. He ultimately wrote more than two thousand pages of this novel, but never published it. However, the novel was published posthumously from voluminous notes he left upon his death. In 1986, his *Going to the Territory* was published, a collection of essays on novelists such as William Faulkner and Richard Wright, the music of Duke Ellington, and the contributions of African Americans to America's national identity. Ellison died in 1994 of pancreatic cancer and was interred in a crypt at Trinity Church Cemetery in the Washington Heights neighborhood of Upper Manhattan.

ELLISON'S *INVISIBLE MAN*: PLOT AND RESPONSE

The narrator, an unnamed Black man, begins by describing his living conditions: an underground room wired with hundreds of electric lights, operated by power stolen from the city's electric grid. He reflects on the various ways in which he has experienced social invisibility during his life and begins to tell his story, returning to his teenage years.

The narrator lives in a small Southern town and, upon graduating from high school, wins a scholarship to a prestigious Black college. However, to receive it, he must first take part in a brutal, humiliating battle for the entertainment of the town's rich white dignitaries. In this context, he is pitted against other young Black men, all blindfolded, in a boxing ring. After the battle, the white men force the youths to scramble over an electrified rug in order to snatch at fake gold coins. The narrator has a dream that night in which he imagines that his scholarship is actually a piece of paper with the crude command: "To Whom It May Concern: Keep this Nigger-Boy Running."

One afternoon during his junior year at the college, the narrator chauffeurs Mr. Norton, a visiting white trustee, out among the old slave-quarters beyond the campus. By chance, he stops at the cabin of Jim Trueblood, who has caused a scandal by impregnating both his wife and his daughter in his sleep. Trueblood's account horrifies Mr. Norton so badly that he asks the narrator to find him a drink. The narrator drives him to a bar that normally serves Black men, a bar filled with prostitutes and patients from a nearby mental hospital. The mental patients rail against both of them and eventually overwhelm the orderly assigned to keep the patients under control, injuring Mr. Norton in the process. The narrator hurries Mr. Norton away from the chaotic scene and back to campus.

Dr. Bledsoe, the college president, rebukes the narrator for showing Mr. Norton the underside of Black life beyond the campus and expels him. However, Bledsoe gives several sealed letters of recommendation to the narrator, to be delivered to friends of the college in order to assist him in finding a job. The narrator travels to New York and distributes his letters, with no success; the son of one recipient shows him the letter, which reveals Bledsoe's intent to betray the narrator, portraying him as dishonorable and unreliable. Acting on the son's suggestion, the narrator seeks work at the Liberty Paint factory, renowned for its pure white paint. He is assigned first to the shipping department, then to the boiler room, whose chief attendant, Lucius Brockway, is highly paranoid and suspects that the narrator is trying to take his job. This distrust worsens after the narrator stumbles into a union meeting, and Brockway attacks the narrator and tricks him into setting off an explosion in the boiler room. The narrator is hospitalized and subjected to shock treatment, overhearing the doctors' discussion of him as a possible mental patient.

After leaving the hospital, the narrator faints on the streets of Harlem and is taken in by Mary Rambo, a kindly old-fashioned woman who nurtures his sense of Black heritage. One day, the narrator witnesses the eviction of an elderly Black couple from their Harlem apartment. Standing before a crowd of people gathered at the apartment, he gives an impassioned speech that incites the crowd to attack the law enforcement officials in charge of the eviction. The narrator escapes over the rooftops and is confronted by Brother Jack, the leader of a group known as "the Brotherhood," a political organization that allegedly works to help the socially oppressed. At Jack's urging, the narrator agrees to join and speak at rallies to spread the word among the Black community. To do so, he must take a new name, break with his past, and move to a new apartment. Using his new salary, he pays Mary the rent he owes her and moves into an apartment provided by the Brotherhood.

The rallies go smoothly at first, with the narrator receiving extensive indoctrination on the Brotherhood's ideology and methods by a white member of the group named Brother Hambro. Soon, though, he encounters trouble from Ras the Exhorter, a fanatical Black nationalist who believes that the Brotherhood is controlled by whites. Neither the narrator nor Tod Clifton, a youth leader within the Brotherhood, is particularly swayed by his words. One day, however, the narrator receives an anonymous note warning him to remember his place as a Black man in the Brotherhood. He is later called before a meeting of the Brotherhood and accused of putting his own ambitions ahead of the group. He is reassigned to another part of the city to address issues concerning women. After giving a speech one evening, he is seduced by one of the white women at the gathering, who attempts to use him to play out her sexual fantasies about Black men. Eventually, he is called back to Harlem when Clifton is reported missing and the Brotherhood's membership and influence begin to falter.

The narrator can find no trace of Clifton at first, but soon discovers him selling dancing dolls on the street, having become disillusioned with the Brotherhood. Clifton is shot and killed by a policeman while resisting arrest; at his funeral, the narrator delivers a rousing speech that rallies the crowd to support the Brotherhood again. At an emergency meeting, Jack and the other Brotherhood leaders criticize the narrator for staging the funeral without permission, and the narrator determines that the group has no real interest in the Black community's problems.

The narrator returns to Harlem, trailed by Ras's men, and is forced to wear a disguise to elude them. As a result, he is mistaken for a man named Rinehart, known as a lover, a hipster, a gambler, a briber, and a spiritual leader. Understanding that Rinehart has adapted to white society at the cost of his own identity, the narrator resolves to undermine the Brotherhood by feeding them dishonest information concerning the Harlem membership and situation. He decides to flatter and seduce a woman close to one of the party leaders in a fruitless attempt to learn their new activities. However, the woman he chooses, Sybil, knows nothing about the Brotherhood, and attempts to use the narrator to fulfill her fantasy of being raped by a Black man. While still with Sybil in his apartment, the narrator receives a call asking him to come to Harlem immediately. The narrator discovers that riots have broken out in Harlem due to widespread unrest. He realizes that the Brotherhood has been counting on such an event in order to further its own aims. The narrator gets mixed up with a gang of looters, and wanders away from them to find Ras, now on horseback, armed with a spear and shield, and calling himself "the Destroyer." Ras shouts for the crowd to lynch the narrator, but the narrator attacks him with the spear and escapes into an underground manhole. Two white men seal him in, leaving him alone to ponder the racism he has experienced in his life.

The epilogue returns to the present, with the narrator stating that he is ready to emerge from underground. He explains that he has told his story in order to help people see past his own invisibility, and to provide a voice for people with a similar plight: "Who knows but that, on the lower frequencies, I speak for you?"

POINTS TO PONDER IN *INVISIBLE MAN*

Ellison's *Invisible Man* addresses many of the social and intellectual issues faced by African Americans in the early twentieth century, including black nationalism, the relationship between black identity and Marxism, and the reformist racial policies of Booker T. Washington, as well as issues of individuality and personal identity. In his speech accepting the 1953 National Book Award, Ellison said that he considered the novel's chief significance to be its "experimental attitude." Before *Invisible Man*, most novels dealing with African Americans were written solely for social protest, most notably Richard Wright's *Native Son* and Harriet Beecher Stowe's *Uncle Tom's Cabin*. By contrast, the narrator in *Invisible Man* says, "I am not complaining, nor am I protesting either," signaling a break from the Black protest novel.

Innovative as it is, *Invisible Man* clearly has forbears going back to the picaresque novel and the *Bildungsroman*. Despite being a successor to these strong literary traditions, Ellison's depiction of a Black man's coming of age in America has not always had an easy reception. When it appeared, with its sophisticated modernist techniques, many critics—especially critics of the left and scholars of the "Social Realist" school—felt that the book had no moral bite. They charged that the work, while a literary achievement, abandoned the crucial struggles of Black people (as seen, for example, in the work of Richard Wright). In his essay, "The World and the Jug," Ellison makes a fuller statement about the position he held about his book in the larger canon of work by an American of African ancestry. In the opening paragraph, Ellison poses three questions: (1) Why is it that critics so often subject African-American literature to inferior or primitive modes of analysis? (2) Why is it that sociology-oriented critics seem to rate literature far below politics and ideology? (3) Why is it that so many commentators on the meaning of Negro life never bother to learn how varied it is?

Placing *Invisible Man* within the canon of either the Harlem Renaissance or the Black Arts Movement is difficult, primarily because it owes allegiance to both and to neither at the same time. When asked to identify his influences, Ellison distinguished between his literary "ancestors" (such as T. S. Eliot, William Faulkner, Ernest Hemingway, Herman Melville, and Fyodor Dostoevsky) and his literary "relatives" (such as Richard Wright and Langston Hughes).

In the beginning of *Invisible Man*, the narration seems to be structured similarly to Dostoevsky's *Notes from Underground*: "I am a sick man," compared to "I am an invisible man." Likewise, Ellison's narrator resembles Ishmael of *Moby-Dick*. Ellison signals his debt to Melville in the prologue to the novel, where the narrator remembers a moment of truth under the influence of marijuana and evokes a church service: "Brothers and sisters, my text this morning is the 'Blackness of Blackness.' And the congregation answers, 'That blackness is most black, brother, most black. . . . '" In that scene, Ellison recalls a moment in the second chapter of *Moby-Dick*, where Ishmael wanders around New Bedford looking for a place to spend the night and enters a black church: "It was a negro church; and the preacher's text was about the blackness of darkness." According to Arnold Rampersad, Ellison's biographer, it was Melville who empowered Ellison to describe the complexity of race and racism introduced so judiciously in *Moby-Dick*.

Invisible Man is an ambitious, even epic, undertaking. It situates its protagonist's search for identity in an American landscape that includes innumerable voices from South and North, Black and white, country and city. Ellison is the great musician of American literature, and his novel ushers jazz music—the improvisational art of the twentieth century—into America's narrative tradition. By examining the protagonist's various encounters with authority figures, both Black and white, we can explore how the theme of invisibility evolves, and measure the remarkable range of voices and perspectives that Ellison packs into his rites-of-passage story.

Ellison precedes his story with a quotation from Herman Melville's novella, *Benito Cereno*. At the end of the story, Delano, the American sea captain, asks Cereno, the captain of a Spanish slave ship, what had cast such a shadow on him, seeing he had survived the ravages of storms and plagues and a slave revolt on his ship, to which Cereno responds, "the Negro," referring to Babo, the rebellious slave who served as the ingenious power behind the scenes.

Like Cereno, Ellison's account of the "invisible man" goes a long way toward dramatizing such matters. The narrator tells us that his own grandfather shocked his family on his deathbed by telling them that he had been "yessing" the white culture all his life, but had done so as an act of independence and insurrection. The narrator recounts this, but he does not understand it. Ellison's narrative inserts an innocent, uncomprehending young boy into scenes of considerable systemic racism, but the young hero is incapable of measuring them as such, having absorbed the lessons his teachers had given him but finding that they blinded him to reality.

An early instance is the "battle royal," the incident arranged by the white male power figures in the Southern community as a kind of entertainment. The incident featured a nude blonde woman gyrating and arousing not only the white male audience but also the young Black boys, who are then blindfolded and ordered to fight one another for the entertainment of the white audience. At a key moment, the protagonist peeks under his blindfold and sees, but cannot quite grasp, the larger strategic arrangements in which he is simply a tool. As a final reward, the Black boys are told to fetch the coins thrown on the rug, but when they do so, they are violently jolted by an electric current in the rug. Their "dance," it turns out, is a brutal mockery of Black stereotyping.

Next, we find the protagonist in college, clearly modeled on Tuskegee Institute, which Ellison attended in the 1930s. Washington's signature philosophy of racial submission is a central issue in the novel. While in college, the protagonist is asked to drive Mr. Norton, a wealthy philanthropic trustee of the college, around the countryside. They stop at the farm of Mr. Trueblood, who is in an incestuous relationship with his daughter. By portraying such scenes, Ellison's work portrays the elemental forces that flow through the human body and through society.

Much of the drama in Ellison's story is rooted in the search for authority. The protagonist begins his pilgrimage by seeking to ingratiate himself with "white fathers." However, in this novel, Ellison explores Black power as vigorously as white power, for the protagonist encounters a series of incidents, some focusing on predictable white figures but also surprisingly involving potent Black figures. In every case, the protagonist rediscovers his "invisibility," his status as a pawn. These bouts of futility and exploitation are counterbalanced by moments of passion and self-discovery, invariably centered on the hero's exploits as a mesmerizing speaker and political visionary, rediscovering his identity as a Black man.

As the narrator of *Invisible Man* struggles to arrive at a conception of his own identity, he finds his efforts complicated by the fact that he is a Black man living in a racist American society. Throughout the novel, the narrator finds himself passing through a series of communities, from the Liberty Paints plant to the Brotherhood, with each microcosm endorsing a different idea of how Blacks should behave in society.

Ellison was writing during the 1930s, 1940s, and 1950s, at the time of Marxism's great appeal among intellectuals, and thus the protagonist's stint with the Brotherhood, a group of organizers and activists with a Communist agenda. The Brotherhood seduces the young man by promising to give the world a new shape and to give him a vital role in it. The Brotherhood wishes to use the narrator as their man in Harlem, as part of their blueprint for history, and we see them making him conform to that blueprint in scenes of Stalinist indoctrination. The material may seem dated, but at the same time we sense that Ellison's choice of the name "Brotherhood" was brilliant, because brotherhood is what this book is about—from the Marxist Brotherhood to solidarity in the Black community, and eventually, to human solidarity.

Ultimately, the narrator realizes that the racial prejudice of others causes them to see him only as they want to see him, and their limitations of vision in turn place limitations on his ability to act. He concludes that he is invisible, in the sense that the world is filled with blind people who cannot or will not see his real nature. Correspondingly, he remains unable to act according to his own personality and becomes literally unable to be himself. Although the narrator initially embraces his invisibility in an attempt to throw off the limiting nature of stereotype, in the end he finds this tactic too passive. He determines to emerge from his underground "hibernation," to make his own contributions to society as a complex individual. He will attempt to exert his power on the world outside of society's system of prescribed roles. By making proactive contributions to society, he will force others to acknowledge him, to acknowledge the existence of beliefs and behaviors outside of their prejudiced expectations.

The narrator is not the only African American in the book to have felt the limitations of racist stereotyping. While he tries to escape the grip of prejudice on an individual level, he encounters other Blacks who attempt to prescribe a defense strategy for all African Americans. Each presents a theory of the supposed right way to be Black in America and tries to outline how Blacks should act in accordance with this theory. The espousers of these theories believe that anyone who acts contrary to their prescriptions effectively betrays the race. Ultimately, however, the narrator finds that such prescriptions only counter stereotype with stereotype and replace one limiting role with another.

The narrator's story demonstrates just how many obstructions his society has erected to prevent African Americans from achieving true equality and the freedom to self-actualize. As an educated man with both the ambition and talent necessary to lead the charge for Black civil rights, the narrator initially believes in the promise of freedom. However, his varied experiences as a young man show him just how illusory this promise really is. The narrator often faces situations and authority figures that reinforce oppressions with roots in the time of slavery. These oppressions consistently keep freedom out of reach.

Aside from the narrator, the character in the novel who best encapsulates the illusory promise of freedom is Rinehart. Rinehart is a surreal figure who possesses several identities, including a pimp, a gambling facilitator, and a preacher. The narrator obsesses over Rinehart's freedom to exist as many different people, and he longs to experience a similar freedom. However, the narrator also realizes Rinehart may not even be real. Moreover, even if he is real, his freedom comes at the cost of needing to hide in plain sight, since every costume he wears is also a disguise. Freedom therefore remains as elusive for Rinehart as for the narrator.

Another important motif in *Invisible Man* is blindness, which recurs throughout the novel and generally represents how people willfully avoid seeing and confronting the truth. The narrator repeatedly notes that people's inability to see what they wish not to see—their inability to see that which their prejudice doesn't allow them to see—has forced him into a life of effective invisibility. However, prejudice against others is not the only kind of blindness in the book. Many figures also refuse to acknowledge truths about themselves or their communities, and this refusal emerges consistently in the imagery of blindness. Thus, the boys who fight in the "battle royal" wear blindfolds, symbolizing their powerlessness to recognize their exploitation at the hands of the white men. The Founder's statue at the college has empty eyes, signifying his ideology's stubborn neglect of racist realities. Blindness also afflicts Brother Jack, who is revealed to lack an eye—a lack that he has dissimulated by wearing a glass eye. The narrator himself experiences moments of blindness, such as when he addresses the

Black community under enormous, blinding lights. In each case, failure of sight corresponds to lack of insight.

The plot of *Invisible Man* focuses on the psychological and moral development of the unnamed narrator, which makes him the novel's protagonist. The narrator reflects on his life from his present situation, removed from society in an underground lair. He tells his story in part to make sense of his experiences and the confusion they have caused him. As a Black man living in a country still pervaded by anti-Black racism, the narrator struggles to comprehend his position in society. He also struggles to understand his own identity. He strives for equality of opportunity and the power of self-determination. Above all, he desires for others to see him in his full complexity. Nevertheless, the blindness of others in his society undermines these desires. Others fail to look beyond his skin color and hence cannot see who he really is. Since the narrator has examined himself through other people's eyes, he too has long failed to see who he really is. Unseen in these ways, the narrator feels invisible. By the end, however, the narrator reconciles himself to his status as an "invisible man." He decides to return to his troubling and divided society, hoping to transform it.

Invisibility can be good, if, as readers of Harry Potter books know, we desire an invisibility cloak to keep us from being seen or detected. However, under normal conditions, people wish to be acknowledged, affirmed, and understood, rather than ignored or devalued. Undesirable invisibility, as Ellison depicts, can take many forms—from cruelty, abuse, and servitude to prejudicial disregard and neglect. Minorities, by way of response, often act in perplexing ways. Some, treated as inferior, respond in retaliatory ways or through groups that are hateful, violent, or injurious. Others simply retreat and become invisible. The unnamed protagonist in *Invisible Man* experiences all such possibilities and perseveres spiritually. Such resilience comes at a cost individually, and must be acknowledged and supported by the larger society, particularly by those in the majority. If spirituality does not support growth in both inner and outer freedom, it is not authentic spirituality.

JOSÉ VASCONCELOS'S *THE COSMIC RACE*

In 1925, Mexican philosopher José Vasconcelos (1882–1959) wrote the influential yet controversial Spanish-language book, *La raza cósmica* (The Cosmic Race) to express a novel thesis: the ideology of a future "fifth race," a synthesis of all the races in the world, with no respect to color, to erect a new universal civilization in the Americas. An opponent of social Darwinism—a scientifically groundless ideology that uses biological concepts of natural selection and survival of the fittest to support authoritarianism, eugenics, racism, imperialism, and totalitarianism—Vasconcelos attempted to refute these theories by affirming his optimistic theory of the future development of a cosmic race.

As a youth, Vasconcelos's family moved from Oaxaca to the border town of Piedras Niegras, where he attended a school in Eagle Pass, Texas. There he became bilingual, which opened doors to the English-speaking world. Later, attending law school in Mexico City, he became involved with a group of progressive-thinking students that opposed Anglo culture while emphasizing the redemptive power of education. In 1913, Vasconcelos joined the movement to defeat the Mexican military regime of Victoriano Huerta. As a result, he was forced into exile in Paris, joining other intellectual and artist expatriates.

After Huerta was ousted in 1914, Vasconcelos returned to Mexico, where he served as Minister of Education and later as rector of the National University and then as Secretary of Public Education. In this latter position, he implemented his vision of Mexico's history, especially of the Mexican Revolution of 1910 to 1920. Under his secretariat, artists such as Diego Rivera, José Clemente Orozco, and David Alfaro Siqueiros were permitted to paint the inner walls of important public buildings in Mexico City, creating the Mexican muralist movement. In 1929, Vasconcelos ran for the presidency, but lost in a controversial election.

He traveled widely across Central and South America, promoting his educational and spiritual ideals. For a time, he was a guest lecturer at Columbia University and Princeton University, though his influence decreased over time in the United States. He later directed the national Library of Mexico and presided over the Mexican Institute of Hispanic Culture. In his final years, he adopted a deeply Catholic political conservatism. In *La raza cósmica*, he argued for the mixing of races as an ethic, searching for the "spiritual basis" of culture.

Although Vasconcelos is often referred to as the father of indigenous philosophy, in recent times he has come under criticism from Native Americans for the negative implications of *"indigenismo"* concerning indigenous peoples. To an extent, his philosophy argued for a new, modern mestizo people, at the cost of cultural assimilation for all ethnic groups.

Vasconcelos's fifth or "cosmic" race embodies the notion that traditional, exclusive concepts of race, culture, and nationality can be transcended in the name of humanity's common destiny. Noting that his social experiment had to begin somewhere, Vasconcelos envisioned that this new civilization would emerge in the Americas with the erection in the South American Amazon basin of an urban Universópolis, from which city trained emissaries would travel throughout the planet educating humanity in an ideology fashioned by Spanish colonialism and Roman Catholic dogma. Vasconcelos believed that the people of the Iberian regions of the Americas (that is, the parts of the American continent colonized by Portugal and Spain) had the territorial, racial, and spiritual factors necessary to initiate the "universal era of humanity."

Reading Vasconcelos as an idealistic college student majoring in Modern Foreign Languages with a concentration in Spanish literature and culture, I was attracted to his radical call for developing a cosmic race. Thinking now about my youthful fascination with Vasconcelos, I must admit that it was naïve, for I only focused on the positive elements of Vasconcelos's thesis, while ignoring negative elements. For example, in espousing synthesis and universalism, was he not subverting uniqueness, including individual and cultural values and beliefs? When Vasconcelos first wrote his essay, it was viewed as a refutation of biological racism, but viewed in the context of Vasconcelos's life and body of work, it becomes evident that his thought was also racist, for, like all humans, Vasconcelos had cultural, religious, and racial biases and preferences. As Nicandro Juárez, Agustín Palacios, and other critics have noted, Vasconcelos was not truly multicultural or nonracist, for, as a social and religious conservative, he espoused European and Anglo-Saxon social, cultural, educational, and institutional bias. While opposing the negative eugenics of social Darwinism, Vasconcelos advocated a "eugenics of aesthetics," which he described as the survival of the beautiful, as compared to Darwin's survival of the fittest. This viewpoint, alongside specific comments by Vasconcelos, suggests that he held some races as better than others.

To speak of a "cosmic race" implies that humanity will become united and reach its spiritual potential as it sheds inferior traits and beliefs through synthesis. The phrase "cosmic race" originally referred to a movement by Mexican intellectuals during the 1920s who pointed out that Latin Americans had the blood of all the world's so-called races: European (white); Asian, including Native Americans (mongoloid); African (black);

and Australian (oceanic), thereby transcending the peoples of the "Old World." Vasconcelos also alluded to the term when he coined the National University of Mexico's motto: "*Por my raza hablará el espíritu*" ("through my race the spirit will speak").

Significantly, Vasconcelos's ideology lost its initial idealism and degenerated into *mestizaje* (racial mixture) and mestizos (an ethnic/racial category for persons of combined European and indigenous American ancestry), rather than the creation of the cosmic race. For example, the Chicano movement transformed the idea of a fifth race into a Mexican national ideology, focusing on creating a society that was less Eurocentric or Western rather than following Vasconcelos's idea to evolve indigenous and mixed races into something better. According to non-racist theories, people of mixed color cannot be racist, because if everyone is mixed, this removes color from culture as a race category. But does it? Isn't *mestizaje*, or racial mixture like blackness, whiteness, redness, and yellowness, itself a race category?

As Herman Melville notes in *Moby-Dick*, whiteness and blackness, viewed symbolically, represent attitudes or visions of the nature of the world. They are not simply polarities or colors on the spectrum, but somehow together encapsulate reality. In describing the albino whale, Melville argues that "whiteness is not so much a color as the visible absence of color, and at the same time the concrete of all colors." As Melville describes it, "whiteness is colorless, yet an all-color." Perhaps this is the best we can say about race, gender, religion, and all other self-designations that make us unique: "I am in all, and all are in me; together, we are the subspecies *Homo sapiens*."

Some people argue that the idea of race is naïve or simplistic. I must admit that at times I too have wondered, if there is not only one race—the human race—and if so, why we cannot simply jump on the bandwagon of racial unity and avoid all the tension and in-fighting caused by debate around race. However, when such thoughts arise, reality quickly takes over, and I realize that eliminating race, like eliminating gender, nationality, religion, creed, and personal values, means eliminating individuality and uniqueness, something we neither can nor should accomplish. As we have seen repeatedly throughout this study, human uniqueness is an extension of personality, and personality springs from spirituality. Individually, humans consist of body, mind, and emotions, but beyond the physical, mental, and emotional realms lies the spiritual realm. Hence, any attempt to threaten, curtail, or eliminate a person's uniqueness is to control their soul, by definition something limited to divine purview.

Modern science regards race as a social construct, an identity based on rules made by society. Therefore, while based partly on physical similarities within groups, race does not have an inherent physical or biological meaning. The term "race" was initially used to refer to speakers of a common language, and then, to denote national affiliation. Only later, during the seventeenth century, was the term used to refer to physical traits. Hence, it is glib to declare skin color mere pigmentation, for beneath pigmentation is race, beneath race is culture, and beneath culture is spirituality.

Spirituality, displayed in uniqueness, is wholesome and unitary, for it is not our lack of differences but rather our differences, rightly shared, respected, honored, and enjoyed, that unite humanity.

NATURALISM, DARWINISM, MARXISM, SCIENTISM, BEHAVIORISM, AND DYSTOPIANISM

Beginning with the Renaissance in the fifteenth century and continuing through the Enlightenment of the sixteenth through nineteenth centuries, there was a gradual yet sustained move away from theism (belief in a loving Creator and sustainer of the universe), through deism (belief in a sovereign watchmaker who no longer acts in history or with humanity), to modern naturalism (belief in no God but rather in a purposeless world where humans are at the mercy of the whims of nature). The downward trend in theological thought from the outset of the Renaissance to naturalism was clearly a movement from theism to atheism. As a result, spirituality lost its theistic base, devolving into secular humanism, a trajectory described by many literary artists pessimistically, using dystopian categories.

As God became less and less important in secular thought, nature became increasingly prominent. In due course, naturalism paved the way for Darwinism, Marxism, and dystopianism. Each of these afford an understanding of reality and a vision for order and harmony in public life. With the rise of Marxism, a new concept of society and the basis of authority emerged. Recognizing no transcendent reality and rejecting belief in anything nonmaterial, Marxism envisioned a coming utopia with a classless society that needed no government. The emergence of such a utopia, however, required a dictatorial state, which would eventually wither away.

The result would be pure communism, a self-determined society freed of any transcendent spirituality.

In response to naturalism and its scientific offshoots, scientism (the belief that people can perfect themselves through the use of scientific methods), behaviorism (the view that since humans are merely condition-able animals, properly controlling their environment can eventually make them perfect), and atheistic materialism, with its utopian idealism, a body of literature arose in the late nineteenth and early twentieth centuries labeled dystopianism. The very word "utopia" involves a pun, for, literally under-stood, it describes a "good place" (eu-topia) that is "no place" (u-topia), an ideal society that has no existence. Affirming a higher wisdom in the order of the universe—whether in God or in nature—dystopian thinkers criticized contemporary utopian thought not only for its idealism, but also as doomed to failure.

An early and popular dystopian author was H. G. Wells (1866–1946), who wrote many kinds of science fiction, including political novels, realistic works, and what he called "scientific romance." Possessed of a fertile scientific imagination, one of Wells's earliest writings was *The Time Machine*, a novella published in 1895. In this story, a time traveler invents a machine that allows him to travel selectively forward or backward through time. Using his device to travel tens of thousands of years into the future, he discovers a kind of grotesque Eden. Earth has become a garden, but humanity has evolved into two bipolar species. One of these species is the Eloi, attractive, civilized, yet compliant humans, and the other is the Morlocks, who are subterranean, predatory, and subhuman. The Morlocks supply the Eloi with food, only to devour them.

Influenced by T. H. Huxley's "cosmic pessimism," an interpretation of Darwin that presented a negative outcome of the cosmic or evolutionary process, Wells, a rather gloomy social thinker, reduced humanity to two types, both competing for power: the ultra-civilized esthetes (Marx's bour-geoisie) and the workers (Marx's proletariat). According to Wells, brain workers and hand workers, as the Victorians called them, or capitalists and laborers, as later economists called them, would never join forces, but the balance of exploitation would turn. In the future, it would be the workers (the Morlocks) who exploited and, literally, consumed the upper classes (the Eloi). Conflict between the classes would continue until the heat death of the planet. According to Wells, evolution would turn backward to the primal soup, devolving without hope for any progress from that point onward. Other evolutionists, including the later Wells, perceived a more optimistic future for humanity, but Wells's novels, particularly his earliest, popularized dystopian ideas.

Other influential dystopian arguments are depicted in E. M. Forster's *The Machine Stops* (1909), an early anti-utopian scientific romance critical of technological progress and totalitarian control, in Aldous Huxley's *Brave New World* (1932)—an explicit polemic against the behaviorism advocated by J. B. Watson and sixteen years later by B. F. Skinner in his fictional utopia *Walden Two* (1948)—in C. S. Lewis's space trilogy (*Out of the Silent Planet*, 1938, *Perelandra*, 1943, and *Out of the Silent Planet*, 1945), and in George Orwell's *Nineteen Eighty-Four* (1948). The future, an interrogator tells Orwell protagonist Winston Smith, is "a boot stomping on a human face forever." An equally dark picture is painted by William Golding in *The Lord of the Flies* (1954), in which a group of children crash-lands on an isolated island in the Indian Ocean and who, in a few months, revert to savagery of the worst kind. This same bleak tendency is found in Anthony Burgess's vision of a welfare system dominated by youth gangs in *A Clockwork Orange* (1962).

For dystopian writers, the future, as T. S. Eliot described it in his 1922 poem, is a bleak wasteland. As it turns out, dystopian authors were far more than pessimists or doomsday prophets, for they warned that society might become a terrible place, not so much from default or the absence of social planning, but from the success of societal plans that rest on false views of humanity. If utopian designs were actually implemented, dystopians argue, they would dehumanize people.

Theists and naturalists differ radically on how to deal with perplexing contemporary moral concerns such as religion, class, gender, and race. These issues continue to divide us today, and human destiny depends on which moral positions people affirm and live by in the future: secular humanism or theistic spirituality.

QUESTIONS FOR DISCUSSION AND REFLECTION

In addition to the questions listed at the end of the preface, answer the following questions, writing your answers in a journal. If you are in a group study, be prepared to share your answers with those in the group.

1.   Explain how Ralph Ellison's life influenced the plot of *Invisible Man*.

2. Explain Ellison's distinction between his literary "ancestors" and his literary "relatives."

3. Explain the variety of meanings behind the term "invisibility."

4. Explain and assess whether racial submission can be subversive or compliant.

5. In the segment on *Invisible Man*, what did you learn about racial prejudice, racial stereotyping, and about living in racist societies?

6. Explain and assess the ideology behind "social Darwinism."

7. Evaluate the positive and negative implications of the ideology behind the desire and need to develop a cosmic race.

8. Explain why some people might find attractive the notion of a "cosmic race."

9. Explain why indigenous peoples and other minorities might find the notion of a "cosmic race" racist.

10. In the segment on José Vasconcelos, what did learn about the meaning and evolution of the term "race"?

11. Explain and assess the implications of the ideology of naturalism, and how "modern" naturalism differs from primal and ancient naturalistic perspectives.

12. Explain the meaning and development of modern dystopian perspectives, and describe some of dystopianism's principal literary exemplars.

Appendix

Franz Kafka's *The Metamorphosis*

PEOPLE OFTEN SYMPATHIZE WITH CHILDREN of missionary parents for living apart from family and friends, deprived of the comforts and amenities available to peers back home in the United States. As an MK (missionary kid), an "only child" born and raised in idyllic Costa Rica, I lived simply and frugally, but in my case, the gains far outweighed the losses. My family did not own cars or televisions, but I had a loving environment, a healthy self-image, and a positive spirituality. In addition, I had many books at my disposal, a curious mind, and an active imagination.

At the age of eight, my parents relocated from the rugged mountain setting of the orphanage they served to the capital city of San José, where my father assumed a new position as supervisor of construction work for the Latin America Mission (LAM). In San José, I lived in the Mission's Biblical Seminary complex, a theological center that prepared Latin America's future church leaders. Students enrolled in the seminary came from many countries to study. In addition to the seminary, the LAM operated a publishing house, a hospital, a large downtown church, and radio station TIFC, the first evangelical radio station in Central America and the second missionary station in the world. Nearby was a Spanish language school, used by many organizations training English-speaking North Americans for service across Latin America.

In this bilingual, multicultural setting, I lived and studied with many outstanding professionals; taking piano lessons with Richard Foulkes, a world-class pianist who also taught theology in the Biblical Seminary; interacting with missionary recruit Joseph Coughlin, founder of Christian Service Brigade, a religious alternative to the Boy Scouts, who was establishing the boys' movement in Latin America; and one year, as a ten-year-old, attending weekly Saturday morning gatherings for missionary kids on the grounds of the TIFC radio station, where I attended a serialized reading of a science fiction tale about a man who, scientifically and inadvertently, was changed into a fly or acquired insect-like qualities. Kids love bugs, reptiles, and animals of all kinds, and hearing this dramatic story read over the course of that year was one of the highlights of my childhood.

Thus far in our study, we have examined the question, "What does it mean to be human" through the lens of spirituality, exploring such topics as gender, race, and sexuality. In this appendix, we consider Franz Kafka's surrealistic short story *The Metamorphosis* (1915), examining the relationship between mind and body and the boundaries between human and animal life.

In his 1912 play *Pygmalion* (best known in the musical adaptation *My Fair Lady*), the famous Irish playwright George Bernard Shaw used another literary genre, the comedy of manners, as a vehicle for what may be called the drama of ideas. The title of Shaw's play was taken from the first-century Roman poet Ovid's *Metamorphoses*, meaning "change or rebirth," which is what concerned both Shaw and Kafka. In Ovid, Pygmalion is a sculptor who falls in love with a statue he has made of a beautiful woman. The statue then comes to life. By generating a human being through art, the artist achieves what is usually reserved for the gods—the creation of another human being.

In the famous encounter between Oedipus and the Sphinx, Oedipus is asked to name the creature that is on four legs in the morning, two legs at noontide, and three legs in the evening. His answer is "man," who crawls on four legs as an infant, walks on two legs as an adult, and uses a cane in old age. For humans, metamorphosis is real, and one of the questions raised by Kafka in *The Metamorphosis* is, "How much change does it take for someone to stop being considered human?"

Kafka speaks to the sense that our world is full of those who are alive but not treated as humans because of religion, race, gender, and age. Kafka's novella might be a text that serves as a rationale for why literature matters. Kafka's work doesn't give us a familiar representation of things that are already known; instead, it reworks the given into a constellation that we have never considered before. In that sense, *The Metamorphosis* occupies a unique place in the history of fiction and will remain a classic as long as people still read.

FRANZ KAFKA

Regarded as one of the major figures of twentieth-century literature, Franz Kafka (1883–1924) was a German-speaking novelist and short-story writer whose work fused elements of realism and the fantastic. Exploring themes of alienation, anxiety, guilt, and absurdity, his works typically feature isolated protagonists facing surrealistic predicaments and incomprehensible socio-bureaucratic powers. His best known works include *The Metamorphosis* and his novels, *The Trial* and *The Castle*.

Kafka's writings, like many dreams and nightmares, are about the frightening world around him, which he often did not understand. A typical situation in his books might be someone who has gone somewhere to convey a message, but he does not know what the message is or for whom it is intended. The people he meets confuse him even more. Sometimes, when people find themselves in strange, nightmarish situations like this, they are described as experiencing Kafkaesque moments. A prominent theme of Kafka's work is father-son conflict; other prominent motifs and themes include guilt, alienation, physical and psychological brutality, terrifying quests, and mystical transformation.

Despite Kafka's pessimism, perplexity, and irrationality—or perhaps because of his enigmatic perspective and style—critical response to Kafka has been mixed. Some critics find his universe too gloomy and depressing, his characters trapped, confused, full of guilt, frustrated, and lacking understanding of their surreal world. Others, such as the poet W. H. Auden, the novelist Vladimir Nabokov, and the literary critic Harold Bloom, are full of praise. Auden, for example, called Kafka "the Dante of the twentieth century," and Nabokov placed Kafka among the greatest writers of the twentieth century. Bloom agreed, writing that "when he is most himself, Kafka gives us a continuous inventiveness and originality that rivals Dante and truly challenges Proust and Joyce as that of the dominant Western author of our century." Harry Steinhauer, a professor of German and Jewish literature, said that Kafka "has made a more powerful impact on literate society than any other writer of the twentieth century," and Kafka's friend Max Brod declared that the twentieth century would one day be known as the "century of Kafka."

Kafka was born into a middle-class German-speaking Jewish family in Prague, the capital of Bohemia, then part of the Austro-Hungarian Empire and today the capital of the Czech Republic. His father, a merchant, was very strict and unkind to his family. Kafka's stories often have fathers who are distant and brutal. Kafka spent most of his life living at home; he never married or became free from his parents. Feeling he lacked self-will and that he did not belong, he wrote about lonely, isolated people dominated by mysterious powers.

Kafka trained as a lawyer at the University of Prague, and it was there that he met Max Brod, a writer who later wrote a biography of Kafka. After his studies, Kafka took a job in an insurance company, but he found office work boring and spent his free time writing. In 1917 he contracted tuberculosis, an illness that forced him to retire in 1922 and led to his death in 1924, at the early age of forty. Various publishers realized the value of his writings and asked to publish his works. Kafka relented on a few items, such as his short story *The Metamorphosis*. In his will, Kafka instructed his executor and friend Max Brod to destroy his unfinished works, including his novels *The Trial, The Castle,* and *Amerika,* but thankfully, Brod ignored those instructions, for Kafka's work has influenced a vast range of writers, critics, artists, and philosophers.

KAFKA'S *THE METAMORPHOSIS*: PLOT

The Metamorphosis, Kafka's allegorical short story, tells the story of salesman Gregor Samsa, who wakes one morning to find himself inexplicably transformed into a huge insect, and subsequently struggles to adjust to this new condition. The tale has been widely discussed among literary critics, with differing interpretations being offered. In adaptations of Kafka's work, the insect is commonly depicted as a cockroach.

Gregor wakes up one morning to find himself transformed into a large, repulsive insect. He initially considers the transformation to be temporary and slowly ponders the consequences of this metamorphosis. Stuck on his back and unable to get up and leave the bed, Gregor reflects on his job as a traveling salesman and cloth merchant, which he detests as being full of "temporary and constantly changing human relationships, which never come from the heart." He would quickly quit his job if he were not his family's sole breadwinner.

While trying to move, Gregor finds that his office manager, the chief clerk, has shown up to check on him, indignant about Gregor's unexcused absence. Gregor attempts to communicate with both the manager and his family, but all they can hear from behind the door is incomprehensible vocalizations. Gregor laboriously drags himself across the floor and opens the door with his mouth, since he has no hands. The clerk, upon seeing the transformed Gregor, flees the apartment. Gregor's family is horrified, and his father drives him back into his room, injuring his side by shoving him when he gets stuck in the doorway.

With Gregor's unexpected transformation, his family is deprived of financial stability. They keep Gregor locked in his room, and he begins to accept his new identity and adapt to his new body. Gregor wakes and sees that someone has put milk and bread in his room. Initially excited, he quickly discovers that he has no taste for milk, once one of his favorite foods. He settles himself under a couch and listens to the quiet apartment. The next morning, his sister Grete comes in, sees that he has not touched the milk, and replaces it with rotting food scraps, which Gregor happily eats. This begins a routine in which his sister feeds him and cleans up while he hides under the couch, afraid that his appearance will frighten her. Gregor grows more comfortable with his changed body. He begins climbing the walls and ceiling for amusement. Discovering Gregor's new pastime, Grete decides to remove his furniture to give him more space. She and her mother begin to empty the room of everything except the sofa Gregor hides under whenever anyone comes in, but he finds their actions deeply distressing.

He desperately tries to save a particularly loved portrait on the wall of a woman clad in fur. His mother loses consciousness at the sight of him clinging to the image to protect it. When Grete rushes out of the room to get some aromatic spirits, Gregor follows her and is injured when she drops a medicine bottle and it breaks. Their father returns home and angrily hurls apples at Gregor, one of which becomes lodged in a sensitive spot in his back and severely wounds him.

Gregor suffers from his injuries for several weeks and takes very little food. His father, mother, and sister all get jobs and increasingly begin to neglect him, and his room begins to be used for storage. The family replaces their maid with a cheap cleaning lady who tolerates Gregor's appearance and speaks to him occasionally. For a time, his family leaves Gregor's door open in the evenings so he can listen to them talk to each other, but this happens less frequently once they rent a room in the apartment to three male tenants, since they are not told about Gregor. One day the cleaning lady, who briefly looks in on Gregor each day when she arrives and before she leaves, neglects to close his door fully. Attracted by Grete's violin-playing in the living room, Gregor crawls out and is spotted by the unsuspecting tenants, who complain about the apartment's unhygienic conditions and say they are leaving, will not pay anything for the time they have already stayed, and may take legal action.

Grete, who has tired of taking care of Gregor and realizes the burden his existence puts on each member of the family, tells her parents they must get rid of Gregor or they will all be ruined. Gregor, understanding that he is no longer wanted, laboriously makes his way back to his room and dies of starvation before sunrise. His body is discovered by the cleaning lady, who alerts his family and then disposes of the corpse.

The relieved father, mother, and sister all take the day off work. They travel by tram into the countryside, during which they consider their finances. Months of spare living have left them with substantial savings. They decide to move to a better apartment. During the short trip, Mr. and Mrs. Samsa realize that, despite the hardships that have brought some paleness to her face, Grete has grown up into an attractive woman, and they think about finding her a husband.

POINTS TO PONDER IN *THE METAMORPHOSIS*

In *The Metamorphosis*, Kafka packages the unwelcome news that control of our bodies is illusory, and makes us wonder what a strange thing it is to live in a body. Like most of Kafka's works, most interpreters tend to give a religious, psychological , or sociological interpretation to *The Metamorphosis*. Beginning with its first sentence, which introduces the wildly irrational metamorphosis, it is clear that the story focuses on the absurdity of life, for the protagonist dwells in a random, chaotic universe. The absurd event is Gregor's waking up to discover he has turned into a giant insect, and since it is so far beyond the boundaries of a natural occurrence—it's not just unlikely to happen, but physically impossible—Gregor's metamorphosis takes on a supernatural significance. Curiously, the story never explains Gregor's transformation. It never implies, for instance, that Gregor's change is the result of any particular cause, such as punishment for some misbehavior. On the contrary, by all evidence Gregor has been a good son and brother, taking a job he dislikes so that he can provide for his parents and planning to pay for his sister to study music at the conservatory. There is no indication that Gregor deserves his fate. Rather, the story and all the members of the Samsa family treat the event as a random occurrence, like catching an illness. All these elements together give the story a distinct overtone of absurdity and suggest a universe that functions without any governing system of order and justice.

The responses of the various characters add to this sense of absurdity, specifically because they seem almost as absurd as Gregor's transformation itself. The characters are unusually calm and unquestioning, and most don't act particularly surprised by the event. (The notable exception is the Samsa's first maid, who begs to be fired.) Even Gregor panics only at the thought of getting in trouble at work, not at the realization that he is physically altered, and he makes no efforts to determine what caused the change or how to fix it. He worries instead about commonplace problems, like what makes him feel physically comfortable. In fact, the other characters in the story generally treat the metamorphosis as something unusual and disgusting, but not exceptionally horrifying or impossible, and they mostly focus on adapting to it rather than fleeing from Gregor or trying to cure him. Gregor's family, for example, doesn't seek out any help or advice, and they appear to feel more ashamed and disgusted than shocked. Their cleaning lady also shows no surprise when she discovers Gregor, and when the boarders staying with the family see Gregor, they are mostly upset that Gregor is unclean and disturbs the sense of order they desire in the house. These unusual reactions contribute to the absurdity of the story, but they also imply that the characters to some degree expect, or at least are not surprised by, absurdity in their world.

In addition to the absurdity of life, another theme involves the relationship between mind and body, and how humans connect and interrelate. Gregor's transformation completely alters his outward appearance, but it leaves his mind unchanged, creating a discord, or lack of harmony, between his mind and body. When Gregor first gets out of his bed after waking, for instance, he tries to stand upright, even though his body is not suited to being upright. He also thinks of going to work, despite the fact that he is unable to do so, and when Grete leaves him the milk, he is surprised to find he doesn't like it, even though milk was a favorite drink when he was human. In essence, he continues to think with a human mind, but because his body is no longer human, he is unable at first to reconcile these two parts of himself.

As Gregor becomes accustomed to his new body, his mind begins to change in accordance with his physical needs and desires. Yet he is never able fully to bring his mind and body into harmony. Gregor gradually behaves more and more like an insect, not only craving different foods than he did when he was human, but also beginning to prefer tight, dark spaces, like the area under his sofa, and enjoying crawling on the walls and ceiling. (Through these details, the story suggests that our physical lives shape and direct our mental lives, not the other way around.) Nevertheless, Gregor's humanity never disappears entirely, and he feels conflicted as a result. This conflict reaches its climax when Grete and the mother move the furniture out of Gregor's room. Gregor initially approves of the idea because it will make his room more comfortable for him physically. Without furniture, he will be able to crawl anywhere he pleases. However, realizing that his possessions, which represent his former life as a human, provide him emotional comfort, he suddenly faces a choice: he can be physically comfortable or emotionally comfortable, but not both. In other words, his mind and body remain opposed to one another. Gregor, unable to relinquish his humanity, chooses emotional comfort, leading him to cling desperately to the picture of the woman in furs.

After Gregor's transformation, his family members struggle with feelings of both sympathy and revulsion. Grete and Gregor's mother in particular feel a great deal of sympathy for Gregor after his change, apparently because they suspect some aspect of his humanity remains despite his appearance. Eventually, however, the stress caused by Gregor's presence wears down the family members' sympathy, and even the most caring of them find that their sympathy has a limit. One of those sources of stress is Gregor's appearance. Grete is so upset and revolted by the way he looks that she can hardly stand to be in the room with him, and his mother is so horrified when she sees him as she and Grete are moving his furniture that she faints.

Like characters in E. M. Forster novels, Gregor cannot connect with those around him. His metamorphosis literally separates him from the human race, as it makes him no longer human. Essentially, he has become totally isolated from everyone around him, including those people he cares for like Grete and his mother. Moreover, the fact that Gregor cannot communicate his thoughts and feelings leaves others without any connection to his human side, and consequently, they come to see him more and more as an actual insect. All these factors combined steadily work against their sympathy, and the family reaches a point where Gregor's presence is too much to bear. Significantly, it is Grete, the character to show the most sympathy toward Gregor, who decides they must get rid of him.

However, as we learn over the course of the story, Gregor's feeling of estrangement actually preceded his transformation. Shortly after waking and discovering that he has become a bug, for example, Gregor reflects on his life as a traveling salesman, noting how superficial and transitory his relationships have become as a result of his constant traveling. Later, Gregor recalls how his initial pride at being able to support his family faded once his parents began to expect that support, and how he felt emotionally distant from them as a result. There is also no mention in the story of any close friends or intimate relationships outside his family. In fact, the alienation caused by Gregor's metamorphosis can be viewed as an extension of the alienation he previously felt as a person.

As we study *The Metamorphosis*, we discover that the story depicts not one but multiple transformations, the most obvious example being Gregor's metamorphosis into an insect. Though Gregor's physical change is complete when the story begins, he also undergoes a related change, a psychological transformation as he adapts to his new body. However, another transformation—perhaps the crucial metamorphosis in the story—is that of Grete. While Gregor's metamorphosis leaves him languishing and ultimately dying, Grete, by contrast, matures as a result of the new family circumstances and assumed responsibility. In the end—after her brother's death—her parents also notice their daughter's transformation, her metamorphosis from a girl into a woman.

As becomes obvious, *The Metamorphosis* sheds great light on family relationships. It is well known that Kafka felt bullied all his life by his father Hermann, a large, powerful man, who had no understanding for his rather effete son. The struggle in *The Metamorphosis*, however, plays out in a different way. Here, the father is depicted as a man who attacks Gregor pitilessly because he believes that this insect will destroy his wife and daughter. Before Gregor's transformation, his father had been a moribund, decrepit figure, but his need to protect his family revitalizes him.

As German critic Gerhard Rieck pointed out in 1999, Gregor and Grete form a pair, which is common in many of Kafka's texts. Typically, one is passive and austere, and the other active and libidinal. Rieck viewed these pairs as parts of one single person (hence the similarity between the names Gregor and Grete), and in the final analysis, as the determining components of the author's personality. In Rieck's estimation, conflict between nations, social groups, and family members is universal because it reflects polarities within each human individual. Internal conflict is dominant in

Kafka's works, not only because it was dominant in Kafka's experience, but because it represents the spiritual struggle at the core of everyone's psyche.

We must always remember that although we know Gregor's thoughts and feelings, he no longer possesses language and cannot communicate with this family. The story is narrated from Gregor's point of view, and readers know—though no one else does—that he is still a sentient, thinking creature. Human language, it seems, is the last badge of our citizenship in the human community, central to what makes us human, and what shows others that we are thinking, feeling creatures. Toward the end of the story, Gregor hears Grete playing music and experiences a great craving, as if music might be the nourishment he craves. Here, Kafka suggests that humans might seek a kind of nourishment that is not material but spiritual. Indeed, the whole story seems to focus on the relationship between body and soul. In Gregor's case, it is the body that has changed, and he has exited the human community. Yet we know that he is still a living, feeling, desiring, loving creature.

At story's end, the dead Gregor is swept out with the trash, and the family is freed of him. The parents look at their daughter and realize that she will marry soon and have children. Can we say, then, that Gregor is like Christ? As Christ's resurrection and ascension prompt the spiritual transformation (rebirth) of his followers, so Gregor's metamorphosis and departure catalyze the psychological and social transformation (rebirth) of his sister and parents.

QUESTIONS FOR DISCUSSION AND REFLECTION

In addition to the questions listed at the end of the preface, answer the following questions, writing your answers in a journal. If you are in a group study, be prepared to share your answers with those in the group.

1. Describe Franz Kafka as an artist, and how his life influenced his literary and philosophical perspective.

2. Explain why Kafka is called "the Dante of the twentieth century."

3. In your estimation, is it preferable to view human beings as a subspecies of the animal kingdom or as a distinct and unique species? Explain your answer.

4.   In your estimation, is Kafka's *The Metamorphosis* more about psychology (the relation of the body and the mind), about sociology (social alienation and social transformation), or about philosophy (the absurdity of life)? Explain your answer.

5.   In your estimation, is Kafka's perspective in *The Metamorphosis* essentially optimistic or pessimistic? Explain your answer.

6.   After completing this book (or class or seminar), has your estimation of modern literature changed? If so, how?

7.   After completing this book (or class or seminar), has your self-understanding changed? If so, how?

8.   After completing this book (or class or seminar), has your relation to God, others, and nature changed? If so, how?

Bibliography

Austen, Jane. *Sense and Sensibility*. Oxford: Oxford University Press, 1966.

Bazin, Nancy Topping. *Virginia Woolf and the Androgynous Vision*. New Brunswick, NJ: Rutgers University Press, 1973.

Beer, John. *A Passage to India: Essays in Interpretation*. Totowa, NJ: Barnes & Noble, 1986.

Brontë, Charlotte, *Jane Eyre*. London: Zodiac, 1946.

Butler, Robert J. *The Critical Response to Ralph Ellison*. Westport, CT: Greenwood, 2000.

Cornils, Ingo. *A Companion to the Works of Hermann Hesse*. Rochester, NY: Camden House, 2009.

Dickens, Charles. *Bleak House*. New York: Oxford University Press, 1948.

Dostoyevsky, Fyodor. *The Brothers Karamazov*. Translated by Constance Garnett. New York: Modern Library, n. d.

———. *The Grand Inquisitor*. Introduction by Charles B. Guignon. Indianapolis, IN: Hackett, 1993.

Eliot, George. *Middlemarch*. 2 vols. New York: Century, 1910.

Ellison, Ralph. *Invisible Man*. New York: Vintage, 1995.

Forster, E. M. *A Passage to India*. New York: Harcourt, Brace & World, 1952.

Fox, Matthew. *Creation Spirituality*. San Francisco: HarperSanFrancisco, 1991.

———. *Original Blessing*. Santa Fe, NM: Bear & Co., 1983.

Gerber, John C. *Twentieth Century Interpretations of The Scarlet Letter*. Englewood Cliffs, NJ: Prentice-Hall, 1968.

Guignon, Charles B. D. "Introduction." In *The Grand Inquisitor*, ix–xliii. Indianapolis, IN: Hackett, 1993.

Guiguet, Jean. *Virginia Woolf and Her Works*. Translated by Jean Stewart. New York: Harvest, 1976.

Hardy, Thomas. *Tess of the D'Urbervilles: A Pure Woman*. New York: Harper & Row, 1966.

Hawthorne, Nathaniel. *The Scarlet Letter*. New York: Norton, 1962.

———. *Tales and Sketches*. New York: Library of America, 1982.

Hesse, Hermann. *Demian: The Story of Emil Sinclair's Youth*. Translated by Michael Roloff and Michael Lebeck. New York: Harper & Row, 1965.

———. *The Glass Bead Game (Magister Ludi)*. Translated by Richard and Clara Winston. New York: Henry Holt, 1969.

———. *Narcissus and Goldmund*. Translated by Ursule Molinaro. New York: Farrar, Straus and Giroux, 1968.

———. *Siddhartha: An Indian Poem*. Translated by Susan Bernofsky. New York: Modern Library, 2006.

——. *Steppenwolf*. Translated by Basil Creighton. New York: Holt, Rinehart and Winston, 1982.

Holmes, Urban T. *A History of Christian Spirituality*. New York: Seabury, 1980.

Johnson, Claudia. *Jane Austen: Women, Politics, and the Novel*. Chicago: University of Chicago Press, 1988.

Jung, Carl G. *AION: Researches into the Phenomenology of the Self*. In *Collected Works*, 9:2. New York: Pantheon, 1959.

——. *Memories, Dreams, Reflections*. Recorded and edited by Aniela Jaffé. Translated by Richard and Clara Winston. New York: Vintage, 1965.

——. *The Structure and Dynamics of the Psyche*. In *Collected Works*, 8. New York: Pantheon, 1960.

Kafka, Franz, *The Complete Stories*. New York: Schocken, 1971.

Korg, Jacob. *Twentieth Century Interpretations of Bleak House*. Englewood Cliffs, NJ: Prentice-Hall, 1968.

LaValley, Albert J. *Twentieth Century Interpretations of Tess of the D'Urbervilles*. Englewood Cliffs, NJ: Prentice-Hall, 1969.

Leatherbarrow, W. J. *The Cambridge Companion to Dostoevskii*. Cambridge: Cambridge University Press, 2002.

McConkey, James. *The Novels of E. M. Forster*. Ithaca, NY: Cornell University Press, 1957.

Miller, J. Hillis. *Charles Dickens: The World of His Novels*. Cambridge, MA: Harvard University Press, 1958.

Miller, Robin Feuer. *The Brothers Karamazov: Worlds of the Novel*. New York: Twayne, 1992.

Mochulsky, Konstantin. *Dostoevsky; His Life and Work*. Translated by Michael Minihan. Princeton, NJ: Princeton University Press, 1967.

Moglen, Helene. *Charlotte Brontë: The Self Conceived*. New York: Norton, 1976.

Muir, Edwin. *The Structure of the Novel*. London: Hogarth, 1938.

Perkins, Moreland. *Reshaping the Sexes in Sense and Sensibility*. Charlottesville, VA; University Press of Virginia, 1998.

Preece, Julian. *The Cambridge Companion to Kafka*. Cambridge: Cambridge University Press, 2002.

Roe, Sue, and Susan Sellers. *The Cambridge Companion to Virginia Woolf*. New York: Cambridge University Press, 2000.

Rohr, Richard. *Eager to Love: The Alternative Way of Francis of Assisi*. Cincinnati, OH: Franciscan Media, 2014.

——. *Falling Upward: A Spirituality for the Two Halves of Life*. San Francisco: Jossey-Bass, 2011.

——. *Immortal Diamond: The Search for Our True Self*. San Francisco: Jossey-Bass, 2013.

——. *The Naked Now: Learning to See as the Mystics See*. New York: Crossroad, 2009.

——. *The Universal Christ*. New York: Convergent, 2019.

——. *What the Mystics Know*. New York: Crossroad, 2015.

Scanlan, James P. *Dostoevsky the Thinker*. Ithaca, NY: Cornell University Press, 2002.

Thackeray, W. N. *Vanity Fair*. Everyman's Library. New York: Knopf, 1991.

Vande Kappelle, Robert P. *Dark Splendor: Spiritual Fitness for the Second Half of Life*. Eugene, OR: Resource, 2015.

——. *Deep Splendor: A Study of Spirituality in Modern Literature*. Eugene, OR: Wipf & Stock, 2021.

BIBLIOGRAPHY

————. *Wading in Water: Spirituality and the Arts.* Eugene, OR: Wipf & Stock, 2021.

————. *Walking on Water: Living into a New Way of Thinking.* Eugene, OR: Wipf & Stock, 2020.

Vasconcelos, José. *La Raza Cósmica.* Mexico City: Porrúa, 2005.

Wellek, René. *Dostoevsky: A Collection of Critical Essays.* Englewood Cliffs, NJ: Prentice Hall, 1962.

Welsh, Alexander. *Thackeray: A Collection of Critical Essays.* Englewood Cliffs, NJ: Prentice-Hall, 1968.

Woolf, Virginia. *Orlando: A Biography.* London: Hogarth, 1970.

Index

androgyny, 140, 141
anima, animus, 20, 29, 140
archetype(s) 19, 25, 29, 31, 96
Aristotle, 16, 99
atheism, 56, 57, 174, 175
Auden, W. H., 181
Augustine, 19
Austen, Jane, 133
  biographical information on, 62, 64–66
  Pride and Prejudice, 64, 65
  Sense and Sensibility, 64, 65, 66–72

Baldwin, James, 161
behaviorism, 175, 176
Bentham, Jeremy, 105
Berdyaev, Nicholas, 54
Bildungsroman, 75, 161, 165
Bloom, Harold, 181
Bloomsbury group, 136, 145
Brod, Max, 181, 182
Brontë, Charlotte, 123
  biographical information for, 72–74
  Jane Eyre, 73, 75–80
  models of religion in, 77–78
Brontë, Emily, 72, 73, 74
  Wuthering Heights, 73, 74
Bunyan, John, 117
Burgess, Anthony, 161, 176

Calvinism, 90
Camus, Albert, 44
Carlyle, Thomas, 104
Cervantes, Miguel de, 118
class(ism), 79, 175

collective unconscious, 19, 158
comedy. *See* humor
Comte, Auguste, 125
Conrad, Joseph, 133
Cowper, William, 64

Dante Alighieri, 181
Darwinism, 93, 174, 175
  social, 171, 172
deism, 174
Dickens, Charles, 63, 75, 117, 120, 123, 131, 132
  biographical information for, 102–6
  Bleak House, 102, 103, 105, 106–12, 120, 132
  A Christmas Carol, 102, 105
  David Copperfield, 75, 102, 103
  Great Expectations, 102, 103, 105, 112
  Oliver Twist, 102, 105
  The Pickwick Papers, 102, 104, 105
  A Tale of Two Cities, 102, 105
Dickinson, Emily, 130
dogma, dogmatism, 97, 124
Dostoevsky, Fyodor, 160, 166
  biographical information for, 43, 44–46, 52–53
  The Brothers Karamazov, 43, 44, 45, 46–60
  and Russian Orthodoxy, 45, 46, 56
dreams, 32, 33, 49
dystopianism, 174, 175, 176

Einstein, Albert, 44
Eliot, George, 63, 75, 123

(*Eliot, George continued*)
  biographical information for, 123–27
  Middlemarch, 124, 126, 127–33
Ellington, Duke, 162
Ellison, Ralph
  biographical information for, 160–62
  Invisible Man, 161, 162–70
Emerson, Ralph Waldo, 82, 83, 125,
  160
enlightenment, 35, 36

Faulkner, William, 44, 162, 166
feminine principle (the Goddess; the
  Virgin), 31–32, 51, 59, 152
feminism, 62, 69–70, 79–80, 91, 92, 98,
  123, 133n1
Feuerbach, Ludwig, 125
Fielding, Henry, 63, 118
first half of life, 20–24, 41
Forster, E. M., 136, 176, 186
  biographical information for, 145–47
  Howards End, 146, 147
  A Passage to India, 146, 147–59
Fox, Matthew, 6
Freeman, Ralph, 27
Freud, Sigmund, 17, 28, 44, 136, 158
Fry, Roger, 136, 137, 145

Galen, 15
Gaskell, Elizabeth, 74
gender, 70, 140–41, 176
  stereotypes, 69, 70, 96, 98
Golding, William, 176
God
  archetype, 19
  image of, 2–4, 6
  knowing, experiencing, 7
  as Reality, 1, 9
  and self-image, 2–3
  views of, 1–3, 7
good and evil, 47, 58–59, 111–12, 157

Hardy, Thomas, 160
  biographical information for, 92–94
  Jude the Obscure, 92, 94, 160
  Tess of the D'Urbervilles, 92, 94–100
Hawthorne, Nathaniel, 96, 110
  biographical information for, 82–83

The Scarlet Letter, 82, 83, 84–92
Hemingway, Ernest, 166
Hesse, Hermann, 27–42, 44, 56, 58
  biographical information for, 27–29
  Demian, 27, 28, 29, 31, 32, 37
  The Glass Bead Game, 28, 40–42
  Narcissus and Goldmund, 27, 28,
    30–33
  Siddhartha, 27, 28, 29, 34–37
  Steppenwolf, 27, 29, 37–40
higher criticism, 124
Hippocrates, 15
Holmes, Urban, 10
Holy Spirit, 9
Hughes, Langston, 161, 166
Hugo, Victor, 131
human and animal nature, 58–59
humor, humorist, 38, 62, 63, 69, 102,
  103, 104, 113, 117, 118, 120
Huxley, Aldous, 44, 176
Huxley, T. H., 175

individuation, 20
Irenaeus, 16
irony, 62, 117, 120

James, Henry, 88, 133, 146
Jesus Christ, 25, 36, 188
  archetype, 25
  and The Grand Inquisitor, 48–49,
    52–54
Johnson, Claudia, 69–70
Johnson, Samuel, 63, 64
Joyce, James, 160, 181
Jung, Carl, 3, 4, 17–20, 24, 25, 28, 30,
  40, 41, 57, 58, 140, 141, 158
  and models of self, 18–20

Kafka, Franz, 44, 180
  biographical information for, 181–82
  The Metamorphosis, 180, 182–88
kingdom of God, 6, 51

Lawrence, D. H., 88, 94, 133, 141
Leary, Timothy, 33
Leavis, F. R., 133
Lewis, C. S., 63, 176
literature, ix, 2, 24, 25

and spirituality, ix, 11–12, 24
Luther, Martin, 54, 55

Mann, Thomas, 29
Marx, Karl, 127, 175
Marxism, 165, 168, 174
Maugham, Somerset, 44, 146
Melville, Herman, 83, 166, 173
Merton, Thomas, 8
metamorphosis, 112, 118, 138, 182–83, 184–88
Mill, John Stuart, 93, 145
Moore, G. E., 136, 145
Muir, Edwin, 111
Myers-Briggs Type Indicator (MBTI), 17–18, 30

Nabokov, Vladimir, 181
naturalism, 77, 174, 176
    definition of, 174
nature as symbol, 91, 97, 98–99
novel
    character and dramatic, 111
    as genre, 63, 72, 104–5
    thesis or propaganda, 108

Oedipus, 180
Orwell, George, 176
Ovid, 180

panentheism, 1
patriarchy, patriarchal, 31, 32, 33, 69, 70, 79
Paul (apostle), 25, 55
Perkins, Moreland, 70
personality, 1, 14
    and change, 4–6
    and imagination, 4–6
    and spirituality, 1–2, 18, 41, 56–60, 173
    and temperament, 14–17, 56–57, 71
    theory, 14–25
Plato, 15, 16
Pope, Alexander, 138, 142, 143
Prescott, Orville, 161
Proust, Marcel, 181
Puritan(ism), 85, 89–91

race, 166. 172–74
    stereotypes, 167, 168, 173, 176
    racism, 161, 165, 166, 168, 170, 172, 173
realism, literary, 62, 63, 118, 126, 132, 132–33, 181
religion, 7, 8
    definition of, 25
    mature, 8, 9
    organized, 125
    task of, 4, 124
Richardson, Samuel, 63
Ricoeur, Paul, 22
Rieck, Gerhard, 187
Rohr, Richard, 21
Russell, Bertrand, 136

Sackville-West, Vita, 136, 140
salvation, 31, 90
Sand, George, 123
Sartre, Jean-Paul, 44
satire, 102, 104, 112, 116, 117, 119
scientism, 175
Scott, Sir Walter, 63, 72, 143
second half of life, 20–24, 33, 42
self, selfhood, 39, 97, 141
    False, 7, 7–9
    shadow, 9n3, 20
    transformation of, 7–9
    True, 3, 7–9, 18, 19
    See also Jung, Carl, and models of self
self-image, 1–4, 27, 96
self-knowledge, 7, 19, 33
sensibility, 10, 34–37
    and sense, 71, 72, 119
sexuality, 31, 140, 141, 146
Shakespeare, William, 44, 99
Shaw, George Bernard, 180
sin, 4, 32, 52, 59, 85, 86, 87, 90, 99
Skinner, B. F., 176
Spinoza, Baruch, 126
spiritual journey, the, 6–7, 20, 36–37
spirituality, 1, 25, 41, 80, 151, 170, 173, 174, 176
    and change, 4–6
    definition of, 6–7
    Hindu, 150–58

(*spirituality continued*)
  global, 151, 153
  and healing, 5–6
  and imagination, 4–6
  and literature, ix, 11–12
  and personality, 1–2, 18, 41–42,
    56–60
  task of, ix, 7
  and theology, 2–3
  transformative, ix, 6, 7–9
  typology of, 10–12
Stowe, Harriet Beecher, 165
Strauss, David, 125
Swift, Jonathan, 112

Thackeray, William, 123. 131. 132
  biographical information for, 113
  Vanity Fair, 113–21, 132
theism, 174, 176
third half of life, 24
Thoreau, Henry David, 82, 83

utilitarianism, 105
utopia, 31, 51, 57, 174, 175, 176

Vasconcelos, José
  biographical information for, 170–71
  La raza cósmica, 170, 171
Victorian(s), 63, 75, 92, 93, 94, 96, 97,
    99, 102, 104, 108, 109, 117, 118,
    120, 121, 123, 124, 125, 126, 131,
    133, 134, 139, 143, 145, 175
  definition of, 79n4

Washington, Booker T., 160, 165, 167
Watson, J. B., 176
Wells, H. G.
  biographical information for, 175
  The Time Machine, 175
Wilde, Oscar, 146
Wollenstonecraft, Mary, 62
Woolf, Leonard, 126, 136
Woolf, Virginia, 44, 94, 130, 145, 147
  biographical information for, 133–37
  Mrs. Dalloway, 133, 135
  Orlando, 133, 137–43
  To the Lighthouse, 133, 134
Wright, Richard, 161, 162, 165, 166

www.ingramcontent.com/pod-product-compliance
Lightning Source LLC
Chambersburg PA
CBHW061733270326
41928CB00011B/2223